Shellfish

Anton Mosimann/Holger Hofmann

Shellfish

The art of shellfish cookery with an illustrated directory

HAMLYN

Contents

Contents

Seafood, what the French call *fruits de mer*, or fruit of the sea – there could scarcely be a more delightful or apt description of the harvest the sea provides. Shellfish and crustaceans have been a favourite theme in cooking for centuries. A popular ingredient in classic cuisine, they are now a favourite of Nouvelle Cuisine, too. Whether one is dealing with the symbols of luxury and high living – lobster, crawfish and oysters – or more widely used, less expensive species like prawns, crabs and mussels, correct preparation is the key. Simplicity and refinement in preparation remain the essential requirements for domestic cooks, chefs and gourmets alike.

This book will tell you all you need to know about the delicate art of preparing and cooking shellfish. *Shellfish* contains not only a range of classic recipes but also a number of Nouvelle Cuisine dishes. Alongside the most elaborate dishes, you will find simpler regional dishes from around the world. The central, basic recipes and the correct methods for preparing seafood are clearly explained with easy-to-follow, step-by-step photographs. These will provide a sound basis for your own creations.

In addition – and this is completely new – we provide you with the necessary background knowledge by means of a comprehensive, scientifically based, richly illustrated directory of seafood. This will not only be an inestimable help when shopping, in helping you to identify the various types of shellfish and crustaceans; it will also serve as a guide to the great variety of new kinds of seafood that are flooding on to the market with the increase in imports from all over the globe.

It is hoped that the directory will help to sort out the worldwide confusion over the correct names of the innumerable species and to bring a greater clarity to price lists and menus. It is, therefore, appropriate that at this point I should express my profound thanks to all my scientific helpers and advisers, without whose valuable help and support this comprehensive listing could not have been compiled.

Finally, I hope that, as you read and use this book, you will soon find it indispensable, both as a cookery book and as a work of reference.

Christian Teubner

THE OLDEST DELICACY KNOWN TO MAN

To trace the history of shellfish back to its earliest origins, one must search in rocks rather than in books. The forms of shellfish and snails, lobsters and crayfish have been preserved as fossils for millions of years. Such fossils can still be found in quarries, on cliffs and on the lower slopes of coastal uplands. Collectors know where to look: anywhere where, millions of years ago, there was sea where now there is land – where once there were waters in which fish, shellfish and crustaceans made their home. When the earth was young, unimaginable forces moved land, formed mountains and altered the shape of the seas. Seas and rivers found new beds, mountains threw up their folds. Sea creatures turned to stone, or left their skeletons embedded in rock, preserving their outlines to the present day.

It is scarcely credible that sea creatures existed millions of years ago, yet the fossils prove that numerous species thrived, including brachipods, cephalopods and starfish. Long before fish existed, it is thought that a wide variety of molluscs were devoured by primitive man. During the Tertiary Age, mankind developed from a four-footed to an upright creature. This allowed him to carry a sharpened spear in his hand, not only to hunt game, but also to spear fish. And, of course, he would also need his hands to pluck oysters from their beds, to grab a crab or to collect shellfish. Whatever nature provided, early man consumed to keep himself alive.

Since man's brain had also increased in size during the Tertiary Age, we can presume that he was able to be selective about which type of seafood he preferred. It has been discovered that human beings were intelligent as long ago as the Neozoic Age – no wonder, if they fed on seafood, which is rich in biologically valuable protein. Protein provides nourishment for every cell of the human body, including the brain cells. According to anthropologists, human speech began to develop in the Early Stone Age and we can therefore assume that our forefathers were able to inform their fellows, not only in sign language but also in a form of words, where the delicacies from sea and river could be found in the greatest numbers.

With the discovery of fire – some 500,000 years ago – humans were finally able to cook anything that did not taste too wholesome raw. Roasted on spits over open fires, many sea creatures were turned into mouth-watering food. As fire became more widely used, the art of cooking began to develop. Man learned to make more of his food. The Ancient Egyptians, for example, enjoyed crustaceans and shellfish in a variety of adventurous dishes. The Ancient Greeks, too, who settled on the shores of the Mediterranean, loved seafood dishes. This preference was not shared, however, by the famous Greek poet Homer, who considered anything that came out of the rivers or seas as 'poor man's food'. An incorrigible city-dweller!

The Ancient Romans were another matter entirely. Their banquets were legendary, not least for the shellfish and crustaceans served in huge quantities as an hors-d'oeuvre. They were also fussy about where their seafood came from. The most popular came from a small town on the Pontine marshes and the coast of Tarrent, or from one of their artificial oyster beds. This was the time when the oyster made

Taschenkrebs
(Cancer pagurus). ⅓.

its grand entrance. Oysters were slurped with as much devotion and enjoyment as today – by the privileged classes, needless to say. The common people had to content themselves with ordinary shellfish, for oysters were expensive even then. Wealthy Romans decorated their dining rooms with mosaics portraying their favourite seafoods: lobster, crawfish, prawns, crabs and – of course – oysters.

One Roman gourmet who was particularly partial to shellfish was Marcus Caelius Apicius (born 25BC). He is the author of the oldest surviving cookery book, which contains recipes for squid, prawns, lobster and shellfish in spicy sauces or made into the Roman equivalent of fritters. He also includes a recipe for crawfish, which clearly shows the tastes of the time; his secret was to use plenty of caraway. In fact, the ninth volume of his book (ten volumes in all) is devoted entirely to seafood.

Whichever century one looks at, seafood has always been a great favourite. This is true of the Gauls of medieval France, for example, who were not only great hunters but also excellent fishermen and merchants. Crawfish and oysters, abundant in their coastal waters, were among their most valuable merchandise. And their main customers were the Romans!

In the eighteenth century, the popularity of seafood dishes reached its zenith in Rococo France. Most highly favoured were oysters, said to have an aphrodisiac effect (a belief which still exists today). They were eaten by the dozen for breakfast. The reputation of Louis XIV improved when rumour had it that he had eaten 400 oysters before his marriage to Maria Theresa. (We are not told how long it took him – or whether it had the desired effect!)

Despite periods of unpopularity for shellfish and crustaceans, the pleasure of eating these oldest of delicacies is today even greater than it has ever been.

Hannelore Blohm

SEAFOOD DIRECTORY

A practical guide to shellfish

The known families of shellfish and crustaceans are so large and various that it would be an impossible undertaking to attempt to include all the species in the world in a directory intended primarily to serve as an introduction to a cookery book. Our aim is to list the main types of crab, prawn, lobster, shellfish and snails that are important as human food, to provide a description of them and to indicate their origins, distribution and significance in the world market. We have also made every effort to give them their correct names, for this seems to be a source of confusion throughout the world.

The difficulty of selecting the right species to include is clear when one considers that there are, for example, some 10,000 different types of lobster, 5,000 different crabs and 2,000–3,000 species of prawn – not to mention over 80,000 shellfish, snails and other molluscs.

For thousands of years, shellfish and crustaceans have been an important element of the human diet; it is only in recent years, however, that they have been exploited commercially to any extent. As fishing methods and techniques have become more and more refined, and transportation and preservation methods have developed, the obstacles to international trade have been steadily eroded. The demand for nutritious and delicious seafood has risen so steeply, however, that many species are now endangered. The situation is exacerbated by the increasing pollution of our seas. Overfishing and pollution have led to a continual search for new fishing areas, new types of shellfish and new sources of supply, but this has not solved the problem; it has only made it worse. One hopeful development is that great efforts are now being made to preserve the number and variety of sea creatures through strict fishing regulations, closed seasons and artificial cultivation of suitable types.

CRUSTACEANS

Decapods

(*Decapoda*)

Prawns, crawfish, lobsters and common crabs, crayfish and hermit crabs, robber crabs, spider crabs, mitten crabs, squat lobsters and stone crabs – despite the differences between these creatures, all of them belong to the great order of decapods. These ten-footed crabs can be divided into two sub-orders:

1. Prawns or long-tailed, prawn-like crustaceans, the *Natantia* or

'swimmers'. The 2,000 species which make up this sub-order live in a great variety of habitats, ranging from the depths of the ocean to freshwater. Most are, however, sea creatures.

Their bodies are narrow and slightly compressed at the sides. The shell (*carapace*) comes to a point at the front (*rostrum*). The antenna (*scaphocerit*) is well developed. The tail section (*abdomen*) is the same length as the carapace. The stunted, leg-like limbs on the tail section (*pleo-*

pods) are usually well developed and support the creature during swimming. Together with the tail fan, the whole tail is longer than the carapace.

Although prawns are swimmers, they are often found on the sea-bed, strutting around on their five pairs of legs or raking through the sand.

2. Crabs and lobsters, the *Reptantia* or 'crawlers'. These are distinguished from the prawns by the flattened shell and the powerful

pincers on the forelimbs. The antennae are lacking or much smaller than those of *Natantia*. The tail section is often shorter than the breastplate. The stunted limbs on the lower body are no longer used for swimming but are used by the females to attach their eggs, which are carried (as with prawns) beneath the tail section.

The crabs can be further subdivided into:

a) Long-tailed crawling crabs, whose best-known representative

is the crawfish from the *Palinuridae* family. Crawfish lack pincers but have antennae longer than the body length. Other well-known members of this group include lobsters and crayfish.
b) Medium-tailed crabs, the *Anomura*, which represent the transition between the long-tailed and short-tailed crabs. Representatives of this sub-order are hermit crabs (sea and land) and stone crabs, which are not true crabs. The medium-tailed crabs usually carry the lower body turned forward under the thorax.
c) True crabs or short-tailed crabs, the *Brachyura*, are the most highly developed of the crabs. These species date from the Jurassic period. Many short-tailed crabs like to camouflage themselves with plants or other objects. Well-known representatives of the sub-order of *Brachyura* are the Common Crab, Swimming Crab and Blue Crab.

The **bodies** of crabs can be subdivided into head, thorax and abdomen. The antennae and jaw segments are considered to be part of the head. The thorax has a few mandible feet and a pair of legs for movement. Sometimes legs are also present on the abdomen.

The **shell** of crustaceans is made of calcium and chitin, which can be reddish, bluish or greyish-brown in colour. Many crustaceans can change their colour to match their background for protection. The shell is often covered with tubercles, hairs for feeling and steering and prickle-like appendages. When these 'growths' are arranged in rows, they are usually used to produce sound.

Growth in crustaceans is not a continuous process, for the shell does not grow with the creature inside it. For this reason, crustaceans produce a hormone which makes them cast their shells. Then a period of growth begins. Beneath the old shell, the crustacean already has the 'new' skin, which lies in folds since it is much too large, to allow the creature to 'grow into it'. At this stage, any

lost limbs begin to grow back. With each shedding of the shell, they grow a little more until eventually they reach their original size.

The unprotected 'soft-shell' crab takes up to three weeks to form a new, larger shell from layers of chitin and calcium; the calcium is taken in from the water. While the crustacean is soft, it will hide under stones or in small cavities. Many crabs are much sought after in this state, especially on the East Coast of the United States, where the soft-shell crabs have a particularly good flavour.

Decapods **move** by swimming, crawling, strutting or raking through soft ground. The first three pairs of legs are mandibles, for feeding. The next five pairs – from which the decapods get their name – are walking legs, although the first pair have evolved into pincers. The pincers are mainly used for feeding, for defence against enemies and for holding onto the partner during mating.

If a crustacean loses its pincers in a fight with a rival or another enemy or if it discards them when danger threatens, to distract the attention of a predator, the first pair of legs are then used for catching and eating food. Lost limbs grow back when the shell is next replaced. The last anterior pair of swimming legs are flattened out and, with the hind end of the abdomen, form the *telson* or tail fan. In times of danger this acts as a rudder, propelling the creature through the water at great speed – backwards! This is extremely useful, as it means that the creature can retreat while keeping the enemy in its sights.

Feeding patterns vary considerably amongst the higher crustaceans. Many are filterers: from the respiration water, carried along by appendages on the legs, and from the sea-bed they extract small vegetable and animal particles. Algae and other plants and small creatures, both dead and alive, are seized in the pincers.

One interesting example is the Harlequin Prawn (*Hymenocera*

picta), which feeds only on starfish, which it lifts up and turns onto their backs. Then it bores into the starfish with its pincers and gradually tears off small pieces of tissue from the opening.

The mandible feet are an important part of the feeding process. They sort out the inedible parts of the prey and get rid of them. The edible parts are then sorted and dissected in a sort of stomach with chitin teeth.

The **sense organs** of decapods are highly developed. They have complex eyes with all-round vision. Many crustaceans can spot a moving object over 15 m (50 feet) away. In species which live in deep water or caves, the sense of touch is highly developed, registering the minutest vibrations. Other species have an amazing sense of direction, using the sun, moon, current, and other natural navigation aids; this allows them to return to their original position after wandering off in search of food, and to find shallower waters in which to spawn.

Reproduction cycles in many crustaceans are governed by the season or by the phases of the moon. During mating, the male holds the female with his pincers. Some of the swimming legs have evolved into reproductive organs. When the female lays her eggs, shortly after mating, they are attached to the legs on the hind part of the body until the larvae have developed sufficiently to swim alone. Larger larvae swim and float extremely well, which enables them to scatter quite widely, increasing their chances of survival.

Crustaceans reach sexual maturity at the age of three or four. Decapods can grow to a very old age. Crayfish, for example, can live for over twenty years if they escape predators. Lobsters can live for fifty, and in some cases even eighty, years.

SHRIMPS/PRAWNS
(*Natantia*)

The sub-order of decapods with the zoological name *Natantia* is found in many related forms in

every ocean. Almost every type of prawn has a relatively narrow body, tapering and slightly curled at the hind end, and relatively long antennae (feelers). Many species of prawn are semi-transparent and greenish-brown, pink or brownish-red in colour. The pigmentation is made up of blue, which is susceptible to heat, and red, which is heat-resistant. When the prawns are boiled, only the red pigmentation remains.

The terms 'shrimps' and 'prawns' used in the fish trade have no scientific basis. They are usually no more than an indication of the size of some of the 2,000–3,000 known species, of which only a few are of economic importance. 'Shrimps' is the term usually applied to small prawns, with over 200 to the kilo (100 to the pound). Most of these are deep-sea creatures. The Grey or Brown Shrimp and the East Asian King Prawn live in shallow coastal waters. In addition to subdivisions based on size and depth of water, one can also distinguish between warm- and cold-water prawns. Cold-water prawns are better quality and therefore more expensive. One can also distinguish between marine, freshwater and brackish-water prawns.

Unfortunately, the use of the terms 'shrimp' and 'prawn' is not consistent throughout the world. The creatures are usually sorted and named by their size but the system is different in Britain and on the Continent and different again in the United States, with its immense fishing grounds, and in India and the Pacific region. The only point common to all is that extremely large prawns are sold as giant, king or tiger prawns. In New York's Fulton fish market, for instance, prawns are sold in pound boxes. Tiger prawns average two per pound, prawns or jumbo prawns up to fifteen per pound. Prawns averaging sixteen to twenty per pound are known as extra large; twenty-one to thirty per pound are large; thirty-one to forty, medium. The name 'shrimps' is used when you get 160–180 per pound.

Fresh prawns make up a relatively small part of the market, compared with the numbers of prawns sold frozen or canned. Fresh prawns from the North Sea, like these, are usually available only on the coast.

Giant prawns and scampi are often confused, although scampi have little in common with the various types of prawns. Seen from the top, prawns have a very narrow tail; viewed from the side, they are wide at the top and taper to a point. The shell on the tail of the prawn is thin and smooth compared with that of scampi. In scampi, the shell is quite thick and tapers to a series of points at the side, as one would expect in a member of the lobster family.

In England, the term 'shrimp' is often used even for large prawns, and the terminology is fairly arbitrary.

In India, the country with the largest cultivating farms (even the water-covered rice paddies are used for breeding prawns), all creatures of this type are known as prawns. Here, the only distinction made is between those that belong to the *Penaeidae* family and those that do not. Indian and Pakistani cultivated prawns are not, however, of the same quality as free-range prawns.

In the United States there are two extremely good methods of cultivating prawns with no loss of quality:

1. Young prawns carried by the tide into shallow coastal waters are kept in special tanks until they grow to market size.

2. Female prawns are caught before spawning and lay their eggs in artificial tanks. This method was developed in Japan, where it has been used with great success.

Large prawns, usually known as king prawns, play an important part in fine cuisine in most countries. Zoologically speaking, they belong to the *Penaeidae* family, mostly to the species

Penaeus and *Metapenaeus*. Because of the similarities between the various species and sub-types, they do not have different colloquial names in the countries where they are caught. This has given rise to a variety of regional or local names, which are often interchangeable.

Even more complicated for commercial purposes are the Latin names, for here too variations have arisen over the years. Unfortunately, there is as yet no authoritative reference book on the scientific names of commercially important crustaceans. In our directory, we have been able to include only the main types of prawns. It is impossible to produce a totally comprehensive list, since new *Penaeidae* types are coming onto the market continually (for all are edible).

Many are of only local importance. The common names of more exotic prawns are in some cases translations from the native language of their country of origin and many have never before been recorded in print.

Prawns are the most widespread and popular crustaceans of all. There is scarcely a country where you will not find them on the menu.

Prawn fishing has developed into quite an industry. Ships the size of this North Sea fishing smack operate close to land. Deep-sea prawns are fished using large, well-equipped, ocean-going ships and are usually boiled and processed on board.

PENAEIDAE

The prawns belonging to this family are relatively large; most measure 10–20 cm (4–8 in) in length and many up to 30 cm (1 ft). The first three pairs of legs end in small pincers, while the two following pairs are of similar length and pointed. One peculiarity of this family is that the females do not carry their eggs around with them under the abdomen but scatter them into the water.

The shell of prawns contains little calcium, so the body is light and well adapted for swimming. *Penaeidae* occur in huge numbers. Since even the true deep-sea varieties are of good to excellent quality, they play an important part in the world prawn trade. As they are so popular, we must look more closely at *Penaeidae* and the main areas in which they are found.

Although shrimps are widely used and much valued in Europe, it is to the United States we must look to see prawns caught, processed and cooked in huge numbers. In the United States, prawns are the best-known and most popular crustacean. Here, the insignificant prawn is known as 'the queen of crustaceans'. The huge West Coast prawn fishing grounds from California northwards to Washington State and Alaska reflect this opinion, as do the East Coast Atlantic fishing grounds from North Carolina southwards to Florida and the Gulf of Mexico. Both coasts are important centres for the prawn industry.

Several types of prawn are known in the United States. The main types from the fishing grounds we have mentioned are included below. It is difficult or even impossible for the man in the street to distinguish between them, for even the names based on colour are not much of a guide. *Penaeus duorarum* is known as Pink Shrimp, but then so are *Pandalus borealis* and *Pandalus jordani*.

The best quality, best-known and most popular *Penaeidae* of the East Coast of America and the Gulf of Mexico are the Lake Shrimp or White Shrimp (*Penaeus setiferus*) and the Caribbean White Shrimp (*Penaeus schmitti*). The first of these, *Penaeus setiferus* (White or Lake Shrimp), prefers to live on the sea-bed at depths of up to 100 m (330 ft). Young ones like to collect nearer to land in river mouths, where they are often caught. Smacks fishing for full-grown prawns may be at sea for up to a fortnight and the catch is immediately put on ice on the boat to prevent it going off in the warm climate. The head, with the intestine, is usually removed first and the tails are landed packed in ice and sent fresh for processing.

Certain types of brown and pink shrimps – such as *Penaeus duorarum* (Pink Shrimp), the most popular of this group – are also well known and liked. Pink Shrimp may be pink, brown or yellow depending on their geographical origin. This species can also be successfully farmed in large tanks. True brown prawns include *Penaeus aztecus* (reddish-brown) and *Penaeus brasiliensis*. Another popular prawn is the deep-red Royal Red Shrimp from the Gulf of Mexico (*Hymenopenaeus robustus*) but this too is sometimes found in a greyish-pink shade, usually at great depths.

The Blue Shrimp (*Penaeus stylirostris*) is found on the west coast of Mexico, where it makes up 90 per cent of the total Mexican catch.

The larger Giant Tiger Prawn (*Penaeus monodon*), the Japanese Kuruma Prawn (*Penaeus japonicus*) and *Metapenaeus mastrersii* are imported into the United States from the Pacific and Indo-Pacific regions.

Blue and Red Shrimp (Prawn)

(*Aristeus antennatus*), Fr. Crevette Rouge, Ger. Afrikanische Tiefseegarnele
A relatively large prawn with a strongly pointed brow and short feelers. In females, the total body length can be up to 25 cm (10 in). Distribution extends from the Portuguese coast to the Cabo Verde islands and also includes the Mediterranean. Related species live in tropical West Africa and in the seas between East Africa and India. The head section is blood-red in colour and the tail almost white with the odd blue fleck. They are found at depths of 200–1,440 m (650–4,725 ft).

Giant Red Shrimp (Prawn)

(*Aristaemorpha foliacea*), Fr. Gambon Rouge, Ger. Rote Tiefseegarnele
A large red prawn fished mainly off the Mediterranean coasts of Spain, France, Italy, Algeria and Israel at depths of 250–700 m (820–2,300 ft). They are also to be found off all Atlantic coasts at depths of 250–1,300 m (820–4,265 ft) and will certainly increase in importance in the future in areas outside the Mediterranean.

Kadal Shrimp

(*Metapenaeus dobsoni*), Fr. Crevette Kadal, Ger. Kadalgarnele
This prawn is caught mainly in the Indian Ocean and off the south coast of Indonesia. The females grow up to 13 cm (5 in) in length, males only to around 7 cm (3 in). In the Indian state of Kerala, this species is cultivated in the paddy fields.

Greasy-back Prawn

(*Metapenaeus ensis*), Fr. Crevette Glissante, Ger. Große Südpazifische Garnele, Jap.

Yoshi-ebi, Indon. Udang Gof Godot, Phil. Hipon Suahe
A large prawn, similar to the Fleshy Prawn, which grows to around 15 cm (6 in) in length. It is found in the Indo-Pacific seas from Sri Lanka to Japan and Australia. The thorax and tail shells are flattened and run along the back like the teeth of a comb. This species is landed mainly in Malaysia, Singapore and Indonesia.

Red Spotted Shrimp

(*Penaeus brasiliensis*), Fr. Crevette Royale Rose, Ger. Rosa Tropengarnele
A prawn of about 20 cm (8 in) with extremely long antennae. They prefer depths of 45–65 m (150–215 ft) and a sand-silt or gravel sea-bed. They are found on the tropical east coast of South America and off the southern United States, especially in the Gulf of Mexico.

Giant Tiger Prawn

(*Penaeus monodon*, formerly *P. carinatus*), Fr. Crevette Géante Tigrée, Ger. Bärengarnele, Schiffskielgarnele, Jap. Ushi-ebi, Phil. Sugpo, Indon. Udang Windu, Chin. Gwai Ha
A large prawn found throughout the Indo-Pacific from East Africa to South-East Asia. Their normal habitat is several miles off the coast at depths of up to 110 m (360 ft). They grow to a length of 15–33 cm (6–13 in). This is the

Pacific prawns, especially from the warm waters around Malaysia and Indonesia, are beginning to make an impact on the market. Usually only the frozen tails are exported, frozen either separately or in blocks or, specially for Japan, filled with water and then frozen. The flavour is not, however, as good as that of prawns from colder waters.

most common and most frequently eaten species in the Indo-Pacific area. The young live in brackish water and swim to the sea when full grown.

Kuruma Prawn, Japanese Prawn
(Penaeus japonicus), Fr. Crevette Kuruma, Ger. Radgarnele, Jap. Kuruma-ebi, Phil. Hipon Bulik
A large prawn that grows to 20–22 cm (8–9 in) in length. It has a yellowish tail, flecked in black, and is found from Japan throughout the whole of the West Pacific to Indonesia and the Red Sea, from where it has made its way through the Suez Canal to the eastern Mediterranean. The young prefer relatively shallow water but when fully grown move to depths of up to 20 m (65 ft). In Japan, they are found at depths of up to 100 m (330 ft).

Fleshy Prawn
(Penaeus chinensis, formerly P. orientalis), Fr. Crevette Charnue, Ger. Hauptmanns-garnele, Jap. Korai-ebi
A long, straight prawn found at depths of up to 80 m (260 ft); fully grown, it can reach 18 cm (7 in) in length. The Fleshy Prawn lives mainly in the coastal waters between Korea and China. In winter, they head further south to the open sea, covering hundreds of kilometres. They are caught throughout the year but the largest catches are during the summer months.

Striped Shrimp (Prawn), Caramote Prawn
(Penaeus kerathurus, formerly P. trisulcatus or P. caramote Risso), Fr. Caramote, Crevette de Maroc, Ger. Furchengarnele, Ital. Gambero Imperiale, W. Afr. Tiger Shrimp
A prawn found in the eastern Atlantic from southern England to Angola and throughout the Mediterranean, on silty sand in river mouths. It prefers depths of 5–40 m (15–130 ft). The females can be up to 23 cm (9 in) long and before laying their eggs they are yellowish-green or yellowish-grey in colour with brownish-purple or greenish-bronze cross-

Giant Tiger Prawns are one of the most commercially important varieties on the world market. These huge prawns (they can grow to 30 cm/1 ft in length) are native to the Indo-Pacific and they play an important part in Far Eastern cooking.

Fleshy Prawns are sold frozen as Prawns or Chinese Prawns. They are exported from China either whole or just as tails. These prawns are of medium size, 15–18 cm (6–7 in), but of extremely good flavour.

Green Tiger Prawn (*Penaeus semisulcatus*). A prawn found throughout the Indo-Pacific region, in very great numbers in the Gulf of Aden, but also in the Red Sea and the Mediterranean, which it reaches through the Suez Canal. It is now fished commercially in the eastern Mediterranean. In the Ganges delta in India, it is cultivated in the rice fields.

stripes. The tail section has a bluish-pink border. The males are smaller and pink in colour, with darker stripes at the hind end.

The best time to catch these prawns is during the late evening, while they are laying their eggs. They are extremely tasty and have been grossly overfished. They were traditionally caught in the Mediterranean but stocks have been so much reduced that Mediterranean countries now rely heavily on imports.

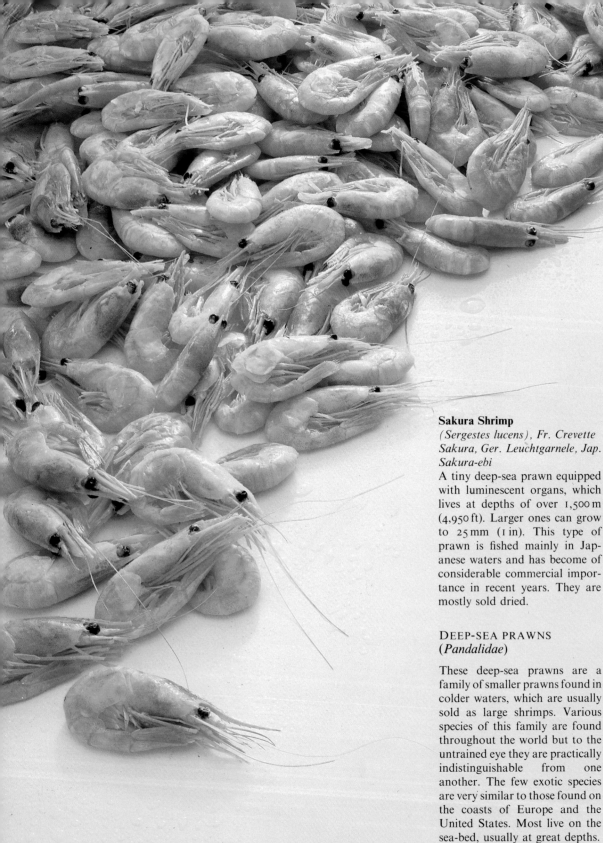

Spitsbergen and the Barents Sea and off the coasts of Iceland and Greenland, as well as off the north-west coast of the USA and off the coast of Alaska.

They are larger than other members of the family at up to 16 cm (6 in) in length. They are a translucent pink colour and inhabit depths of 100–250 m (330–820 ft) or more. Other species, which are slightly larger, are found in the warmer waters of the North and Indo-Pacific.

Pandalus borealis is unusual in that it is hermaphrodite. The prawns begin life as males but spend the second half of their lives as females, when they lay 1,000–3,000 eggs. In cold waters, they spawn in autumn. To protect the eggs from being damaged by the cold, the female carries them beneath her body until the following spring. When the water temperature rises and there is more food about, the larvae hatch. Prawns in warm waters do not have this problem and hatching takes place within a few weeks of spawning.

The main fishing seasons are between March and October. Since the aptly-named Deep-sea Prawn lives in deep water, it can be caught only with trawl nets. They do not keep well, so they are usually cooked and frozen on board ship.

Sakura Shrimp

(Sergestes lucens), Fr. Crevette Sakura, Ger. Leuchtgarnele, Jap. Sakura-ebi

A tiny deep-sea prawn equipped with luminescent organs, which lives at depths of over 1,500 m (4,950 ft). Larger ones can grow to 25 mm (1 in). This type of prawn is fished mainly in Japanese waters and has become of considerable commercial importance in recent years. They are mostly sold dried.

DEEP-SEA PRAWNS (*Pandalidae*)

These deep-sea prawns are a family of smaller prawns found in colder waters, which are usually sold as large shrimps. Various species of this family are found throughout the world but to the untrained eye they are practically indistinguishable from one another. The few exotic species are very similar to those found on the coasts of Europe and the United States. Most live on the sea-bed, usually at great depths.

Deep-sea Prawn, Pink Shrimp, Northern Shrimp

(Pandalus borealis), Fr. Crevette Nordique, Ger. Tiefseegarnele, Grönlandgarnele, Nordmeergarnele, Nordische Garnele, Dan. Rejer, Nor. Reker, Dut. Diepzeegarnaal

The Deep-sea Prawn is one of the specialities of the North Sea. The best fishing grounds lie in the deep Norwegian fjords up to

Aesop Shrimp, Pink Shrimp

(Pandalus montagui), Fr. Crevette Esope, Ger. Rosa Garnele *(Krabbe)*

A prawn which is fished mainly in shallow water off the English coast but whose habitat extends as far as the southern North Sea. About 5 cm (2 in) long, this prawn prefers a firm sea-bed. The main fishing season lies between April and September. This is the most common native British prawn but is not much fished. To the layman, it is practically indistinguishable from the Deep-sea Prawn (above).

Deep-sea prawns are usually sold deep-frozen but are nevertheless of exceptional quality. Most come from the northern seas around Greenland and Spitsbergen. The flavour and consistency of cold-water prawns are far superior to those of prawns from warmer waters.

SERGESTIDAE

A family containing some thirty-five types, of which most species average 12–113 mm ($\frac{1}{2}$–$4\frac{1}{2}$ in) long. They are found in large shoals in the open sea. Smaller types swim on the surface at night, so they are relatively easy to catch, although only one species is currently caught in any numbers.

Mediterranean Deep-sea Prawn

(Parapandalus narval), Ger. *Mittelmeer-Tiefseegarnele*
The varieties of *Parapandalus* prawn are easily distinguishable from *Pandalus* prawns by their elongated, saw-toothed rostrum. They are the sub-tropical and tropical counterpart to the northerly *Pandalus* varieties. This species is usually found in deep water in the Mediterranean or the nearby warmer waters of the Atlantic. They are being fished commercially in increasing numbers, especially in the Canaries and Madeira and on the Atlantic coast of southern Europe. The catch is usually sold locally.

Camarón, Chile Prawn

(Heterocarpus reedi), Ger. *Camarón, Chilegarnele (Krabbe)*, Span. *Camarón, Camarón Nailon, Gamba*
Found in the Indo- and South-east Pacific, this prawn is 6–12 cm (2½–5 in) long. When sold, it is usually named after its country of origin. Chilean Camarónes, which have an excellent flavour, are beginning to make their way onto European markets.

PALAEMONIDAE

The various *Palaemon* species of prawn, smaller than *Pandalus* and *Aristeus* varieties, are found in the warmer waters of the moderate zones. They were previously classified as *Leander*. The *Palaemonidae* family can be divided into two distinct groups, according to their habitat: one group prefers salt water, the other lives in fresh water, brackish water or river mouths. They are known respectively as freshwater and salt-water prawns.

Several members of the family are found along European coastlines. Some, like *Palaemon serratus*, prefer seawater while others, such as *Palaemon longirostris*, are found in the estuaries of large rivers.

One member of the family, *Palaemon adspersus*, lives in brackish water. Although this prawn can be found in the North Sea, it lives mainly in the Baltic and is usually called the Baltic

Camarón is the Chilean name for this deep-sea prawn from the South Pacific (*Heterocarpus reedi*). They are of similar quality to deep-sea prawns from the North Sea and are usually sold boiled and peeled. They are always imported frozen.

Prawn. It is up to 6 cm (2½ in) long and lives among seaweed and algae. They are caught in shoals and usually canned.

Many members of this family are found in fresh water in South America and the Antilles. In South-east Asia they are farmed in the paddy fields. The main farmed varieties are the *Macrobrachium* types, which include the Oriental River Prawn and the Rosenberg Prawn. Of lesser commercial importance, but excellent flavour, are the freshwater *Atyidae* prawns. Distribution of these larger freshwater varieties extends from the warm Indo-Pacific to the Caribbean, the southern USA and the north of South America.

The *Palaemonidae* are extremely adaptable. Many can be found in underground rivers, for example in the Balkans. These types have practically lost their sense of sight but have a well-developed sense of touch. Others live in symbiosis with sponges, sea anemones, corals and certain types of fish. One Caribbean variety, *Periclimenes petersoni*, flags down fish with its antennae, cleans their scales and gills of parasites and even enters the mouth to clear away unwanted food debris. Since freshwater

prawns often have a slightly musty flavour, they are not usually preserved but sold fresh. The first two species listed below are examples of very similar types living in very different waters.

Baltic Prawn

(Palaemon adspersus, formerly *Leander adspersus* and *L. adspersus ssp. fabricii)*, Fr. *Bouquet Balte*, Ger. *Steingarnele, Ostseegarnele*, Dan. *Roskilde Rejer*, Nor. *Strandreker*, Swed. *Tångräka*, Dut. *Steurkrab*, Span. *Camarón Baltico, Esquilla, Gamarillo*
Similar in shape to the Deep-sea Prawn but with a shorter rostrum, transparent body and dark brown stripes. Males grow up to 6 cm (2½ in), females to 8 cm (3 in). The Baltic Prawn lives amongst vegetation on the seabed at depths up to 60 m (200 ft), and at greater depths in winter. It prefers sheltered bays and fjords. The main areas of distribution are around Denmark, along the Baltic coast, as far as the Eastern Atlantic, Mediterranean and Black Sea. The main fishing season is in summer. At one time, this prawn was fished commercially on the German Baltic coast but nowadays it is hardly fished at all.

Pink Shrimp, Common Prawn

(Palaemon serratus, formerly *Leander serratus)*, Fr. *Crevette Rose, Bouquet, Salicoque*, Ger. *Sägegarnele, Rosa Krabbe*, Port. *Camarão Mauro*, Span. *Gamba, Esquilla, Gambaretto Commune*
A transparent prawn with a longer rostrum than the Baltic Prawn, this species can reach 12 cm (5 in) long. It is normally found in heavily vegetated, rocky waters on the south and west coast of England, the Danish North Sea coast, the Atlantic coasts of France, Spain and Portugal and in the Mediterranean. Related species can be found in similar coastal conditions throughout the world. As well as being sold for human consumption, these prawns are used in Great Britain as salmon bait. In France and some other Mediterranean countries, where they are sold live, these prawns are considered the best of all.

Oriental River Prawn

(Macrobrachium nipponense, formerly *Palaemon nipponensis)*, Fr. *Bouquet Nippon*, Ger. *Japanische Garnele*, Jap. *Tenaga-ebi*
This medium-sized prawn, about 7 cm (3 in) long, has a distinctive humped back and elongated rostrum. It lives in brackish and fresh water in Japan, northern China, Taiwan and Vietnam. Attempts have been made to farm them in Japan.

Rosenberg Prawn, Giant River Prawn

(Macrobrachium rosenbergii), Fr. *Bouquet Géant*, Ger. *Rosenberg-Garnele*, Indon. *Udang Galah*
This large, Indo-Pacific prawn is one of the best-known in Southeast Asia. With its extremely thin, elongated pincers, it is not unlike the European Scampi (*Nephrops norvegicus*), although the pincers of the Rosenberg Prawn are dark in colour and are usually removed before sale. The tasty tails are around 10 cm (4 in) long. As with all freshwater prawns, they should never be eaten raw as they are hosts to the lung leech.

Rosenberg Prawns have been

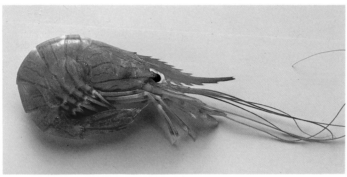

The Pink Shrimp or Common Prawn is extremely popular in Europe. These prawns, 8–10 cm (3–4 in) in length, are sold fresh or boiled and are considered by the French and Italians to be the best prawns on the market. People on the Atlantic coast of France enjoy catching them at low tide in hand-nets, to boil and eat.

farmed in Singapore for a long time and, more recently, in Israel, where they are sold as Rosenberg Shrimps.

FRESHWATER PRAWNS (*Atyidae*)

Camacuto Shrimp
(*Atya scabra*), Fr. *Saltarelle Camacuto, Cacador* (*Guadeloupe*), Ger. *Süßwassergarnele*, Port. *Conca, Camarão de Pedra*
The largest of the *Atyidae* family at 7 cm (3 in) long, this shrimp is found both in the Caribbean (Guadeloupe and Antilles) and in the tropical waters of the mainland from North America and Mexico to Brazil. It is much sought-after for its fine flavour. One of the main areas of local consumption is northern Brazil.

SAND PRAWNS (*Crangonidae*)

The sand prawn family is of great commercial significance, since it includes the Grey or Brown Shrimp. The *Crangon* family includes thirty species found mainly in northern waters which are cold to moderate, in both the North Atlantic and North Pac-

ific. Apart from the two varieties included here, scarcely any other *Crangon* variety is fished, probably because they are very small. This could change in the future, though, if other, more popular types of prawns become scarce through overfishing.

They differ from other types of prawns in that their first, highly developed pair of legs are not pincered claws but shaped like a small hammer. They can live up to 20 km (13 miles) from the coast as well as in the depths of the ocean. Distribution is from the eastern Atlantic, the North Sea and the Baltic to the Mediterranean and the Black Sea.

Grey Shrimp, Brown Shrimp, Sandy Shrimp, Common Shrimp
(*Crangon crangon*, formerly *Crangon vulgaris*), Fr. *Crevette Grise*, Ger. *Nordseegarnele, Deutsche Nordseekrabbe, Granat, Dut. Gewone Garnaal, Ital. Gambero della Sabbia, Port. Camarão*
These shrimps average 5–7 cm (2–3 in) long and have a transparent, grey body and – unlike the Deep-sea Prawn – a short, flat rostrum.

The popular Grey Shrimp is a creature of the shallows, a typical soft-sand dweller, and so is constantly exposed to changes in temperature and in the salt content of the water, but it has adapted well to these problems. As the tide ebbs, it is carried out to sea and returns to the sandbanks with the incoming tide. During the day it likes to burrow into the sand or mud with only its eyes and antennae showing. At night it takes on a darker colour for camouflage and goes in search of food such as krill, worms, shellfish, algae and other vegetable matter. Providing that they are not caught, Grey Shrimp can live to three years of age. With the females laying thousands of eggs twice a year, they are well adapted for survival.

Commercial fishing for the Grey Shrimp, which occurs on a large scale in the North Sea, is carried out from smacks equipped with two large nets. The main season is summer and autumn.

The Rosenberg Prawn is a well-known freshwater prawn, 20 cm (8 in) long with thin pincers. They are from the Indo-Pacific and are widely sold in the Far East. The frozen tails are increasingly being exported, as they have a delicious flavour and are nice and plump. Rosenberg prawns have been successfully farmed for many years.

The shrimps larger than 5 cm (2 in) are suitable for eating; the catch is sorted by size and boiled on board ship. Those that are too small for eating are eventually turned into animal feed and fertiliser.

California Shrimp
(Crangon franciscorum), Fr. Crevette Californienne, Ger. Amerikanische Sandgarnele
A small shrimp of the northern Pacific, and a relative of the Grey Shrimp, the California Shrimp is fished commercially on the coast between San Francisco and Vancouver. It is the main shrimp to be found in the fish markets of San Francisco.

The Grey or Common Shrimp exists in profusion in shallow North Sea waters, and is a culinary favourite in most European countries.

LOBSTERS/**CRABS** (**CRAWLERS**) (*Reptantia*)

The sub-order *Reptantia* can be divided into three groups: the long-tailed crawling crabs, which include the pincerless crawfish or Spiny Lobster and the related Squat Lobster as well as lobster and crayfish; the medium-tailed crabs (*Anomura*), which include Langostinos, Hermit Crabs and Stone Crabs; the most highly developed crabs, the short-tailed or true crabs (*Brachyura*).

Long-tailed crawling crabs

CRAWFISH (*Palinuridae*)

This section includes descriptions of three of the known species of the *Palinuridae* family. At first glance, all three are very similar, but they can be distinguished by the following features:

In *Palinurus*, the highly developed frontal plates protrude, while the rostrum is reduced to a small thorn.

In *Panulirus*, the rostrum is again no more than a thorn but the breastplate (*carapace*) ends in a plain, sharp edge at the centre.

Members of the *Jasus* species, however, come to a triangular

Lobster and crayfish – symbols of luxury. It has proved difficult to meet the ever-increasing international demand for these, the most refined of crustaceans, and this has led to continually escalating prices. Strict controls in the producing countries and encouragingly successful attempts at farming should help to provide sufficient stocks to meet demand in the future.

point at the front. On either side of the rostrum are two large frontal spines, whose hollow underside protects the eyes, whereas in members of the *Palinurus* and *Panulirus* families the eyes can move freely beneath the frontal horns.

To the untrained eye, a crawfish looks like a lobster that has lost its claws. Despite its lack of claws, however, the crawfish is well able to defend itself. To scare away enemies it can produce a creaking noise with its jointed antennae. It has been discovered that crawfish also 'creak' at each other when mating.

In order to catch and consume its prey in the absence of pincers, the crawfish has a kind of 'shell-opener', which looks something like the blade of a knife and by means of which the crawfish prises shellfish off the rocks and breaks them open.

Crawfish live on rocky coasts in moderate, sub-tropical and tropical waters. In summer, they can usually be found at depths of between 30 and 100 m (100–330 ft) but in winter they go deeper. They usually hunt for food (shellfish and other small animals, both dead and alive) at night. By day, they hide in clefts in the rock or in coral reefs with only their thin antennae protruding into the water to monitor their immediate surroundings.

During the mating season, crawfish head for shallow water. Immediately before mating, the females shed their shells. The eggs are laid only every other year. They are orange to coral-red in

A guaranteed method of testing whether a crawfish is alive before you buy it is to touch the protective horns above the eyes. A fresh, live crawfish will immediately wriggle.

colour and are carried under the tail. The females seek out a calm bay for spawning, so that the spawn can develop in peace.

Since crawfish tend to hide in inaccessible places during the day, fishing methods are unusual and varied. Sometimes they are caught by divers (mainly in tropical waters) but usually they are trapped in baskets tied to ropes. The fishing season extends from April to late September. Often – as in Ireland and the United States – crawfish and lobster are caught, packed and transported together.

Spiny Lobster
(Palinurus mauretanicus), Fr. Langouste Rose, Langouste du Portugal, Ger. Portugiesische Languste, Mauretanische Languste, Afrikanische Languste, Rote Languste, Port. Lagosta
This crawfish grows to 75 cm (30 in) long and to 5–6 kg (11–13 lb) in weight. The thorny shell is a light brick-red, without spots. It has striking antennae, with clearly defined red and white rings, and irregular, light-coloured spots along the edges of the tail section. Its area of distribution overlaps that of the European Thorny Lobster on the Atlantic coasts of Portugal and North Africa and the Mediterranean, but this crawfish is also found as far south as the mouth of the Congo River. They like to live among rocks at greater depths than the European crawfish (around 100 m/330 ft).

Thorny Lobster, Spiny Lobster
(Palinurus elephas, formerly P. vulgaris), Fr. Langouste Rouge, Langouste Bretonne, Ger. Europäische Languste, Stachelhummer, Ital. Aragosta, 'Grillo di Mare' (Venice), Port. Lagosta Vulgar, Span. Langosta
The Thorny Lobster of Europe differs from other crawfish in its two rows of white flecks on the tail section, arranged one on either side of each tail segment. The Thorny Lobster is also a much deeper red in colour and has dark-red rings on its antennae. It can grow to 45 cm (18 in)

You can get some idea of the freshness of a crawfish simply by looking at it. The tail should always be rolled inwards. When you pick the crawfish up, it should beat its tail about vigorously. If it also makes a creaking noise, you can be sure it is absolutely fresh. Crawfish are embedded in damp wood shavings for transportation. Gourmets insist that they should first be wrapped in paper to prevent the smell of the wood from spoiling the delicate flavour of the meat.

The Spiny Lobster is inferior in quality to the Thorny Lobster. One easy way of distinguishing between the two is to remember that this crawfish has no white spots on the tail section. The Spiny Lobster is one of the largest species in its family and full-grown specimens can weigh up to 6 kg (13 lb); they are usually sold before they grow so large, however, when they reach 800–1,500 g (1¾–3¼ lb).

long. It is found from Scotland and southern England, along the French Atlantic coast, to the Mediterranean and the Atlantic coast of north-west Africa. It likes shallower water than the Spiny Lobster and is usually found between 40 and 70 m (130–230 ft).

Florida Spiny Lobster
(Panulirus argus), Fr. Langouste Brune, Ger. Amerikanische Languste
This American crawfish is found in greatest numbers along the Atlantic coast from North Carolina to Mexico, but it is also widespread throughout the west Atlantic from the Bermudas and Bahamas to the Caribbean (especially Cuba) and along the coasts of Central America to Rio de Janeiro.

In shape and colour it is similar to the European and African species, but the Florida Spiny Lobster has the large white flecks on only the second and sixth tail segments. At around eleven to twelve years old, the body length reaches up to 45 cm (18 in) and the weight around 4 kg (9 lb). The antennae can be up to 70 cm (27 in) long.

One peculiarity of this species is its seasonal migration; hundreds of these crawfish goose-step as much as 100 km (60 miles) across the sea-bed to reach an area with better food. This means that huge catches can sometimes be made in areas where crawfish were previously unknown.

These normally nocturnal creatures go on their migratory march during the day. It was discovered a few years ago that crawfish have a special noise which they make during migration.

The United States imports crawfish from Mexico, Japan, South Africa, Australia, New Zealand and a few Caribbean countries, with the tails usually reaching the shops in cans or frozen. In the United States more than anywhere else, crawfish are regarded as an integral part of the lobster industry.

California Spiny Lobster
(Panulirus interruptus), Fr. Langouste Californienne, Ger. Pazifische Languste, Span. Langosta Roja
One of the crawfish from the North American Pacific coast (chiefly off California and the west coast of Mexico). This species differs slightly from that described above in the construction of its tail sections and the shape of its head. It is considerably longer than European and African crawfish.

Painted Rock Lobster
(Panulirus versicolor), Fr. Langouste Verte, Ger. Grüne Languste, Japanische Languste, Malay. Karang, Indon. Udang Barong
This crawfish is distinguishable from those already described by its much longer, tapering antennae and its striking coloration. Its deep greens and blues are emphasised by a white line along the rear edge of each tail segment and white stripes on the legs. Although they are by no means smaller than other crawfish, they prefer shallower waters – between 5 and 30 m (15–100 ft). They are found on the east coast of Africa, the northern coast of Australia and in warm Pacific waters.

Western Rock Lobster, Crayfish
(Panulirus cygnus), Fr. Langouste Australienne, Ger. Australische Languste
A crayfish found mainly on the west coast of Australia. There is nothing unusual about its shape and size, or its deep-red colour. The only slight distinction is in the formation of the head and tail. This species can weigh up to 4.5 kg (10 lb) but most of those caught tend to be around 500 g (18 oz).

Egg-carrying crawfish should never come onto the market, but if you should happen to get one this is a great bonus, for the eggs are excellent in sauces. There is some controversy over whether the best meat comes from the male or the female. Female crawfish have large, flat legs on the tail, under which they carry their eggs. In the male, these legs are narrow.

The best European crawfish are caught on the west coast of Ireland, an area which provides us with both lobster and crawfish of excellent quality. While crawfish of 3–4 kg (6–9 lb) are not caught every day, they are by no means rare (see right). Typical of the European Lobster are the light spots on either side of the tail segments.

Crawfish

are a delicacy all over the world. They are found in varying sizes and colours in every ocean. They are valued everywhere for their excellent flavour and this demand has depleted worldwide stocks. With modern farming methods, however, it is to be hoped that we will be able to continue to enjoy these delicious crustaceans far into the future.

The American Crawfish is very similar to the European one. The only difference is that the typical white spots are found only on the second and sixth tail segments. It is usually the tails only (sold as lobster tails) that are exported frozen to Europe, mainly from Cuba.

Ornate Rock Lobster

*(Panulirus ornatus), Fr.
Langouste Ornée, Ger.
Ornatlanguste*

This crawfish, found throughout the Indo-Pacific region, is green in colour with white lines on the two pairs of hind legs and the tail segments. The shell is more irregular than that of most crawfish and the first third of the white antennae is tuberous. These crawfish like stony or rocky sea-beds at depths of up to 50 m (165 ft).

Cape Crayfish, Rock Lobster

(Jasus lalandii), Fr. Langouste du Cap, Ger. Kaplanguste, Afrikanische Languste, Rote Languste

This type of crayfish is found all along the coast of South Africa but is most numerous on the west coast. It is of great commercial importance in South Africa, with production running at 6,500 tonnes (6,384 tons) per annum, 90 per cent of which is exported. The Cape Crayfish is usually sold fresh (after being stored in cages on the sea-bed) but some are sold canned.

Like most other lobsters, the Cape Crayfish lives amongst

Painted Rock Lobster is the name of this colourful crawfish. In its native Asia, it is prized more for its flavour than its colour. Even boiled, it is still visually attractive.

The most attractive crawfish (shown here, *Panulirus polyphagus*) are caught on tropical coasts. The fishermen of Panyee, a picturesque village built on piles on the west coast of Thailand, catch them without traps or nets. In Asia, crawfish are widely sold on the home market and bring quite high prices. Far-Eastern cuisine makes much of crawfish in delicious variations.

rocks. Since it grows very slowly – taking thirty to forty years to reach its maximum length of around 40 cm (16 in) – stocks could easily be depleted, so for several years strict fishing regulations have been in force. The species may be caught only between November and June and then only if the shell is at least 89 mm ($3\frac{1}{2}$ in) long. It takes about nine years for the crayfish to reach this size. They are sexually mature when their carapace reaches 70 mm ($2\frac{3}{4}$ in) for males and 80 mm ($3\frac{1}{4}$ in) for females. The prescribed minimum length of 89 mm ($3\frac{1}{2}$ in) therefore guarantees that they will have been capable of reproduction before being caught.

A smaller version of the Cape Crayfish is found on the south-west coast of Africa. In Luderitz Bay, in Namibia, natives and settlers use a trick in catching them which makes use of their inherent rivalry. Shellfish or other bait which crayfish like are attached to a large wire or plastic ring. This is suspended in the water from rocks or a boat. Only when two or three crayfish have taken the bait is it pulled out of the water, since rivalry will then prevent any of them from relinquishing the bait, whereas a crayfish on its own will let go when the ring is pulled up.

Eastern Crayfish, Sydney Crayfish, Rock Lobster

(Jasus verreauxi), Fr. Langouste Tasmane, Ger. Ostaustralische Languste

This is the largest crayfish in the world (weighing over 7.5 kg/16 lb!). It resembles the Cape Crayfish, but lives in the moderate waters off the south coast of Australia and New Zealand.

SLIPPER OR SQUAT LOBSTERS

(Scyllaridae)

The slipper or squat lobsters, a family containing over fifty different species, all have a relatively flattened body. The shell of the upper body is wide, with sharply toothed edges. The five pairs of legs end in claws. Unlike the

The Eastern Crayfish, a member of the *Jasus* family, is usually exported to world markets from New Zealand and Australia as frozen 'lobster tails'. Live ones are occasionally flown to Europe.

crawfish with their elongated, thin antennae, the antennae in squat lobsters are reduced to short, wide plates of shell, pointed at the front and sides. These are thought to have some purpose in warding off enemies and are also used for digging when searching for food. Two short feelers ending in claws extend from the centre of the nose. The eyes are inset under the edge of the shell.

Squat lobsters like to live in coastal rocks, especially under overhangs into which they crawl headfirst. They are also found in coral reefs.

The species *Thenus*, *Parribacus* and *Ibacus* are found in the Indo-Pacific.

Slipper Lobster, Squat Lobster, Scyllarian

(Scyllarides latus), *Fr. La Grande Cigale, Cigale de Mer, Ger. Großer Bärenkrebs, Ital. Cicala di Mare, Magnosa, Port. Lagosta da Pedra*
The Slipper Lobster is rust-red on the top with a yellow underside. On the first tail segment behind the breastplate are two striking red spots, which continue into rings on the legs. This species can grow up to 45 cm (18 in) in length and to around 2 kg (4½ lb) in weight. They are found throughout the Mediterranean and the warm-to-moderate east Atlantic, often close to shore in up to 10 m (33 ft) of water. Slipper Lobsters are generally caught less frequently than other large crustaceans.

For those in the know, the meat of the Slipper Lobster is a real delicacy. Since it often finds its way into the nets of fishermen looking for other catches, it is often undervalued, but its tail meat is actually extremely tasty.

Small Slipper Lobster, Squat Lobster, Scyllarian

(Scyllarus arctus), *Fr. La Petite Cigale, Ger. Kleiner Bärenkrebs, Ital. Cicala di Mare, Magnosella, Span. Cigala, Cangrejo, Port. Lagosta da Pedra*
The Small Slipper Lobster has the same clumsy shape as its larger cousin. The back is deep-brown with a red fleck at the centre front of each tail segment, but the colour can change for camouflage. These creatures prefer to live on stones or coarse sediment at depths of 5–25 m (15–80 ft).

The Small Slipper Lobster is 7–12 cm (3–5 in) long. They live in the Mediterranean and nearby eastern Atlantic. These lobsters are very popular locally; they are usually cut in half lengthways and grilled before eating.

LOBSTERS
(*Homaridae/Nephropsidae*)

The lobster resembles the fresh-water crayfish in external appearance. The right pincer is usually thicker and more highly developed, since it is this one that is chiefly used for holding and cracking food or enemies. The other pincer is narrower and is used to break up the prey and carry it to the mouth.

Some lobsters, however, do have the powerful pincer on the left. These are either 'left-handed' lobsters or those that have lost their right pincer at an early age, so that the left develops into a cracking pincer to replace it. In older creatures, the pincer regrows in its original shape after the shell has been cast.

Lobsters like cooler waters and a rocky sea-bed. Their colour varies from region to region to match that of their habitat. The back may range in colour from a marbled blue, through greenish-blue to dark violet. The sides and underside are yellowish, spotted with red. Old lobsters, especially from American waters, can grow up to 70 cm (27 in) long and over 9 kg (20 lb) in weight.

As with all crustaceans, lobsters shed their shells periodically as they grow, more frequently when young than when they are mature (nine times in the first year, four times in the third year, every two years when adult). As soon as these greedy creatures put on weight, a kind of leathery skin forms beneath the shell, until the growing body eventually cracks the shell. Within the space

The Asian Slipper Lobster, *Thenus*, known in Australia as the Moreton Bay Bug, is very popular locally but not considered 'marketable'. It is rarely to be found on sale – probably because the tail, which contains the most delicious meat, is small by comparison with the body.

In zoological terms, *Homarus americanus* and *Homarus gammarus* differ only in minor details. When they are sold, the main differences are those of age or size: The Northern Lobster (above right) usually has larger, more fleshy claws and a wider tail than the European Lobster (above left).

of half an hour, the lobster arches its back to split open the shell and then crawls out. After shedding its natural protection, the lobster crawls into a hole in the rock. It takes about three weeks for the skin to harden into a new, made-to-measure shell.

The lobster is a timid animal that hides in holes and under stones by day and searches for food by night. In summer it lives near the coast, in winter at depths of up to 50 m (165 ft).

Since they grow very slowly, lobsters are not sexually mature until the age of six. By this time, the males are about 18 cm (7 in) long, the females slightly larger. Their average weight is around 350 g (12 oz). To guard against overfishing, most countries have introduced regulations which prohibit catching lobsters smaller than 21 cm (8 in) long. If small fry end up in the nets or baskets, they must be returned to the sea.

Female lobsters spawn every

other year and carry an enormous number of eggs under their tails – often up to 100,000. Once the larvae have hatched, it takes from two to three weeks for them to develop into young lobsters. This process takes slightly longer in colder waters.

Lobsters are most meaty just before they cast their shells and during the following month or two. The claws of the male are especially sought-after, as they contain more meat than those of the female. On the other hand, the tail of the female is slightly wider (and more fleshy) than that of the male. In many parts of the world, the female tail is considered the greatest delicacy.

Lobsters are usually caught in baskets lowered into the water on ropes. These baskets widen out from the opening so that the lobster can get in but not out. In some places, the lobsters are caught in trawl nets.

Since lobsters are normally sold live, they must be stored and transported accordingly. Great

care is necessary to avoid damaging them in transit. Methods of storage are very similar throughout Europe, the United States and Canada; the only difference is in the size of the containers used. Once the lobster is caught, its pincers are tied together to prevent it hurting the others. Then they are stored in wooden or plastic cases at the sea's edge. Slats in the cases allow the water to flow through to provide the lobsters with constant, fresh seawater. In Europe, these cases hold only a few dozen lobsters at most, while those in the United States and Canada can hold as many as 4,000.

The live lobsters are transported in cases, strong cartons or plastic bags, with ventilation holes. The boxes are packed with straw or wood shavings or occasionally sawdust. When the lobsters are being sent to a very hot country, ice is placed under the straw or wood shavings. Long distances are usually covered by air. When lobsters are sent in large, closed canisters, they are packed in chemically prepared water which gradually gives off oxygen. Packed in this way, lobsters can be sent as far as from Canada to Australia.

European Lobster

(Homarus gammarus, formerly H. vulgaris), Fr. Homard Européen, Ger. Europäischer Hummer, Ital. Astice, Lupo di Mare, Elefante di Mare, Span. Bogavante, Lubrigante, Port. Lavagante, Dut. Zeekreeft, Nor./Swed./Dan. Hummer

The largest crustacean in European seas (it can grow to 60 cm/23 in long and 5–6 kg/11–13 lb in weight). Its area of distribution extends from the Norwegian, Swedish and Danish coasts to France. Most European Lobster are fished in seas around Britain. This lobster is also found around the coasts of Portugal, Spain and the Mediterranean. In northern waters, its limit is set by a water temperature of 5°C (41°F).

The meat of this crustacean has long been popular. Since demand has continued to rise in recent years and some traditional fishing grounds, such as those around Heligoland, are almost fished out, the European lobster today supplies only 50 per cent of demand, with catches standing at between 3,000 and 4,000 tonnes (2,945–3,930 tons) per annum. Europe therefore imports lobsters from the United States and Canada. France also imports from Britain, where the demand is less.

Northern Lobster

(Homarus americanus), Fr. Homard Américain, Ger. Amerikanischer Hummer

This lobster, found on the east coast of the United States from Labrador to North Carolina, is very similar to the European Lobster. It is slightly larger, ranging from greenish-blue to reddish-brown in colour, with dark green speckles on the shell. The Northern Lobster is of greater commercial importance than the European Lobster, for not only is much of the European demand supplied from the USA and Canada, but there is also a huge market for it in North America itself. Around 40,000 tonnes (39,285 tons) a year are caught, chiefly off Newfoundland and Maine. The state of

Female lobsters taste better! This is the opinion of gourmets who prize the deep-red roe, known as the 'coral', as a special delicacy. Seen from above, it is difficult to tell males from females. Females have a slightly wider tail, but you can only see this if you have a male to hand for comparison.

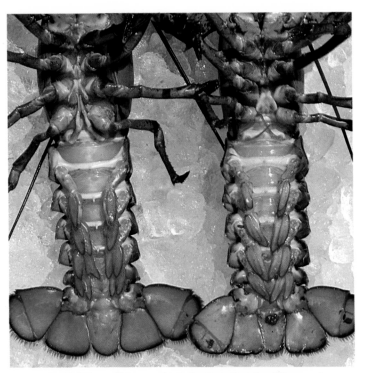

Male or female? You will have to look closely to find the difference. In males, the first pair of hind legs have changed into small, pointed rods which function as reproductive organs. Here (above left), they are folded forwards under the body. In the female (above right), this pair of legs is still present but much smaller. The other, flatter rear legs are used for carrying the eggs.

Maine is famous for its lobster, supplying all the great American cities, with an enormous tonnage going to New York. To guarantee a regular supply, there are large storage facilities on the Canadian coast, the main one being at St Andrews, where several hundred tonnes of live lobsters are kept in salt-water tanks.

Despite the huge American market, trade in lobster is even greater in Canada. The Canadian lobster market is the greatest in the world and lobster is one of the mainstays of the entire Canadian fishing industry. Trade in live lobsters is not only extremely lucrative, it is also capable of expansion. It is much cheaper and easier, however, to export boiled or frozen lobsters. Almost two-thirds of Canadian lobster production goes, live or boiled, to the USA, France or Belgium. In Canada itself, there is a large market for selected lobster meat, either frozen or canned. Only the best meat is used for this. In many places, lobster is divided into two grades: 100 per cent lobster or 50 per cent lobster/50 per cent best-quality fish. If the fish content exceeds 50 per cent, it may no longer be sold as 'lobster'.

With such a huge industry and so much foreign currency depending on one single crustacean, it is hardly surprising that large areas on the American and Canadian coasts have been overfished. To overcome this problem, great efforts have been made to promote artificial farming. Since lobsters grow very slowly, it is still too early to predict whether these efforts will prove commercially successful.

The market leader: Northern Lobster

When you go into a good restaurant in Europe to eat lobster, there is about a 50/50 chance that you will be served a lobster flown in from the North American Atlantic coast. Its European relative, *Homarus gammarus*, has long been unable to answer demand on its own and as a result a highly frequented airbridge has been established across the North Atlantic to fill the gap with American lobster.

The Northern Lobster is by far the most hardy species on the market. Although relatively strict regulations have had to be introduced to protect stocks, it can still be found in huge numbers. It is most plentiful in Canadian waters, off Newfoundland and Labrador, so that Canada now has the largest lobster industry in the world. They even supply those great lobster-eaters, the Americans, although American production is equally impressive. Maine, the northernmost of the New England states on the American Atlantic coast, is famous for its Northern Lobster. It began to be fished commercially there as early as 1840. At that time, with no refrigeration, it could be sold only fresh on the spot, but by 1854 it was possible to can and export lobster meat.

Today, Maine Lobster is not only famous, it is also extremely popular in America. This is to some extent due to the fact that it is caught in such numbers that it is relatively inexpensive, although it is still the most expensive crustacean in America. In Europe, the difference in price between the more expensive European Lobster and the cheaper Northern Lobster is equalled out by freight costs. Large-scale imports from the United States and Canada have done nothing to change the fact that, in Europe, lobster is an extremely expensive delicacy.

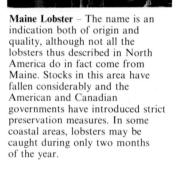

Maine Lobster – The name is an indication both of origin and quality, although not all the lobsters thus described in North America do in fact come from Maine. Stocks in this area have fallen considerably and the American and Canadian governments have introduced strict preservation measures. In some coastal areas, lobsters may be caught during only two months of the year.

Relocating their own baskets is no problem for fishermen, for all the buoys are marked with personal colour codes. The same symbol must be clearly displayed on his boat, so that checks can be made that he is raising only his own baskets.

The minimum size laid down under the protection measures of the American state of Maine must be strictly followed. Any lobster caught must measure at least 80 mm ($3\frac{1}{4}$ in) from the eyes to the end of the breastplate, otherwise it has to be returned to the water. This minimum length corresponds to a weight of 500–600 g (18–21 oz). Lobsters of this size are known as 'one portion lobsters'.

Lobster fishing is the work of small, independent fishermen working from motor boats. They sink 300 to 400 lobster baskets off the coast, marking them with buoys. The baskets are checked at regular intervals.

Not every basket holds a lobster, or at least, not one of suitable size; more often than not they contain starfish, sea urchins or a Jonah Crab. Unless the fisherman wants them for his own consumption, such creatures are usually returned to the water.

Bait must be attractive to lobsters and the fishermen know what they like. Fish carcasses are tied with string or wired to the inside of the basket. In some areas, pieces of fresh cow hide are used as bait or cans of cat food with holes pierced in them, for these can be used over a long period of time.

One compartment of the basket holds a lobster large enough for sale, but a second lobster is too small and has to go back into the sea. The second compartment is filled with fresh bait.

A wooden wedge prevents the lobster from using its claws. Regrettably, this method is still widespread in America. The wedge, which is pushed into the joint of the pincer, causes not only pain but also inflammation and disease if left in for long.

The gourmet's favourite: European Lobster

Gourmets on both sides of the Atlantic agree that lobster is one of the finest culinary delicacies in the world. Only the crawfish has been able to make any impression on the lobster's long-standing reputation.

Since modern transportation methods brought *Homarus americanus* onto the European market, the European Lobster has been faced with competition from a member of its own family. European gourmets were called upon to decide which was best. Naturally, they chose our native lobster, yet the Northern Lobster is eaten in far greater numbers. European Lobster stocks fall far short of demand. Many of the former European Lobster fishing areas have been fished empty; only Ireland, England and Scotland still hold good stocks, although supplies from Norway are increasing.

Especially fine European Lobsters come from the west coast or Ireland, fetching high prices on the European market. Ben Hugmann, buying agent and exporter, goes round the fishing villages of Connemara every week in summer to buy fresh lobster. When he arrives, as here in Letterfrack, it is a special day for the local fishermen.

European Lobster is therefore still available, throughout the year, even though the summer months are the real lobster season. In Ireland, for example – while there are no time limits on fishing and lobster could, in theory, be caught throughout the year – good catches tend to take place in the summer. Fish merchants keep lobster in seawater vats to ensure a continuous supply, but it is a fact that the quality of the lobster deteriorates the longer it is kept in the vats. Since lobsters take in no food in captivity, they are living on their own reserves; it follows that in the months preceding the new fishing season, i.e. in the spring, you will not get top quality lobster.

An egg-carrying female should, in theory, not be caught at all, yet lobsters like this one, carrying thousands of eggs, repeatedly come onto the market. The potential loss to lobster stocks is self-evident. Fishermen have a brilliant excuse – when the tail is folded under, the eggs cannot be seen.

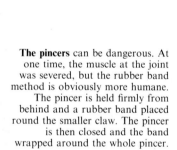

The pincers can be dangerous. At one time, the muscle at the joint was severed, but the rubber band method is obviously more humane. The pincer is held firmly from behind and a rubber band placed round the smaller claw. The pincer is then closed and the band wrapped around the whole pincer.

'German writing' is the name given by Irish fishermen to this strange-shaped growth on lobster shells. It is, indeed, reminiscent of the ornate style of Gothic type. The growths are the homes of small worms, and have had sufficient time to form on this adult lobster because it has not shed its shell for some time. The small, round formations on the head and pincers are made by Sea Pocks. Neither of these creatures has any effect on the quality of the lobster meat.

The Norway Lobster or Dublin Bay Prawn is better known by its Italian name of *Scampo* (plural: Scampi). This delicious member of the lobster family is often confused with the Giant Prawn (see page 14), although they are by no means similar in appearance.

Scampi, Danish or Norway Lobster, Dublin Bay Prawn, Lobsterette

(Nephrops norvegicus), Fr. Langoustine, Scampi, Ger. Kaisergranat, Tiefseekrebs, Scampi, Swed. Havskräfta, Dut. Diepzee Kreeft, Noorse Kreeft, Span. Lagostino, Maganto, Port. Lagostim, Ital. Scampo, Scampolo

Compared to its relative, the lobster, this creature has a much narrower body, is shorter and has thinner pincers. The claw itself takes up only the top third of the first segment of the limb. The top of the narrow pincer is angular, with light-coloured nodules along the inside edge which continue onto the inside edge of the pincer itself. Scampi have a pair of antennae, longer than the pincers, and a pair of shorter, pronged feelers. The shell is fairly smooth and, like the claws, a uniform salmon-pink in colour. The two front pairs of legs end in small pincers, while the hind legs end in claws. The pincered legs are a deeper red. Unlike darker-coloured crustaceans, Scampi scarcely change colour during cooking.

Since the claws are of no culinary interest, the tails alone are usually sold, although occasionally you will find whole Scampi, fresh or boiled. Scampi are often sold under the misleading name of 'crawfish tails'. It is, however, impossible to confuse Scampi with crawfish or slipper lobsters, for the tails of these species are much wider and have thick, dark-coloured, speckled shells with characteristic grooves.

In the trade, the tails of Mantis Shrimps are often sold as Scampi, for they are not dissimilar, although they do not have the same characteristic grooving.

Scampi vary in length according to their sex. Males can measure 24 cm ($9\frac{1}{2}$ in) from the rostrum to the fanned tail, but females rarely exceed 20 cm (8 in). On average, Scampi are between 12 cm (5 in) and 14 cm ($5\frac{1}{2}$ in) in length.

As the Latin name indicates, Scampi were first identified in Norway, but they can be found along the entire Atlantic coast from the North Cape to Morocco, as well as in the western Mediterranean and the Adriatic. The main catches are made between southern Norway and England, between Ireland and the French coast and in the Adriatic.

These creatures like a soft, silty sea-bed at depths of 50–800 m (165–2,625 ft). Like the lobster, the Scampi is nocturnal, protecting itself by day by burrowing into the silt and hunting its prey by night. Sexual maturity occurs between the ages of three and five, when the Scampi are 8–10 cm (3–4 in) long. Females spawn only every other year and the eggs are fertilised after spawning. As with most other lobster-like crustaceans, the eggs are carried beneath the tail until the larvae hatch after eight to nine months. The first changes of shell occur at brief intervals, so that after the third change the Scampi are around 11 mm ($\frac{1}{2}$ in) long.

Scampi are caught mainly in trawl nets. In the north, it is customary to boil them on board ship and to separate the tails. The European catch is around 15,000 tonnes (14,730 tons) per year; half of this is caught by French fishermen.

Scampi also follow the rule that applies to many crustaceans: the colder the water in which they live, the finer the flavour. So the most sought-after Scampi are those from Iceland, Scotland and Ireland.

FRESHWATER CRAYFISH

There are over 300 different crustaceans in the world found only in freshwater and 250 of these are native to North America. In the state of Louisiana alone, there are 29 different species. In Africa and much of Asia, on the other hand, freshwater crayfish are practically non-existent; instead, they have freshwater crabs.

The largest crayfish in the world, which can weigh up to 6 kg (13 lb), is found on the Australian island of Tasmania, while the smallest (found in America) measures only 3 cm (1 in) long. The main crayfish families are the *Astacidae*, the *Cambaridae* and the *Parastacidae*. While the *Astacidae* and *Cambaridae* are found only in the northern hemisphere, the *Parastacidae* are native to the southern hemisphere. The main European crayfish are the Freshwater Crayfish (*Astacus astacus* and *Astacus leptodactylus*), the Crayfish (*Austropotamobius torrentium* and, in some areas, *Pacifastacus leniusculus*) and the Cambarus Crayfish (*Orconectes limosus*).

In the United States, crayfish are of great economic importance. The main types there are *Pacifastacus*, the Louisiana Swamp Crayfish (*Procambarus clarkii*) the Cambarus Crayfish (*Cambarus*) and *Cambarellus*. They live mainly in lakes or slow-flowing rivers and in marshland. Many hide among stones or water plants; others dig holes, sometimes out of the water near a lake or river. Tunnels lead downwards to open out into a water-filled chamber below the level of the water table. Other passages are often used to store food.

The tunnels are dug with the pincers, which are pushed into the soil like forks. Displaced soil is taken to the tunnel entrance and packed down with the claws to form the characteristic 'chimney' of dried soil, which is often as high as 30 cm (1 ft). At times of drought and in winter, the crayfish seals the entrance from the inside. At other times, it comes out at night to search for food.

Nowadays, crayfish are available throughout the year. Overfishing and disease have almost completely wiped out some species, but crayfish are now being successfully farmed in various parts of the world.

The two American types which sell best, *Pacifastacus* and the Louisiana Swamp Crayfish, are widely farmed. Louisiana produces an amazing 4,500,000 kg (10,000,000 lb) of farmed crayfish per year and farming is now on the increase in Missouri, Texas, Mississippi, Alabama and Arkansas.

Methods of trapping and transporation tend to vary from one continent to another, but some methods are universal. In many places, crayfish are caught with crayfish 'plates'. These are round nets fastened to a metal or willow ring. The bait, usually fish or frogmeat, is fixed in the centre of the ring. The plates are placed on the river bed and held from the bank by a rope. When it is pulled in, the net tightens to prevent the crayfish from escaping. Crayfish baskets of wire mesh or thread are also used and willow eel-pots are also suitable.

Live crayfish can be transported in various ways. Two of the main methods are as follows: Plastic bags are filled with crayfish, oxygen and water in equal proportions and placed in padded, solid boxes. When transported by air, the bags are not filled too full, to allow for differences in pressure.

More frequently, crayfish are transported layered in damp, shredded paper in 5 kg (11 lb) boxes. Wood shavings are not as good as paper, for the smell of the wood can get into the crayfish. Crayfish can survive for up to 48 hours out of water. In hot weather, plastic bags full of ice are included just before despatch.

Crayfish of the Northern Hemisphere (*Astacidae/Cambaridae*)

Freshwater Crayfish
(*Astacus astacus*), *Fr. Ecrevisse, Ger. Edelkrebs, Solokrebs, Ital. Gambero di Fiume, Span. Cancrejo de Rio, Dut. Rivierkreeft*
This species, coloured olive-green, grey-black or brown, sometimes with a bluish shimmer, has a wide, thick breastplate of similar length to the tail. The pincers, which are reddish on the underside, are strong and symmetrical. The feelers are shorter than the body, often no longer than the breastplate. They are usually longer in males than in females. The first pair of legs (*pereiopodes*) end in small pincers, the two rear pairs in claws. The male grows to 15 cm (6 in) long and around 140 g (5 oz) in weight, while the female is 12–13 cm (5 in) long and 80–100 g (3–4 oz).

At one time, freshwater crayfish could be found throughout Europe, from western Russia, southern Scandinavia and England to the Balkans. They like clean, oxygenated, chalky, slow-flowing rivers or lakes with a not-too-silty bed. They avoid fast-flowing or cold water.

They not only hide from enemies after casting their shell (ten to fourteen days) but also seek refuge at other times amid vegetation, under stones and in holes in the ground. The crayfish also burrows into the river bank if the soil is not too hard, using his tail as a shovel. These tunnels are between 15 and 20 cm (6–8 in) long and the same width as the crayfish.

Only at dusk will the crayfish come out of hiding to look for food – worms, insects, small fish and other water creatures. They also feed on water plants. Mature, strong males will attack females or young crayfish, or even other adult males who have cast their shells.

Like all lobster species, the crayfish carries its eggs under its tail until the young hatch. The hatched young, the front parts of whose bodies are still full of yolk, remain attached to the mother until the yolk is used up.

Since crayfish disease first appeared in Europe over a hundred years ago (1878), stocks have been decimated and despite efforts to replace them with the more resistant American Crayfish numbers have never returned to previous levels. Attempts have also been made to farm crayfish in disused gravel pits or other enclosed waters free of scavenging fish, but these have met with only limited success to date.

Boiled crayfish. On the left is *Astacus astacus* with its powerful pincers; on the right, *Astacus leptodactylus*. The latter is the most widely sold crayfish nowadays, although it does not compare with the former in either flavour or meat content.

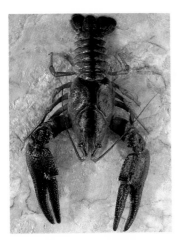

The Freshwater Crayfish (*Astacus astacus*) is rarely found for sale. It is seldom caught but if you should see it on offer don't hesitate to buy. The meat, especially that of the huge claws, has an excellent flavour.

Crayfish disease has not only affected stocks, it has also increased water pollution. There are no statistics available on catches or stocks. According to a survey carried out in West Germany in 1962, the total catch of all types of crayfish was no more than 1,618 kg (3,560 lb), only a small percentage of which was composed of *Astacus astacus*. In contrast, it is estimated that at the turn of the century several hundred tons of crayfish were caught in Germany every year. In 1870, crayfish was still an everyday food. Sixty crayfish, each 80 g (3 oz) in weight, cost 30 to 40 pfennigs. By 1925, the price had risen by a factor of more than 50, to 17 to 25 marks. Today, these crayfish are an extremely expensive delicacy.

(Astacus leptodactylus), *Fr. Ecrevisse*, *Ger. Galizierkrebs, Teichkrebs, Sumpfkrebs, Schmalscherenkrebs*
This crayfish has several notable features which distinguish it from other European or North American crayfish. The greyish-olive green shell is considerably lighter and the underside, legs and the tips of the pincers have a reddish shimmer. It has unusually elongated, narrow claws (which con-

tain little meat) and long antennae. The shell and claws are rough, like emery paper. The breastplate juts out more than those of other crayfish and is relatively soft.

Like all other members of its family, this crayfish turns red when boiled. The colour pigmentation of the shell consists of a blue which is not heat-resistant and a red which is, so that the red is not destroyed by boiling.

Astacus leptodactylus is found in eastern Europe, in the European and central Asian regions of the Soviet Union to the Urals, as well as in the Middle East and south-central Asia, including the Caspian Sea. It is also found to a limited extent in German waters, as it is immune to crayfish disease. In northern Germany, particularly Schleswig Holstein, these crayfish have been imported from Turkey but are used for fattening rather than breeding.

Through canals linked to the Volga, the Freshwater Crayfish has also found its way to the Gulf of Finland and Gulf of Bothnia. It is found as far out as the brackish water at the mouths of large rivers. It is unusual in that it seeks its prey by day and night, which means that it can be caught in daylight. Reproduction and growth are quicker than is the case with *Astacus astacus*, but this may be due to different climatic and water conditions.

Today, this crayfish plays an important role in supplying demand in France, Germany and Scandinavia. The main source of supply is Turkey, where a successful crayfish fishing industry has been established in the lakes around Bursa. The crayfish are kept in water in 5-kg (11-lb) baskets until sold. The main customer is France where, unlike Germany and Scandinavia, the preference is for smaller crayfish of 50–60 g (2–2½ oz). Crayfish from eastern Turkey and the Iranian border are usually sent to Istanbul for shelling and freezing. To protect the crayfish and the industry which has been built up around it, Turkey has introduced close seasons, which vary from

year to year. In the 1960s, the close season lasted for only one month but today it extends from early January to mid-June. Nevertheless, Turkish crayfish are becoming increasingly smaller, now averaging around 60 g (2½ oz) compared with 80–100 g (3–4 oz) twenty years ago.

Crayfish

(Austropotamobius pallipes), *Fr. Ecrevisse*, *Ger. Dohlenkrebs*
A relative of *Astacus astacus* found in cold, fast-flowing rivers of western Europe, including Switzerland, France and other Mediterranean countries, and Britain. Only in Italy and Spain is it of any commercial importance and there the market is a local one. In the Iberian peninsula, central England and Ireland it is the only native crayfish found.

(Austropotamobius torrentium), *Fr. Ecrevisse*, *Ger. Steinkrebs*
This crayfish, which is a protected species in Germany, is similar in shape to *Astacus astacus* but is rarely longer than 7–8 cm (3 in). They prefer mountain lakes and clear-flowing rivers with a sandy or rocky bed. They are found in the mountains of central Germany to the Mosel, in the lower Alps of northern and eastern Switzerland, and in the Austrian Alps and the Balkans. This crayfish is too small to be of any commercial significance.

(Pacifastacus leniusculus), *Fr. Ecrevisse*, *Ger. Signalkrebs*
Originally from California, this crayfish from the *Astacidae* family is a native of North America. It gets its German name from the white or bluish-green stripes on the pincer joints. With its wide tail, it is similar in shape to *Astacus astacus*, although it is usually larger. Colour ranges from greenish-black to reddish-green with a light brown underside.

In America, this crayfish inhabits high, cold mountain lakes at depths of up to 40 m (130 ft). Its distribution is limited to a coastal strip between the Pacific and the Rocky Mountains. The quality of this crayfish and its

Pacifastacus leniusculus is easily distinguishable from other crayfish with its white or bluish-green stripes on the pincer joints. This is an American native but occasionally finds its way onto the European market.

suitability to the prevailing conditions caused the Swedish fishing federation to stock Swedish lakes with large numbers of them to replace the once-common *Astacus astacus*, especially in lakes too cold for the European Crayfish.

There are differing opinions on whether it is worthwhile to introduce this crayfish into Europe. At present, they may be introduced only into enclosed waters and then only when it can be shown that they cannot get out to spread further afield. In German lakes and rivers, both warm and cold, this crayfish has shown itself to be more resilient than *Astacus astacus*.

As far as eating quality is concerned, *Pacifastacus leniusculus* is an excellent representative of the family and is one of the most popular of the American crayfish.

Cambarus Crayfish

(Orconectes limosus, formerly *Cambarus affinis)*, *Fr. Ecrevisse*, *Ger. Amerikanischer Flußkrebs, Kamberkrebs*
The *Cambarus* family includes over seventy species. The Cambarus Crayfish, at 7–10 cm (3–4 in) long, is relatively small. The breastplate is relatively narrow and the antennae short. The pincers are slightly stunted and

The Red Swamp Crayfish (*Procambarus clarkii*) is a hardy native of the southern United States. It is especially numerous in the extensive mangrove swamps of Louisiana, which gives this bright red crayfish its alternative name of Louisiana Swamp Crayfish. In the USA it is usually sold as 'crawfish', a term which in other English-speaking areas is usually reserved for small lobsters. The state of Louisiana is the main crayfish producer of the United States.

contain little meat. The tips of the pincers are yellowish-orange, while the ends of the legs are light red. Each tail segment has two brownish-red spots.

The Cambarus Crayfish is as adaptable as *Astacus astacus* and lives in lakes, lagoons, bays, canals and streams. It will tolerate marshy conditions and even fairly polluted water. It does not dig tunnels but likes to bury itself in mud with only the nose, eyes and feelers showing. In winter, it heads for deeper water. Like all North American crayfish, it has so far proved immune to crayfish disease.

In 1890, 100 Cambarus Crayfish were introduced into Germany near Berneuchen to replace the *Astacus* types wiped out by crayfish disease. They spread westwards along the Oder, Warthe and Netze to the Spree and Havel, spreading at a rate of around 10 km (6 miles) per year. By the 1950s and 1960s, they had found their way into the rivers of western Germany and Poland, where they are found today alongside the *Astacus* types.

In France, they were introduced into a tributary of the Loire between 1911 and 1931 and over the years they have made their way into the Seine and the Marne. By the end of the Second World War, they had reached the upper course of the Rhine and the Moselle by way of the Rhine-Marne and Rhine-Rhône canals. Here they linked up with their brothers spreading from the east. The Cambarus Crayfish is also found in Savoy, particularly in the Lake of Annecy.

The Cambarus Crayfish feeds mainly on water plants, insects, larvae and other small creatures. In winter they look for sheltered water 3–4 m (10–13 ft) deep, but still continue their search for food. The newly hatched crayfish attach themselves to the mother's legs until after the second change of shell. After that, development is so swift that by the end of their

first summer they are sexually mature. Adults cast their shell three times a year.

When this crayfish is threatened, it does not try to swim away with hefty lashings of its tail like *Astacus astacus*, but adopts a defensive stance, pressing the tail to the body and wrapping the legs around it while the pincers are braced against the body.

In North America, the Cambarus Crayfish is found east of the Rocky Mountains from Canada to Florida. It is inferior to *Astacus astacus* in both size and flavour, but the quality can be considerably improved by keeping them in clear water for a time. Only the tails are eaten.

Louisiana Swamp Crayfish, Red Swamp Crayfish

(*Procambarus clarkii*), Fr. *Ecrevisse Rouge*, Ger. *Louisiana Flußkrebs*

A dark red, freshwater crayfish, found in the southern states of the USA, this is America's most widely sold crayfish, thanks to intensive farming methods.

Besides its colour, its main characteristic feature is its heavily pearlised pincers. This crayfish has been introduced into Spain, East Africa, Japan and Hawaii and has been so successful that the American trade has been hit by overproduction abroad.

CRAYFISH OF THE SOUTHERN HEMISPHERE (*Parastacidae*)

Madagascar Crayfish

(*Astacoides madagascariensis*), Fr. *Ecrevisse Malgache*, Ger. *Madagaskarkrebs*

This crayfish of the *Parastacidae* family is extremely large. Its four sub-types are found in a wide diversity of water conditions in the south of the island of Madagascar. It is also found in rivers in the forest region at heights of up to 2,000 m (6,560 ft). It is sold in quantity in local markets, and has plenty of meat.

Murray River Crayfish

(*Euastacus armatus*), Ger. *Großer Australkrebs*

This east Australian crayfish is the second largest freshwater crayfish in the world, growing to up to 50 cm (20 in) in length. It is found in the rivers of New South Wales, Queensland and Victoria as well as in Tasmania. It is also sometimes sold fresh in the markets of Melbourne and Sydney.

Marron

(*Cherax tenuimanus*), Ger. *Australkrebs*

This is the third largest freshwater crayfish in the world and is found exclusively in southwest Australia. Normal specimens weigh up to 2 kg ($4\frac{1}{2}$ lb) and the occasional one has been caught weighing up to 2.7 kg (6 lb).

Distinguishing marks include five wedge-shaped ribs on the head and two characteristic prickles on the end of the tail. Its fine flavour makes it much sought-after in Australia, so that strict regulations have been introduced to protect it. As well as a close season (early May to mid-December), any marron caught must have a minimum carapace length of 76 mm (3 in). They may be caught only for private consumption; fishing for commercial purposes is prohibited.

Marrons have been farmed since 1976. Since they grow relatively quickly (reaching the minimum size within a year) and seem to thrive in artificial pools, marron farming is becoming increasingly popular even for private purposes. In recent years, great efforts have been made to improve methods and techniques to allow eventually for commercial production. There is great interest in the possibility of importing marrons to Europe and the USA.

Other Australian crayfish, all found in the western region, include the Gilgie (*Cherax plebejus* and *Cherax glaber*) and the Yabbie (*Cherax destructoralbidus*), which is similar to the European Crayfish, *Austropotamobius torrentium*. The Yabbie is

not a native of western Australia but was introduced into the area from east and south-east Australia. All three species can survive long periods out of water, burrowing into the soil or digging themselves a burrow.

New Zealand Crayfish
(Paranephrops spp.), Ger. Neuseelandkrebs
Three members of this small family of freshwater crayfish are found on the southern island of New Zealand. One of them (*P. planifrons*) is also found on the northern island.

Murray Lobster
(Astacopsis gouldi), Ger. Tasmanischer Krebs
This crayfish, which lives in the rivers of Tasmania, is the largest in the world and can weigh up to 6 kg (13 lb). It is also found in eastern Australia.

South American Crayfish
(Parastacus spp.), Ger. Südamerikanischer Flußkrebs
This relatively small crayfish is found in lakes and rivers throughout South America. Four of the ten *Parastacus* types found there are native to northern Argentina, Uruguay and southern Brazil. Six types are found in the rivers of Chile.

In its native land of Australia, the Marron is much sought-after but it is becoming increasingly scarce. Strict regulations have been introduced to protect it. This delicious crayfish is ideal for farming and the number of Marron farms is constantly on the increase, although at present annual production is only a few thousand kilogrammes, insufficient to supply the demand. Efforts by the Australian government to promote Marron farming are encouraging the hope that it will eventually become possible to import Marrons into Europe and the United States.

Medium-tailed crabs
(Anomura)

In physical shape, the medium-tailed crabs represent a transitional stage between the long-tailed and short-tailed (true) crabs. A good example is the *Galatheidae* family, usually sold in Europe as 'langostinos' with the addition of the country of origin (e.g. Chilean langostinos).

The members of the large stone crab family (*Lithodidae*), which carry their tails turned forward, resemble the true or short-tailed crabs (*Brachyura*).

Another group of *Anomura* are the hermit crabs (*Paguridae*), which usually make their home in empty shells and which are found both in water and on land.

Langostinos, Squat Lobsters
(*Galatheidae*)

The relatively broad and compact breastplate, with its sharp edges and furrowed surface, is characteristic of this family of medium-tailed crabs. The pronounced rostrum is triangular or sharply pointed. The first pair of legs are extremely elongated and end in small pincers. The strong, compact tail is the same length as the breastplate. Members of this family can be found in all seas and at all depths from the Arctic to the Antarctic. The most commercially important varieties are the two species described here, which tend to be confused with one another.

Langostino, Red Crab
(*Pleuroncodes monodon* and
Cervimunida johni), Ger.
Langostino, Chilekrabbe, Span.
*Langostino Amarillo, Langostino
Chileno, Langostino Colorado,
Langostilla*
These two types of squat lobster, which grow to between 20 and 25 cm (8–10 in) in length, are found mainly in the south-east Pacific. *Pleuroncodes monodon* is caught mainly on the Chilean coast, where it is known as Langostino Colorado or Langostino Zanahoria. It is much sought-after for its fine flavour.

Langostinos are nocturnal

creatures, which hide by day between or under stones. In the course of their nightly search for food, they rake the ground with

their third pair of feet and use the second pair to extract any food particles.

Fresh langostinos are available only in their native Chile. The boiled langostino tails are always exported frozen. The meat is much sought-after for its excellent flavour. The ratio of edible meat to overall size is poor, however – around 1:10.

Frozen langostino meat is often sold wrongly labelled as 'scampi' despite the fact that the small langostino tails have no similarity to *Nephrops norvegicus*.

Deep-sea Squat Lobster
(Munida rugosa), Fr. *Galathé,
Puce de Mer*, Ger. *Tiefwasser-
Springkrebs*
This squat lobster from the
Galathidae family is sold in local
fish markets along the French
Atlantic coast. Occasionally, it
finds its way into Parisian markets but demand is limited. To the
layman, it resembles the Chilean
Langostino Colorado (see inset
picture page 40) but it is, in fact, a
member of a different family. It
lives in depths of 40–70 m
(130–230 ft) and, including the
pincers, is about 20 cm (8 in) long.
It is found in the North Atlantic
from Norway to Madeira and in
the Mediterranean.

HERMIT CRABS
(*Paguridae/Coenobitidae*)

Hermit Crab
(Pagurus spp., formerly
Eupagurus), Fr. *Bernard
l'Hermite*, Ger. *Einsiedlerkrebs,
Eremitenkrebs*, Dut.
Heremietkreeft
Although this totally asymmetrical crab has an armoured head
and breastplate, the tail is soft
and unprotected. The two hind
pairs of legs are stunted. Its
physical shape is well adapted to
living in empty shells, with the
spirals of its unprotected tail
following the twists of the shell in
which it is hidden. When danger
threatens, the crab draws back
completely into its house, sealing
the entrance with the larger of its
two pincers. As the Hermit Crab
grows, it has to move from time
to time to a larger house.
The 100 different species which
make up the *Pagarus* family are
found in every sea up to the
Arctic. The main crab of northern Europe is *Pagurus bernhardus*, which is very popular in
some areas of France.

Robber Crab
(Birgus latro), Ger. *Palmendieb,
Kokosräuber, Diebskrabbe*
This, the largest of the hermit
crabs, is a land crab and so has
lung-like hollows in its breastplate. It can grow to 30 cm (1 ft)
long and up to 2–2.5 kg (4½–5½ lb)
in weight. This asymmetrical

crab, with its reddish and dark-
brown flecks, has extremely large,
strong pincers. The entire tail is
protected by a strong shell. This
evolved hermit crab no longer
lives in empty shells but in holes
in the ground, feeding on coco-
nuts as well as dead animals. This
species is even able to climb palm
trees, in order to knock down the
nuts. It is this activity that gives it
its name.

Hermit crabs: *Pagurus bernhardus* (above) is a unique crustacean that only
rarely comes onto the market, which ensures that gourmets prize its fine
meat all the more. Its physical shape is fully adapted to life in an empty
shell. Only the claws, legs and upper body are plated, for the tail is fully
protected by the shell in which it makes its home.

Stone crabs are of great commercial importance, but unfortunately they
rarely reach us other than as canned crabmeat. The meat is of excellent
quality, but only when you have been fortunate enough to eat a freshly
boiled king crab in Alaska, Chile or Japan can you fully appreciate its
remarkable flavour. As is the case with other deep-sea crabs, live stone
crabs cannot be transported over long distances.

The Robber Crab lives mainly
on the tropical islands of the
western Indo-Pacific. On many
islands it is now extinct, due to
widespread use of insecticides.

STONE CRABS (*Lithodidae*)

Judging from outer appearance,
the stone crabs could easily be
placed among the true crabs, so
they are also referred to by
scientists as 'mock crabs'. Yet
they are, in fact, medium-tailed
crabs and should be classified
with hermit crabs. It is thought
that stone crabs in fact evolved
from hermit crabs. In the course
of their evolution, the soft-
skinned tail became smaller and
folded under the body. In addition, the fifth pair of legs grew
stunted and now serve only for
cleaning the gills. Behind the
pincers, which serve as the first
pair of walking legs, there are
only three strong, long pairs of
legs.
Members of the *Lithodidae*
family live in various seas. They
can be found in the North Pacific
and North Atlantic, along the
west coast of America to the
southern Pacific and in the
southern Atlantic. Stone crabs
prefer cold water and they can
even be found in Arctic coastal
waters. The warmer the water,
the greater the depth at which
they will be found.
One unusual feature of the
stone crabs is their mobility, for
they can cover around 2 km
(1¼ miles) a day. In late winter,
they begin to head for the coast,
where the females shed their
shells before mating. After mating, they head back for deeper
water. Females carry, on average,
240,000 fertilised eggs under their
fan-shaped tails. It takes almost a
year for the larvae to hatch. At
first, the larvae are free-
swimming but after the fourth
change of skin, when the chalky
shell has formed, they lose the
ability to swim and remain on the
sea-bed.
One method of catching stone
crabs is with nets arranged like a
fence along the sea-bed. These are
often 100 m (330 ft) long and have
a mesh of 20–30 cm (8–12 in). In
Alaska, steel baskets weighing
over 300 kg (660 lb) and measuring around 1.5 × 1.5 × 1 m (5 ×
5 × 3 ft) are lowered onto the sea-
bed. These 'pots' are baited with
herring. One ship can lay 50 to

41

King crabs can reach a considerable size. Dr John F. Karinen, oceanographer and expert on stone crabs at the Auke Bay Laboratory in Alaska, is shown holding a fifteen-year-old male whose shell measures around 15 cm (6 in) across. Older crabs are much sought-after by fishermen, as they change their shells only every other year and therefore contain plenty of meat. Strict regulations in America allow only male crabs with a shell width of at least 137 mm ($5\frac{1}{2}$ in) – corresponding to around seven years of age – to be caught. Catching females is prohibited.

100 baskets at a time. In some coastal areas, intensive fishing has markedly depleted the stocks of stone crabs, so less familiar types of stone crab are now being fished to compensate.

Red King Crab, Japanese Crab, Russian Crab, Alaska King Crab *(Paralithodes camtschatica), Ger. Königskrabbe, Japankrabbe, Kamschatkakrebs, Kronenkrebs, Dut. Koningskreeft*

This king crab, which is famous for its size and fine flavour, has been caught and sold in huge quantities in the northern Pacific and Bering Sea since the early 1950s. The fishing industries are run by the USA, Japan and the USSR. The reason it took so long to acquire its present commercial importance is that it has to be caught at depths of several hundred metres. Nonetheless, these countries have developed a flourishing industry in the North Pacific. The trawlers, fitted out as factory ships, and their crews have to withstand gales, icy winds and extremely high seas, for the main fishing season falls during the winter months. Every year, 200 such ships set out from Alaska. The catch is not usually processed on board ship but is brought live with a minimum of delay to factories on the coast, where the crabs are immediately cleaned, boiled and frozen. Processing of the crabs is strictly regulated.

It is only the males that are caught, for these are much larger and meatier than the females. They are usually caught at eight to nine years old when they are about 1 m (3 ft) in overall length and 2.75–4.5 kg (6–10 lb) in weight. A fifteen-year-old king crab can weigh as much as 12 kg (26 lb). Canned crabmeat is also imported into Europe from the Soviet Union. Top-quality canned crabmeat should contain only the meat of the king crab.

The shell of the Red King Crab runs to a triangle at the front and has sharp spines along the sides and back. Between the stemmed eyes, the forehead ends in a pointed rostrum, on either side of which are two feelers of double the length of the eye stem. On the far side of the eyes are two long antennae.

The three hind pairs of legs end in sharp claws. The pincers are long but quite narrow. The shell, legs and claws are red on the upper side, but ivory-coloured on the underside.

Almost the entire creature (claws, legs and body) is edible, yielding 32 per cent of the total weight in meat.

As well as *Paralithodes camtschatica*, other species are caught off the Alaskan coast and in the Bering Sea. These include *Paralithodes brevipes, Paralithodes platypus* (Blue King Crab) and *Lithodes aequispina* (Golden King Crab).

Canned king crab meat comes mostly from factories in Alaska or Chile, but Japan and the Soviet Union also export it; the Russian version is sold as Kamchatka Crab. Boiled king crab legs, and sometimes whole crabs, are also available frozen.

The legs of the king crab contain the finest meat. This Southern King Crab, known in Chile as Centolla, is available in Europe boiled and frozen. The meat has an excellent flavour and is first-rate in any cold dish. Quite apart from the flavour, the size alone makes this crab extremely impressive.

Southern King Crab
(Lithodes antarctica), Ger. Antarktische Königskrabbe, Span. Centolla
This king crab, found mainly on the southern coasts of Chile and Argentina and in the Antarctic, is the southern equivalent of *Paralithodes camtschatica*. Its shell is covered with sharp prickles and measures about 15 cm (6 in) across. It lives in coastal waters at around 150 m (490 ft), but can be found at depths of up to 600 m (1,970 ft). In Chile, it is usually canned for sale as 'crabmeat' (about 70 per cent). Only about 5 per cent of the catch is eaten fresh; the rest is frozen. In 1979, approximately 2,300 tonnes (2,260 tons) were landed in Chile.

A similar species found in the same areas as the Southern King Crab is *Paralomis granulosa*, which is known in Chile as Centollón and in Argentina as Falsa Centolla.

Northern Stone Crab
(Lithodes maja), Ger. Nördliche Steinkrabbe
Another relative of the Red King Crab, this crab lives in the north and east Atlantic and in the North Sea. Its thick, brick-red to earth-brown shell can measure up to 20 cm (8 in) across and, with the legs, it can be up to 1 m (3 ft) across. It is not of commercial importance, however, since it contains relatively little edible meat.

The Golden King Crab, like the Red King Crab a member of the stone crab family, is found off the coast of Alaska and in the Bering Sea. It is difficult to distinguish between these two species but the Golden King Crab is lighter in colour with slightly longer prickles.

Blue King Crab. You will have to look closely to see its pale blue coloration. The best place to look for it is on the pincers. The Blue King Crab is also fished off Alaska and the quality of the meat is just as good as that of other king crabs.

Short-tailed/true crabs (*Brachyura*)

The *Brachyura* are the most highly developed of the crabs. Characteristic features of this sub-group of the *Reptantia* are the truncated head and breast section and the tail section, which is reduced to a short, flat, evenly segmented tailplate folded under the body. In females, this tailplate is wide and rounded and forms a cavity for carrying fertilised eggs.

The *Brachyura* group consists of a number of families, categorised according to the shape of the head and breast section. Some types, such as the Wool Crab of the *Homolidae* family, disguise themselves by carrying living or dead creatures or plants on their backs. The largest living crab, the Japanese Giant Crab, which with legs extended can measure 3 m (10 ft) across, is another short-tailed crb.

It is chiefly the meat from the claws, legs and body that is used for human consumption, together with the liver and roe. Some species, however, such as the Blue Crab, can be eaten whole if they are caught immediately after casting their shell and are still quite soft. These are then sold as soft-shell crabs.

HOMOLIDAE

Giant Crab
(Paromola cuvieri), Ger. *Großer Rückenfüßler*
An orange-red giant crab, whose breastplate is almost circular and whose legs are relatively thin and long. The last, truncated, pair of legs are folded over onto the back. Long legs give this crab a total width of around 90 cm (35 in), but the body length is only 10–18 cm (4–7 in).

This deep-sea crab is found in the Mediterranean, but also as far north as Iceland and in the warmer areas of the eastern Atlantic. Its meat is considered a great delicacy, but it is not much fished and is sold only locally.

Its flesh is considered a real delicacy, yet *Paromola cuvieri* is rarely caught and then is sold only locally. Its long legs give it an overall width of around 90 cm (35 in).

BOX CRABS (*Calappidae*)

Box Crab
(Calappa granulata), Fr. *Crabe Honteux*, Ger. *Große Schamkrabbe, Hahnenkammkrabbe* Ital. *Gallo*
This crab, which grows to 10 cm (4 in) wide, has a hemispherical, strongly domed shell and striking toothed pincers. The rear edge of the shell has pointed indentations. The front pair of truncated legs can be placed close to the body. The shell is light-brown

Cangrejo de la Santa Virgin – this is what they call this sea spider, *Mithrax spinosissimus*, in Cuba. This crab (photographed in Haiti) is found throughout the Caribbean, but is sold only locally.

with carmine-red flecks on the back and the outside of the pincers. Box Crabs live on sand in all warm seas at depths of 30–100 m (100–330 ft). During the day they dig themselves in, protecting their breathing tubes from grains of sand by folding their pincers over their 'face'. At night they search for food, mainly shellfish, which they crack by using their pincers like a tin opener.

The **Sheep Crab** is another member of the *Majidae* family. It is found in large numbers only off the coast of California. To date, this sea spider has been of no commercial importance but with the decline in stocks of king crabs things could change.

SEA SPIDERS (*Majidae*)

Sea Spider, Spiny or Spinous Spider Crab, Thornback Crab
(Maja squinado), Fr. *Grande Araignée de Mer, Grampelle*, Ger. *Große Seespinne, Teufelskrabbe*, Ital. *Maia, Granzo, Granzevola*, Span. *Centolla, Crana, Cabra*, Port. *Santola, Arola, Burro*, Dut. *Spinkrab*
This spider-like crab has a highly domed backplate, the rear portion of which is evenly rounded. The surface of the shell is rough and uneven, with sharp spines along the front edge. The shell is 13–15 cm (5–6 in) long and brownish-red in colour. The legs are bright red. The narrow, graceful pincers are like pointed forceps. The walking legs, which are all of more or less the same length, end in sharp claws. The Sea Spider is found from the south coast of England, down the entire Atlantic coast of Europe as far as North Africa, as well as in the Mediterranean. They like sand or rocks overgrown with seaweed at depths from 20 m (65 ft). They feed mainly on water

The most common European sea spider is *Maja squinado*. This *Araignée de Mer* plays an important part in French cooking, for its meat is delicious and much sought-after by gourmets. It is nevertheless not of great commercial significance.

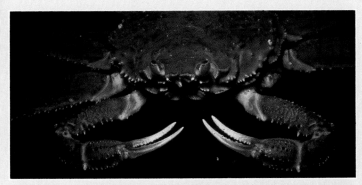

The Snow Crab (otherwise known as the Queen or Tanner Crab) is of top quality. At first, it was caught and sold mainly in Japan but more recently it has begun to be widely fished and marketed in the USA and Canada. Canned as crabmeat or with the tasty claws sold fresh or frozen, it is now a worthy rival of the king crab.

The long-legged Snow Crab was at first sold as Queen Crab – a counterpart to the popular king crab. Since it was already familiar as Snow Crab imported from Japan, however, this is the name that has stuck.

an effort to maintain stocks, and traders have fallen back on the Snow Crab. New techniques have been developed for removing the meat. The home market was developed to compete with imports from Japan.

According to statistics compiled by the FAO (United Nations Food and Agriculture Organisation) in Rome, in 1977 44,602 tonnes (43,805 tons) of Snow Crab were caught in the USA, compared with 21,000 tonnes (20,625 tons) in Japan. The Snow Crab is smaller than the king crabs. A full-grown crab can measure 18 cm (7 in) across the shell and weigh around 2.5 kg (6 lb). About 20 per cent of the bodyweight is edible meat. The Snow Crab is also found in the North Atlantic, off the coast of Canada.

plants. During the summer months, they live only a few metres beneath the surface, but in winter they like at least 50 m (165 ft) of water.

At mating time, in summer, they form large colonies. Fertilisation takes place immediately after the female has moulted. The males remain nearby for several weeks to protect the females until their new shells have formed. The eggs are laid six months later and are attached to the rear legs of the female for a further six months before the larvae hatch. The long legs of the adult Sea Spiders make movement difficult.

Snow Crab, Queen Crab, Tanner Crab
(Chionoecetes opilio and *C. bairdi, C. tanneri, C. japonicus), Ger. Nordische Eismeerkrabbe, Schneekrabbe*
These large, long-legged sea spiders, found in large numbers in the North Pacific – mainly off Alaska, in the Bering Sea and north of the Bering Strait – are sold as Snow Crabs rather than Spider Crabs in the USA. The names Tanner Crab and Queen Crab are also used.

While Snow Crabs have long been popular in Japan, they found few takers at first in the United States, mainly because the meat is difficult to get out of the shell. Since 1967, however, fewer king crabs have been caught, in

These delicious Snow Crab claws can be found only in their boiled and frozen form on the European market. The flesh is quite easy to remove.

Directory of Crustaceans

EDIBLE CRABS (*Cancridae*)
Common Edible Crab, European Rock Crab, Puncher
(Cancer pagurus), Fr. Crabe Tourteau, Crabe Poupart, Crabe Dormeur, Ger. Taschenkrebs, Ital. Granciporo, Favollo, Span. Cambaro Masero, Port. Caranguejo Moure, Dan. Taskekrabbe, Swed. Høvring, Nor. Krabbtaska, Dut. Zeekrab
The twenty species that make up the *Cancer* family are found in the coastal waters of cold to moderate seas. The Common Edible Crab, *Cancer pagarus*, is found from the Lofoten Islands to the Moroccan coast, throughout the North Sea and occasionally in the western Mediterranean and the Adriatic.

In its shell the Common Crab looks as if it is lying between two large, flat dishes. At the sides and front, the shell has toothed markings. There are short antennae between the eyes.

The stemmed eyes and antennae can be drawn in and hidden in small openings in the shell. The first of the five pairs of legs have developed into gripping and cracking pincers, while the four rear pairs, each made up of four bristly segments, end in claws. They are brown to brownish-purple and almost black at the tips. The top shell ranges from brown to reddish-brown and the underside is yellowish.

These crabs can reach a weight of 6 kg (13 lb), when the shell will be around 30 cm (1 ft) across. On average, however, the shell will measure around 20 cm (8 in). The favourite habitat of the Common Crab is a cleft in the rock in up to 100 m (330 ft) of water. This provides good cover in the search for food, although the crab often buries itself in mud or sand. It grips small creatures, slow-moving like itself – such as snails, molluscs or sea urchins – with its strong pincers. The pincers are also used to ward off enemies.

As the moulting and mating season approaches, the male crab looks for a female and up to a week before the moulting he grips her between his legs to help the moulting along. A few hours after moulting, mating takes place and a few days later the female is set free. There is one unusual aspect of this species' mating: the female can store the sperm in her body for up to three years, so when necessary the eggs produced at several moultings can be fertilised without the presence of a male. The eggs are laid between October and January. The spawn, which can number millions of eggs, remain attached to the underside of the female until the summer. Then the larvae hatch and two months later, after several moults, they will measure 4 mm (0.2 in). Then the swimming larva stage comes

to an end and they begin to creep along the sea-bed. At a year old, the small crabs measure about 3 cm (1 in) across. They are sexually mature at five years old, when they are about 12 cm (5 in) across.

In comparison to the impressive size of the shell, the body of the Common Crab contains relatively little meat, but the liver and roe have an excellent flavour and are considered a real delicacy. Most of the meat is in the claws and the breast section. The Common Crab (like all crustaceans) should first be boiled and then served either hot or cold.

These crabs are caught in lobster pots attached to ropes and they occasionally find their way into the nets of the prawn fishermen. The popularity of this crab has led to overfishing in some areas, so that some countries have introduced regulations on seasons and minimum sizes. Some 20,000 tonnes (19,640 tons) of crab are caught in Europe every year, with France contributing 8,000–9,000 tonnes (7,860–8,820 tons) and Britain 10,000 tonnes (9,800 tons).

The Common Edible Crab is particularly popular in France. For the Frenchmen of the Atlantic coast, it is something of a national dish. The British, too, eat a lot of crab, although not as much as the French.

The Common Edible Crab, when correctly prepared, can be a real treat. The meat content, however, is relatively low, with the best meat hidden in the strong claws. The liver, too, has an excellent flavour and is highly prized by gourmets. The strong shell is excellent for filling and browning under the grill, or as an attractive container for a crab salad.

46

Dungeness Crab, California Crab, Market Crab

(Cancer magister), Fr. Crabe Americain, Ger. Kalifornischer Taschenkrebs

The most popular crab on the west coast of the United States is found along the entire Pacific coast from Alaska to Mexico, but the main fishing grounds are around San Francisco. The Dungeness Crab is of similar size to the Common Edible Crab, but its shell is almost trapezium-shaped. The eyes are close together and the feelers slightly shorter. The pincers are slightly narrower and the legs longer and more flexible. The brownish-green shell grows to 20–25 cm (8–10 in) across, with a weight of around 800 g (1¾ lb). Larger crabs can be found, however, around 30 cm (1 ft) across and weighing up to 2 kg (4½ lb).

Although only some 25 per cent of the weight is edible meat, the market demand for this crab is rising continuously. To prevent overfishing, the authorities have set limits on permitted catches. It is prohibited to catch females (they are, in any case, much smaller) and any males caught must measure at least 17 cm (6½ in). If females or small crabs are caught in pots or nets, they must be set free.

The life-cycle and reproductive habits of this creature are very similar to those of the Common Edible Crab.

Cancer magister was first caught commercially in 1880 but large-scale fishing was not developed until 1920, when improvements in freezing techniques were introduced. If you want to eat Dungeness Crabs fresh, you will have to go to the west coast of America, for this is the only place that they are available. All Dungeness Crabs leave the west coast either frozen or conserved in some other way. They are not allowed to be transported fresh, even to other parts of the United States.

Dungeness Crab – the California Crab (*Cancer magister*) – is by far the most popular crustacean on the west coast of the United States and has been adopted almost as an heraldic device in San Francisco. During the summer months, a crab dinner on Fisherman's Wharf, the harbour area of San Francisco, is a must for both local people and tourists.

In typically uncomplicated American style, the crabs are boiled and sold in the open air. You can take them away or eat them on the spot. For those that want to eat them straightaway, they are sold with the claws ready-cracked, so that the fine meat is easy to get at. The restaurants on Fisherman's Wharf offer a variety of crab dishes but it is the Chinese cooks in nearby Chinatown who really know how to cook crab. Gourmets can rely on them to come up with something really delicious.

Increased demand has taken its toll. Although there is no shortage of Dungeness Crabs on the stalls of Fisherman's Wharf, they have in fact become relatively scarce and are now protected by strictly regulated close seasons. The catching of females is prohibited and males must measure at least 15 cm (6 in) across the shell.

Common Rock Crab
*(Cancer irroratus), Ger.
Felsenkrabbe*
This elliptical crab (the shell is one and a half times as wide as it is long) is found along the entire Atlantic coast of the USA from Labrador to Florida and the Bahamas. They are most numerous off the coast of New England and in the Gulf of St Lawrence.

The shell is a striking pale yellow, with small red or violet spots. At the front of the shell are nine flat, tooth-like notches and the pincers are relatively soft. The males are larger than the females, with a shell width of up to 18 cm (7 in), compared to 12 cm (5 in) for females.

Little is yet known about the lifestyle of these creatures. They are of little commercial importance and are mainly caught as a by-product by lobster fishermen, since they occasionally feed on lobsters.

Jonah Crab
(Cancer borealis), Ger. Jonah-krabbe
It is difficult to distinguish the Jonah Crab from the Common Rock Crab, for the front of the shell again has nine toothed notches and again the colour is pale with red spots. In the Jonah Crab, however, the colour becomes darker, nearer brownish-red, the further north you go. The surface of the shell and of the strong claws is very rough.

The Jonah Crab prefers clear water and depths of 180 m (590 ft) and more. It is found from Nova

Scotia to Florida. The meat is delicious, but sales tend to be restricted to local markets.

ROUND CRABS
(Atelecyclidae)

This family takes its name from the characteristic, almost circular shell, which can measure up to 20 cm (8 in) in diameter. Round crabs are found in every sea. The two species described below are the most important as far as eating and trade are concerned.

Edible Round Crabs
(Telmessus sp. and Erimacrus isenbecki), Ger. Eßbare Rundkrabben, Jap. Kurigani, Kegani
For a long time, these two types of crab were caught only in Japan and they are still available there in local fish markets. Nowadays, they are sold throughout the world as 'crabmeat'. The canned meat is produced mainly in the Soviet Union and the United States.

SWIMMING CRABS
(Portunidae)

Like that of the Common Edible Crab, the bodies of swimming crabs are flat, but swimming crabs usually have long prickles along the edges. The chief peculiarity of these crabs is the shape of the fifth pair of legs, with the end section thickly covered with hairs and widened into a sort of paddle. These legs make the crabs excellent swimmers (even sideways), an ability which is used

Swimming crabs of the *Liocarcinus* family are of little culinary interest, as the meat content is extremely small. In Brittany, however, the Hairy Swimming Crab (*Liocarcinus puber*) is considered a delicacy and can be found in local fish markets. The meat may be difficult to extract but it has a really fine flavour.

both for escape and for catching food. Swimming crabs are active hunters, specializing in the capture of fish; they swim straight up to their prey and seize it. This is made easier by the lightness of their body structure, for the delicate shell contains little calcium. Only the extremely sharp pincers are reinforced along the edge to make them more solid.

Swimming crabs usually live in coastal waters, preferably on

sand or mud into which they can burrow. A few species are also found in brackish water.

Common Shore Crab, Green Shore Crab, Harbour Crab
(Carcinus maenas), Fr. Crabe Vert, Crabe Enragé, Ger. Gemeine Krabbe, Gewöhnliche Strandkrabbe, Ital. Carcino, Ripario, Granchio Marino Comune, Span. Cangrejo de Mar, Cranc d'Herba, Port. Caranguejo Morraceiro, Nor/Swed/Dan. Strandkrabbe, Dut. Strandkrab
This is one of the smallest crabs suitable for human consumption. Although a member of the swimming crab family, it does not have the typical paddle feet; the last pair of legs end rather in lanceolate digging feet. The pincers are small but strong, the flat shell reaches 8 cm (3 in) wide and 4 cm (1½ in) long.

This species is a creature of the shoreline shallows. As the tide ebbs it may be carried seawards, but often it burrows into the sand

The Jonah Crab comes onto the American market less frequently than the Common Rock Crab, but both are of outstanding quality. They are usually prepared in the same way as the Common Edible Crab.

Carcinus aestuarii or **Common Shore Crab**. This swimming crab, which is found in similar form in all European coastal waters, is popular in Italy as a soft-shell crab, caught immediately after moulting and deep-fried.

Pu Dao is the Thai name for the Swimming or Star Crab (*Portunus sanguinolentus*), with its three striking red spots. It is found throughout the Indo-Pacific from East Africa to Japan and Australia.

or hides beneath seaweed or stones to await the incoming tide.

The Shore Crab is the most common crab of the North Atlantic from the North Pole to the Spanish Atlantic coast. A closely related species, *Carcinus aestuarii*, is found in the Mediterranean and on the Black Sea coast. Commercially, however, the Shore Crab is of only local importance. In Italy, less frequently than in the past, it is eaten whole, deep-fried in oil if caught when soft – immediately after moulting. In France, too, the Shore Crab is popular and small quantities are even exported. In England, it has long been considered a poor man's dish.

Swimming Crab, Velvet Crab
(Liocarcinus sp, formerly also Portunus sp), Fr. Etrille, Ger. Schwimmkrabbe, Ital. Gambaro, Grancella
Various *Liocarcinus* species live in shallow water and in depths up to 70 m (230 ft) along the coasts of the Atlantic from the Lofoten Islands through Britain and France to Morocco, as well as in the Mediterranean. There are also a few tropical species.

The trapezium-shaped shell with its sharply toothed front edge is brown and reaches around 10 × 12 cm (4 × 5 in). The stemmed eyes are wide-set and between them are two short antennae and feelers. The pincers are short, clumsy and rough. The hind pair of legs is fin-like. These creatures can change colour to match their surroundings.

Blue Swimming Crab, Sand Crab
(Portunus pelagicus, formerly Neptunus pelagicus), Ger. Große Pazifische Schwimmkrabbe, Indon. Rajungan, Malay. Ketam Renjong, Phil. Alimasag, Chin. Far Haai
This large swimming crab is found chiefly in the Indo-Pacific but has also made its way through the Suez Canal into the eastern Mediterranean. It is one of the most commercially important crabs in the Indo-Pacific.

The males are larger than the females, with shells up to 25 cm

Striped Crabs and Blue Swimming Crabs are part of the everyday catch of fishermen in the tropical waters of South-East Asia. Both have really tasty meat, although there is not much of it. They are mainly boiled to make stock or occasionally grilled or fried. A special feature of the Blue Swimming Crab (*Portunus pelagicus*) is its unusual colouring. The males are light blue with white markings, the females brown and white.

(10 in) across. A weight of 750 g (more than 1½ lb) is by no means unusual. The meat is used mainly for canned crabmeat. The marbled, blue or brown and white shell is straight on either side of the head and at the rear, and the whole front edge is thickly set with spines. The pincers are extremely narrow.

Swimming Crab, Star Crab
(Portunus sanguinolentus, formerly Neptunus sanguinolentus), Ger. Pazifische Rotpunkt-Schwimmkrabbe, Thai. Pu Dao
The main distinguishing feature of the Swimming Crab is three round, purplish-red spots on the rear of the greenish-yellow shell. It is found throughout the

Indo-Pacific. Like all large *Portunus* crabs (the shell reaches 20–25 cm/8–10 in), it is fished commercially and often sold together with the Blue Swimming Crab.

Lady Crab, Sand Crab, Calico Crab
(Ovalipes ocellatus), Ger. Ladykrabbe
A small crab of the American Atlantic coast, found mainly on the coast of the southern states and Mexico, the Lady Crab lives in sand in up to 18 m (60 ft) of water. The shell is almost white with red spots and up to 8 cm (3 in) wide. It is found in the largest numbers around New Orleans, where it is widely sold.

Striped Crab, Masked Crab
(Charybdis cruciata), Ger. Kreuzkrabbe, Indon. Rajungan Karang, Chin. Hung Haai
A crab of the Indo-Pacific and China Sea. Its trapezium-shaped shell can grow to 10–15 cm (4–6 in) wide. The smooth shell has a striking pattern of stripes, which resembles a mask. In Thailand it is known as Zebra Crab.

The pincers, which are longer than the other legs, have sharp prickles. As in most swimming crabs, the fifth pair of legs end in paddles. The Striped Crab lives on sand, into which it burrows up to 2 m (6 ft) deep.

49

Blue Crab, Peeler, Soft-shell Crab

(Callinectes sapidus), Fr. Chancre Nageron, Ger. Blau-krabbe

The Blue Crab plays an important part in the American and Mexican fishing industries. It is found on the American Atlantic coast from Massachusetts to Florida and out to the Bahamas, as well as being plentiful in the Gulf of Mexico. It is found in lesser numbers as far north as Nova Scotia, and south as far as northern Argentina. This extremely good swimmer has also been introduced into other seas, so that they are found in the Mediterranean and the Aegean as well.

Although many types of crab are sold in the USA, the Blue Crab is the best known and most widely popular. This is due partly to the excellent quality of the meat, but mainly to the fact that it is the tastiest and meatiest of the soft-shell crabs. During moulting, when the crabs cast their old shells, they increase their size by up to one-third. These soft, meaty crabs are immediately taken out of the water to be sold as the famous Soft-shell Crabs. The right moment must be finely judged, for the new shell grows very quickly if they are left in salt water. As Soft-shell Crabs have become more and more sought after, quite an industry has grown up. The Blue Crabs are caught and kept in large vats until they reach the right size and have moulted.

In shallow water, Blue Crabs are usually caught in small nets which are dragged over the sea-bed. In deeper water, large baskets or wire cages filled with bait are used. Most of the catch is sold fresh, but much is also frozen or canned.

Blue Crabs are true swimming crabs, with the fifth pair of legs ending in flat, oval paddles. The shell is usually 10–20 cm (4–8 in) across and is trapezium-shaped at the rear. The front part of the shell is semicircular, with sharp prickles around the edge. The pincers are slim and usually much longer than the walking legs.

Blue Crab, commercially the most important crab on the east coast of America. These extremely tasty swimming crabs are caught in large numbers on the coast of Virginia and particularly in Chesapeake Bay, which gives them their alternative American name, Virginia Crab. The male Blue Crab is shown on the left and the female on the right.

Soft-shell crabs are best-sellers in the American crustacean market in May and June. While freshly moulted crabs are sold in other countries, such as the Common Shore Crab in Italy and France, the fine soft-shell Blue Crabs from Chesapeake Bay are a market leader and are now exported to Europe.

After twelve to eighteen months and fifteen moultings, the crabs are sexually mature and they live for three to four years.

Mangrove Crab, Mud Crab, Serrated Crab

(Scylla serrata), Fr. Crabe des Paletuviers, Ger. Mangroven-krabbe, Indon. Kepiting, Malay. Ketam Batu, Phil. Alimangong Palaisdaan, Chin. Chang Haai

This large swimming crab, found in the tropical Indo-Pacific, is the most important for trade and eating in South-east Asia. The shell grows to 20 cm (8 in) across and weights of 1.5 kg ($3\frac{1}{4}$ lb) are not unusual. The claw meat is especially good and the large pincers can measure 15 × 6 cm (6 × $2\frac{1}{2}$ in).

There are sharp spines along the front of the shell but the top is completely smooth. These crabs range from olive to brown in colour. As the name implies, their favourite habitat is mangrove swamps.

In Japan and Thailand, the meat is canned and exported as 'crabmeat'.

HIGHER STONE CRABS (*Xanthidae*)

With over 900 species, the *Xanthidae* is the largest of the crab families. Characteristic features are the thick, hard shell and huge pincers. Xanthides are heavy creatures and move very slowly. They are found in all seas but are most plentiful in tropical waters.

Tasmanian Giant Crab

(Pseudocarcinus gigas), Ger. Australische Riesenkrabbe

With a weight of up to 15 kg (33 lb) and shell length of around 30 cm (1 ft), the Tasmanian Giant Crab is the largest member of its family. It is found mainly on the south coast of Australia at depths of 90–450 m (300–1,475 ft). Until recently it was landed only as a by-product but now it is fished in its own right.

Books often refer to the Japanese Giant Crab (*Macrocheira kaempferi*) as the largest of all crabs but it cannot claim the largest shell, for that of the Tasmanian Giant Crab is larger – although, with its legs extended, the Japanese crab has the largest span, measuring as much as 3 m (10 ft).

Stone Crab
(Menippe mercenaria), Ger. Große Steinkrabbe

The characteristic heavy, oval shell of the Stone Crab grows to around 13 cm (5 in) across and is purple to dark brown or reddish with brown spots. The body is around 5 cm (2 in) thick, giving the Stone Crab a rounder appearance than other crabs. The thickly haired legs have red and yellow bands and end in sharp claws. The large pincers have black tips.

Stone Crabs live for around ten years. They are found on the Atlantic coast from North Carolina to Florida, in the Gulf of Mexico and in the Caribbean. They are largest and most numerous in southern Florida.

The favourite habitat of the Stone Crab is near small bays or

Stone Crab claws are a delicacy in America. They are always sold preboiled, as otherwise the meat is difficult to get out. The delicious claw meat is excellent for any cold crab dish. It is to be hoped that Stone Crab claws will one day find their way onto the European market.

The Mangrove Crab, or Serrated Crab as it is known in South-east Asia, is one of the most popular crustaceans of the region. The meat content is relatively high (it has large, meaty claws) and the quality is excellent.

river mouths, in deep holes in the mud or sand, or under rocks or mangrove roots. It is a crab of considerable commercial importance and is caught on a large scale, mainly with traps or baited wire baskets. Almost all of the edible meat is in the large claws, so fishermen often break off the claws and then set the crabs free. New claws grow after about eighteen months. Losing its claws does not seem to worry the crab, which uses the second pair of legs for gripping food instead of the pincers. The regenerated second pincers do not grow as large as the pair that were lost, however.

The claws are boiled immediately after catching and then either chilled and sold fresh, or frozen. Unboiled claws cannot be frozen, for the meat will not then come away from the shell, so only pre-boiled claws are sold.

Italian Stone Crab
(Eriphia verrucosa), Fr. Eriphie, Ger. Italienischer Taschenkrebs, Ital. Favollo, Port. Caranguejo Mouro

This member of the higher stone crab family is similar in shape and size to the Common Shore Crab, but with larger pincers. The wide brow (rostrum) is set with short, strong teeth. The pincer legs have short bristles. The shell is reddish-brown with yellow spots and reddish-brown tubercles. As with the lobster, the pincers are differently shaped, one being for cracking, the other for cutting.

The Italian Stone Crab, whose shell grows to 10 cm (4 in) across, likes to live in holes in the rock or under stones in up to 10 m (33 ft) of water. They are sold locally throughout the Mediterranean and are very tasty, although not very meaty.

51

This smooth Coral Crab (*Carpilius corralinus*) is a native of the Caribbean. Its favourite habitat is a coral reef. They are sold in local fish markets with other related species.

The Italian Stone Crab is sold locally in Mediterranean countries. The meat content is relatively low, but the quality makes it a firm favourite with Italian gourmets.

FRESHWATER CRABS (*Potamidae*)

Many types of crabs can survive for a time in brackish or fresh water, but there are others which live exclusively in fresh water. These include the *Potamidae* family. They are found in the tropics and subtropics of the Old World. *Potamidae* and other families of freshwater crabs are found near the tropics in the same areas as the smaller species of freshwater crayfish.

In Mediterranean and Balkan countries, freshwater crabs live in rivers, streams and lakes. In tropical countries, they are also found in jungle under piles of damp leaves or rocks. A number of freshwater crabs have evolved into land crabs and breath moist air. In South America, the Congo and the Caucasus there are crabs that dig down to the water table, so that they have a water-filled home to which to retreat in periods of drought.

As with the crayfish, the life cycle of the freshwater crab goes through no larval stage. Tiny, but fully formed, crabs hatch from the eggs carried under the tail. The lifestyle and behaviour patterns of these crabs are as varied as the surroundings in which they live. Even the shape of the shell varies considerably. Usually they are oval, wider than they are long, but the shell may be round or rectangular.

Italian Freshwater Crab
(*Potamon fluviatile*), *Fr. Crabe d'Eau Douce, Ger. Italienische Flußkrabbe, Ital. Granzo Tenere*
This round-shelled freshwater crab is found in a few of the inland waters of Italy, especially in Lakes Albano and Nemi, south-east of Rome. It lives in shallow water between tree roots and stones. It is eaten only locally, preferably immediately after moulting, when it is soft.

The Mitten Crab is a delicacy in China, where it is known as Shanghai Crab. In Europe, it is less highly thought-of. This crab, which alternates between sea and fresh water, gets its name from the woolly mittens which cover the pincers of the male (in females, they are hardly noticeable). It is only in the water (inset right) that the mittens can come fully into use.

DEEP-SEA CRABS
(*Geryonidae*)

Deep-sea Red Crab

(Geryon quinquedens), Ger.
Rote Tiefseekrabbe
This deep-red crab is a member of the relatively small family of deep-sea crabs (*Geryonidae*). Its strong legs make it a good runner. The shell is rounded with five blunt teeth, as the Latin name indicates. On the rostrum are four more pointed teeth. The shell reaches a maximum of 18 cm (7 in) across.

Deep-sea crabs like cold water and a muddy sea-bed or occasionally stones. They are found along the American Atlantic coast from Nova Scotia to Brazil.

The deep-sea crabs are of limited commercial value, although they have begun to be fished regularly in recent years. The flesh is similar in both appearance and flavour to King Crab.

There is a similar deep-sea crab in the east Atlantic, *Geryon maritae*. In Namibia another type, *Geryon chuni*, is fished commercially and exported, mainly to Japan.

ROCK CRABS
(*Grapsidae*)

Rock Crab

(Grapsus grapsus), Ger.
Tropische Springkrabbe
A medium-sized crab with a roundish shell and relatively close-set eyes. The pincers are small, relative to the body, and have spoon-shaped tips. They are used to scrape up algae. The Rock Crab is one of the few crabs that live on the tide-line, where it feeds on algae covering stones and rocks.

The Rock Crab is found on the east and west coasts of central and southern America, from southern California to Chile and from Florida to Brazil. Rock Crabs are difficult to catch and are therefore sold only locally, mainly as octopus bait.

Chinese Mitten Crab

(Eriocheir sinensis), Fr. *Crabe Chinois*, Ger. *Wollhandkrabbe*
The Mitten Crab, which gets its name from the woolly claws of the male, is one of the species that can move at will from seawater to fresh or brackish water. This is because it is able to maintain the salt content of the blood at a fixed level, independently of the water that surrounds it.

Regularly every year, all males larger than 45 mm (2 in) across head for the sea in about July. They can cover 8–12 km (5–7½ miles) a day. If obstacles bar their way in the water (weirs, for example), they go round them overland. When they reach the lower course or mouth of the river, they form a barrier which the females will have to cross

when they arrive slightly later. Then mating takes place. The young hatch in May or June of the following year. After producing their young, the mothers usually die. The young Mitten Crabs develop in the water near the coast. As early as the last

larval stage, at three months, they migrate to the mouths of large rivers and, as they develop and grow, they move further and further upstream.

This native of Chinese rivers is thought to have been introduced into the harbours of the North Sea in 1912. From there, it entered rivers and canals and can now be found in France, Belgium, Holland, Germany and Scandinavia. Since they reproduce frequently and congregate *en masse*, they are considered pests in Europe. They decimate freshwater fish stocks, eat fish caught in nets and traps and damage dykes and dams on the coast.

At one time, Mitten Crabs were caught when they came out of the water to pass a weir, but

Because of its striking blue colour, the Caribbean Land Crab (*Cardisoma guanhumi*) is known in Florida as the Blue Land Crab. The white, slightly sweet meat has a very delicate flavour and compares favourably with its sea-dwelling namesake, the Blue Crab. Occasionally, especially around Christmas time, Paris restaurants include the Caribbean Land Crab on their menus. These are imported from the Antilles.

now they are usually contained by electrified fences across the river. Most of those caught are used in fertilizer. There is little fishing for Mitten Crabs.

Attempts to market Mitten Crabs in Germany have remained unsuccessful. They were sold up

to ten years ago, mainly to Chinese restaurants, but nowadays they never come on the market in Europe, although in China they are a great delicacy.

LAND CRABS
(*Gecarcinidae*)

The *Gecarcinidae* family comprises seventeen species. These crabs have completed the transition from sea to land. In the most highly developed species, the gill cavity has evolved into a type of lung. To breed, however, they have to return to the sea, for the larvae can develop only in water. Nevertheless, they can often be found far inland. They are usually caught during migration. Land crabs are found in all tropical countries. They are mainly vegetarian but also eat dead meat, so in many areas they form a sort of 'waste-disposal unit'.

Land Crab

(Cardisoma spp.), Fr. *Crabe Terrestre*, Ger. *Tropische Landkrabbe*, Span. *Cangrejo Terrestre*
The *Cardisoma* family includes seven types found from the Cape Verde Islands to Angola, from Florida to Brazil, on the west coast of central and southern America and in the tropical Indo-Pacific. The crabs dig deep holes in which to hide by day. By night, they go in search of food, often covering huge distances. They search for leaves and fallen fruit, staying close to the hole.

The egg-bearing females migrate in huge swarms at full moon to the sea, to deposit their larvae in the water. The full moon is their sign that the time is right, for then the tide will be particularly high. Mating and development of the eggs takes place on land, but the larvae have to develop in seawater.

The meat of the land crab is very tasty, but it is sold only on the local market.

**Blue Land Crab, Caribbean
Land Crab, White Crab,
Mulatto Crab**
*(Cardisoma guanhumi), Fr.
Tourlourou (Antilles), Ger.
Karibische Landkrabbe, Span.
Cangrejo Azul*
The flesh of this extremely large
land crab is white and quite sweet
and is similar to that of the Blue
Crab. In southern Florida, where
they were found in large numbers
up until the 1950s, blocking roads
as they migrated, crabs of up to
500 g (18 oz) have been caught.
The shell is up to 9 cm ($3\frac{1}{2}$ in) long
and 15 cm (6 in) wide. The pin-
cers, especially on the male, are
large and strong.

This crab is found from Florida, through the Caribbean islands to Brazil. It lives up to 2 km
($1\frac{1}{4}$ miles) from the sea in fields,
woods and overgrown hills, in
holes in the ground which it digs
up to 2 m ($6\frac{1}{2}$ ft) deep. The local
people keep them in cages and
fatten them on corn, bananas and
palm seeds. In general, they are
difficult to catch but a good time
is during the migration of the
females when, like all *Cardisoma*
species and the tropical Land
Crab described above, they head
for the sea at full moon in huge
groups.

Red Land Crab
*(Gecarcinus ruricola), Fr. Tour-
lourou (Antilles), Ger. Gemeine
Landkrabbe*
This land crab, found on all the
Caribbean islands, lives far from
the coast in the hills and mountains, in holes which it digs for
itself. Its trapezium-shaped or
squarish shell measures on aver-
age 9 cm ($3\frac{1}{2}$ in). Both pincers are
equally developed and the four
hind pairs of legs end in sharp
claws. They are mainly caught
and eaten in autumn, when they
are at their best.

A related species in the Indo-
Pacific, *Gecarcoidea lalandii*, is a
diurnal creature, retreating to its
hole only during the hottest parts
of the day or in heavy rain.

Other related species inhabit
islands in the Pacific and Atlantic. Their lifestyle is similar to
that of *Gecarcoidea lalandii*, although some are nocturnal.

The highly developed crabs of
this family with their awkward-
looking legs can run extremely
quickly in a sideways direction.
They live on tropical and sub-
tropical sandy beaches and dig
holes up to 2 m ($6\frac{1}{2}$ ft) deep. At
mating time, the males of several
species build tall pyramids of
sand as a signal for the females.
They have extremely good eye-
sight, with their eyes on the ends
of folding stems.

Fiddler Crab
*(Uca spp.), Fr. Crabe Violiniste,
Ger. Winkerkrabbe*
The *Uca* family consists of sixty-
five species, found on the coasts
of every warm sea. Its common
name derives from its unusual
courtship display. In males, one
of the pincers is much enlarged
and this is used to gesture to the
female. Each species of Fiddler
Crab has its own form of gestures, some waving the pincer
rhythmically in the air and others
using both pincer and legs to
achieve a really balletic display.
Males also use the pincer to make
threatening gestures when de-
fending the entrance to their hole.
Females, on the other hand, have
two eating pincers of equal size.

It is only the enlarged pincers
of the males that are of interest as
food, for they contain the best
meat. In Andalusia, it is customary to break the claws off the
males of the local species, *Uca
tangeri*, and then to release them.
It takes a year for the pincer to
redevelop and the new one will be
slightly smaller. The claw meat is
used in hors d'oeuvres. In Japan,
Fiddler Crabs are salted and
served with rice.

Mangrove Crab
*(Ucides cordatus), Fr.
Mangrove Crabe, Ger.
Atlantische Landkrabbe*
A land crab found in tropical
eastern America. The meat of this
crab is much sought-after. Local
people starve the crab for a few
days before cooking it, since it
feeds on the poisonous manzan-
illo tree.

Ucides occidentalis, a similar
species, is found on the west coast
of America between southern
California and Peru.

Other
Crustaceans

One third of all crustaceans, some
10,000 species, belong to the ten-
footed crustacean or decapod
family. This is the best-known
group of crustaceans, as it includes most of the edible species.
The following sections contain
some of the less familiar, edible
crustaceans, which do not belong
to the decapod group, the most
famous of these being the Mantis
Shrimp.

MANTIS SHRIMPS
(Stomatopoda)

Mantis Shrimp
*(Squilla mantis), Fr. Squille,
Prie Dieu, Ger. Gemeiner
Heuschreckenkrebs, Fang-
schreckenkrebs, Ital. Canocchia,
Pannocchia, Cicala di Mare,
Span. Galera, Castañeta, Dut.
Sprinkhaankreeft, Jap. Shako,
Phil. Tatampal, Palpatok, Chin.
Taan Ha*
Many different species make up
the *Squillidae* family, one of them
being the Mantis Shrimp, the
largest non-decapod crustacean
of the Mediterranean. The name
derives from their similarity to a
Praying Mantis (*Mantis re-
ligiosa*). The similarity lies in the
long, highly developed grasping
legs, which resemble the first pair
of legs of the Praying Mantis.

The Mantis Shrimp is 20–
25 cm (8–10 in) long, with an
extremely short carapace and a
long, wide tail. The second pair of
legs, the grasping legs, have a
powerful jack-knife mechanism
that enables the Mantis Shrimp
to grasp its prey (prawns, fish,
molluscs).

It is found in the coastal waters
of warm seas in 20–100 m
(65–330 ft) of water in overgrown
sandy silt, into which it likes to
burrow.

Mantis Shrimps are caught at
night in strong trawl nets, especially on the Italian coast. In
South-east Asia three main types
are fished: *Harpiosquilla raphidae*
is the largest and most popular,
followed by *Harpiosquilla harpax*
and the smaller *Oratosquilla
nepa*.

In America, Mantis Shrimps
are not fished commercially, although they are found on both
the Atlantic and Pacific coasts.
Italians sell the flavoursome tail
meat under the much-abused
name of 'scampi'.

CIRRIPEDES
(Cirripedia)

This order of lower crustaceans
includes the sea pocks and barnacles, of which only the latter
has any culinary importance in
Europe. Sea pocks are eaten only
in Chile, where the large *Mega-
balanus psittacus* is collected from
the rocks to sell locally.

GOOSE BARNACLES
(Lepadidae/Scalpellidae)

For the layman, it is difficult to
believe that these strange creatures are crustaceans, for they
look much more like molluscs.
The flat body is enclosed by a
chalky shell, supported on a
fleshy stalk. They attach themselves to floating objects, such as
spars of wood or seaweed, and
can survive only in relatively
clean water. Goose barnacles
should not be confused with the
shellfish which the Americans call
duck clams, although the Americans sometimes sell them under
the same name.

Barnacle, Goose Neck
*(Lepas anatifera), Fr. Barnacle,
Ger. Große Entenmuschel, Dut.
Eendenmossel, Port. Perceve,
Span. Bellota de Mar, Percebe,
Ital. Balani, Pico*
This member of the crustacean
family sits on a brown stalk up to
5 cm (2 in) long. It clings to
planks, bottles or other floating
objects. It is not the barnacle
itself which is eaten, but its stalk.
The leathery outer skin peels off
easily after cooking.

Rock Barnacle
(Pollicipes cornucopia), *Fr. Pousse-pied, Ger. Felsenenten-muschel, Span. Percebe*

Similar in shape to the Barnacle, but with each side of the shell composed of several plates, the Rock Barnacle is found on the tide-line of warmer coasts. It clings not to moving objects but to rocks. Rock Barnacles are collected chiefly in Spain and Italy and sold in fish markets. They are also found in the Pacific from the Aleutian Islands to Chile. In Chile, they are regarded as a delicacy and are sold both fresh and canned.

EUPHAUSIACEANS
(Euphausiacea)

The small euphausiaceans, only millimetres long, could easily be confused with shrimps but they are not decapods. There are around 100 species but only one is of interest here, *Euphasia superba*, which we know as 'krill'. These creatures differ from the decapods in that their lateral gills are not covered by the shell and they have no pincers. They have luminous organs, usually ten, situated at the base of the eye-stalks and legs and on the tail segments. As with glow-worms, these luminescent organs are activated by the nervous system.

Their lifestyle is holoplanctic, i.e. they spend their whole life swimming free in the water. They congregate into huge shoals. One of the largest shoals ever recorded was sighted in the Arctic and it covered several square kilometres and a depth of 200 m (650 ft). It would weigh an estimated 10 million tonnes (9,800,000 tons). They are found in open water in every sea, where they form an important part of the plankton.

Krill
(Euphausia superba)

Krill hit the headlines a few years ago when it was first suggested that their huge numbers could be utilized for human consumption. Estimates of possible annual yields vary between 30 million and 160 million tonnes (29,400,000–156,800,000 tons). The thinking behind the lower estimate is to leave an allowance to protect the whale, which feeds exclusively on Krill. With over 60 per cent protein content, Krill would make an excellent human foodstuff. At present, however, it is used mainly for animal feed, for all attempts to turn Krill into a tasty food have failed. In Japan, it is made into a pâté, in the USSR into 'ocean paste'. It has been tried in Europe in cheese spreads.

Mantis Shrimps. These are mostly sold in local markets, for the numbers caught are small. If you do find these attractive creatures for sale, buy them: the tail is very meaty and full of flavour. They are often sold as 'scampi'.

MOLLUSCS

In any discussion of molluscs, it is invariably bivalves which first spring to mind – although this large order in fact includes such varied groups as snails, mussels and squid. Given the confusing variety of molluscs found around the world, only the main ones can be described here. They have been arranged not so much according to any zoological table as according to their availability and importance in the kitchen.

All molluscs are invertebrates with bodies divided into four sections: the head with the mouth opening and often highly developed sense organs, such as tentacles and eyes; the muscular foot, which provides for movement; the intestinal sac, which contains the digestive organs, and the 'mantle', which encloses the mantle cavity and secretes the shell. Respiration in most molluscs is through gills, although in land snails the mantle cavity has developed into an air-breathing lung.

With the exception of the oyster, in most molluscs the sexes are separate. In many bivalves, eggs and sperm are expelled into the water, where fertilization then takes place. The first stage of development is a larval one, in which swimming larvae form part of the plankton before sinking to the sea-bed to continue their development.

The most striking feature of most molluscs is the shell, which not only provides protection and sturdiness but also replaces muscles. The shell usually outlives the animal it houses and is often all the evidence we have of a particular animal. These shells consist of calcium carbonate, which is secreted by the mantle. Carbon dioxide from respiration helps to loosen calcium in the sea-bed, which is then ingested with food. The shells of molluscs consist of three layers: on the outside is an organic layer, which protects the underlying calcium layers against the dissolving effect of acids. Below this are two thick calcareous layers. The great wealth of shapes and sizes ranges from tiny shells 1 mm (0.04 in) in length to the shell of the giant clam, which can be well over 1 m (3 ft) in length and weigh up to 50 kg (1 cwt). In addition, there is the wide variety of shapes and colours. These shells have always been a source of fascination for collectors, with the prettiest and most unusual being catalogued or turned into jewellery. Sea shells are also still used in some primitive cultures as everyday utensils, such as knives, spoons and dishes.

BIVALVES
(Bivalvia)

With around 8,000 species, bivalves are the second largest class of molluscs. The shell consists of two shells, or valves, joined by a dorsal hinge. When closed, the shells completely cover the shellfish. On one side is a hinge, formed by interlocking teeth on either valve. The two halves of the shell are closed by a muscle made up of two parts: one part is used to close the shell quickly, but this uses a lot of energy and soon becomes tired; the other half expends little energy and is able to keep the shell closed for weeks on end. Both reactions are essential for the animal's survival – the quick closure as a protection against enemies and the prolonged closure as a protection against 'siege' and to prevent enemies, such as starfish, from prising the shell open. A few figures will demonstrate the energy expended: in the oyster, the quick-acting mussel can bear a stress of 500 g/sq cm (7 lb/sq in) compared with 12 kg/sq cm (170 lb/sq in) for the retaining muscle!

As a rule, bivalves are immobile. When they do move, it is by means of the foot, which is stretched as far forward as possible, and then anchored to the ground, so that the creature can drag itself slowly forward. Some species, however, are incapable of movement. These include edible mussels and oysters. Mussels, for instance, have byssus threads which anchor them to the rock.

There are other species which dig or bore their way into peat, wood or rock. There are a few bivalves, like scallops, which are able to swim.

Strict quality controls ensure that shellfish are sold in perfect condition. Nevertheless, watch out for the following:
- Uncooked shellfish should always be closed.
- Shells should open during boiling. If they don't, the flesh is inedible.
- Shellfish should always be eaten fresh. If you can't be sure of freshness, don't eat it.

Bivalves, the best filter factories in the ocean

The gills of a bivalve are quite remarkable. They are contained in a cavity formed by the mantle and covered with 'cilia', or fine hairs, which conduct the water over the surface of the gills. The gills fulfill a dual role. They not only allow respiration but also filter the water taken in to remove any suitable food particles, which are then passed to the mouth. The filtering capacity varies, depending on the type and size of the bivalve and on the surrounding conditions. A small, edible mussel filters about 2 L (3½ pts) water per hour at a water temperature of 14 C (57 F), the European oyster as much as 12 L (21 pts) at 15 C (59 F) and the American oyster over 18 L (4 gals) at 20 C (68 F) and more than 37 L (8 gals) per hour at 24 C (75 F). This amazing filtering ability cleanses the water of sediment and waste material, which makes bivalves a sort of 'health inspectorate' of the ocean, benefitting the whole of marine life. On the other hand, this can be far from beneficial to people who eat shellfish. In heavily polluted waters, shellfish can build up dangerous substances in their bodies, which leads to food

poisoning when they are eaten. Strict control of commercial fishing helps to minimize the risk, however.

MUSSELS (*Mytilidae*)
Edible Mussel, Blue Mussel
(*Mytilus edulis*), Fr. Moule, Mouscle, Ger. Miesmuschel, Pfahlmuschel, Seemuschel, Ital. Mitilo Comune, Muscolo, Cozza, Span. Mejillón, Mocejone, Port. Mexilhão
The blue-black edible mussel, 5–10 cm (2–4 in) in length, was referred to by the Ancient Greeks quite simply as the Edible Mussel. Distributed throughout the oceans of the northern hemisphere, it is one of nature's greatest gifts to man. Its tasty flesh is highly nutritious, rich in mineral salts, iron, vitamins A, B, C, D and protein. Where no mussels are naturally available, they can almost always be artificially cultivated in mussel farms. In their natural habitat, they are found at depths of up to 10 m (33 ft). They are found on rocks, stakes and other underwater features. Shallow coastal areas usually have vast mussel beds, which can extend over several square kilometres.

The Edible Mussel is not attached to the rock by its foot but by means of byssus threads. Byssus is a paste-like substance produced by a gland at the base of the foot. When spun into threads, it becomes horny and can withstand a great deal of pressure. When the mussel wants to attach itself to the surface beneath, it presses the tip of its foot on the chosen spot. This produces a sticky secretion which is pressed onto the surface by the foot. The gland then produces one byssus thread after another and each is pressed onto the sticky patch.

Nowadays, the best mussels come from artificial farms. Since they multiply very quickly – one single mussel can eject 5–12 million eggs into the water for fertilization two or three times a year – farming is not difficult.

Compared with the vast European market, sales in the United

States and Canada are relatively low. Here the accent has been mostly upon the export of live shellfish.

Considering the versatility, nutritional value and low cost of mussels, consumption seems likely to rise even in the United States, thus widening the market considerably.

Relatives of the Edible Mussel

Within the *Mytilidae* family, one can distinguish several species and types which are distributed worldwide as well as being concentrated in a few specific locations. On the Pacific coast, from Alaska southwards, is found *Mytilus californiensis*. South-east Asia is home to the bright green *Mytilus smaragdinus*, 8–10 cm (3–4 in) long. In this region, mussels are dried after boiling and then fried or bottled. The Thais like to dip the dried mussels in sugar before frying them. In the Mediterranean, the most common species is *Mytilus galloprovincialis*, the Blue-bearded or Sea Mussel. Here you will also find the Bearded Horse Mussel (*Modiolus barbatus*), whose dark shell is covered with fringes that trail over the edge of the shell. Another interesting Mediterranean mussel is the Date Mussel (*Lithophaga lithophaga*), which produces acids to make holes in limestone rocks, in which it lives.

Mussel farms and mussel sowing

Where mussels are artificially bred, this is known as a mussel farm. The mussel farm can be organized in a number of ways, depending on the coastal features. There are two main methods used, each of which can be varied according to specific circumstances. Either the mussels attach themselves to lines hanging in the water or to piles hammered into the sea-bed – so that they live in open water between the surface and bed of the sea – or they are 'sown' on the sea-bed. Holland relies almost entirely upon the latter method, while in Spain thick ropes are hung in the water. In Italy, grass or hemp ropes are used and in France poles or shrubs are rammed into the sea-bed.

The Dutch method of cultivation is generally considered the most up-to-date. Here, the process begins with the so-called 'sowing'. When the free-swimming larvae attach themselves to the sea-bed as small mussels, they form normal mussel banks. The sea currents that carry the tiny mussels to specific spots where they settle side by side play a decisive part in the establishment of these banks.

Twice a year, in May and in September/October, these mussel banks are fished. Each of the licensed mussel farmers is assigned his own area. The baby mussels collected are first 'sown' on the sea-bed in shallow water. Later, when the mussels have grown to a size of 3–4 cm (1–1½ in), they are transferred to deeper water. Each farmer has his own allotment, leased from the State.

When the mussels are big enough for the market (5–7 cm/2–3 in), they are collected from the sea-bed in trawl nets and then kept in so-called 'wet stores'. These are small areas of coastal seawater leased from dealers. Here the mussels spend between 8 hours (in summer) and 24 hours (in winter) to allow them to get rid of sand and other impurities taken in during the netting process. Depending on the source and quality of the mussels, they will keep for between one and three weeks. Artificial cultivation not only guarantees quality but, together with modern refrigeration methods and re-frigerated transport, provides a practically all-year-round supply.

The old adage that you should only eat mussels when there is an 'r' in the month originated to avoid mussel poisoning during the summer months, from highly poisonous dinoflagellates which enter the mussel's filters with the water and which can build up a high concentration of poison. The risk of mussel poisoning was once much greater than it is today, with our sophisticated storage and transport methods.

In New Zealand, the green *Perna canaliculus* is caught and sold in enormous quantities. This tasty mussel from the *Mytilidae* family is gradually capturing a world market.

Dutch producers in the mouth of the Schelde are known as mussel farmers. The sea-bed cultivation has little in common with fishing, despite the fact that the collection of the tiny 'mussel seedlings' as well as the 'sowing' and 'harvesting' is carried out by boat.

Mussels for export

The Dutch describe their extensive cultivation of mussels as a unique mineral resource. High quality Dutch mussels are now an export of great economic importance. While mussels are farmed in many parts of the world, the only large-scale cultivation is in Europe. Pride of place goes to Spain, with around 150,000 tonnes (147,000 tons) per year, followed by Holland with around 100,000 tonnes (98,000 tons). In Europe, around 300,000 tonnes (294,000 tons) of mussels are bought every year, with the French alone accounting for 80,000 tonnes (78,400 tons). Holland exports mainly to France and Belgium, while most Spanish mussels end up in Italian saucepans.

Holland's mussel centre is at Yerseke, which has the most up-to-date methods of cultivation. Dutch mussels have become a byword for quality – mainly, as in Spain, because of constant State-imposed and voluntary health controls.

Heavy trawl nets are used to harvest the mussels from the sea-bed. This method has been perfected to such a degree that a ship with a two-man crew can harvest several tonnes in the space of three hours.

Galicia, in north-west Spain, is the country's largest mussel producer. Thick ropes up to 8 m (26 ft) in length are covered with baby mussels and then enclosed in a thin, wide-meshed netting. The ropes are then suspended in the water from anchored floats.

The growing of mussels on ropes is a fairly labour-intensive method, for the mussels have to be moved two or three times as they grow. When they are about 3 cm (1 in) in length, they are removed from the ropes for the first time and transferred to new ropes, which are again enclosed in netting and suspended in the water.

Mussel farming in Spain

Cultivating mussels on hanging ropes is a method which works particularly well in Rías, a part of the Spanish Atlantic coast which is not unlike the Norwegian fjords. The sheltered situation of this calm bay and the constant exchange of water through the ebb and flow of the tide encourage the build-up of plankton, the mussels' main food. Today there are over 3,000 firmly anchored floats along the coast of Galicia, from which the mussel-covered ropes are suspended. Because of the extremely favourable conditions in Rías, the mussels grow very quickly so that, after two or three moves of position as they grow, they reach a commercial size of 7 cm (3 in) in length after only eight to nine months. This compares extremely favourably with mussels grown elsewhere – in Britain or Canada, for instance – which take four to five years to reach this size.

The ropes, which can weigh up to 120 kg (264 lb), are hauled into boats and stripped of their harvest. Mussels to be sold fresh are washed, and usually packed, on board. The rest go to preserving factories along the coast, where they are boiled, sorted and finally hand-shelled. It is almost impossible to shell mussels by machine, as the flesh is extremely delicate.

The ropes hang free in the water from anchored floats, to avoid disturbing the sea-bed. The calm, sheltered bays of the Rías on the Atlantic coast of Spain, with water constantly changed by the ebb and flow of the tide, provide ideal conditions for the mussels to grow.

Large metal baskets are used to haul the heavy ropes on board, when the mussels have reached commercial size of at least 7 cm (3 in). Spanish mussels grow faster and are usually larger than Dutch mussels or American ones from the Maine coast.

The mussels are washed on board the boat by machines, which use seawater. Spanish mussels are already free of sand, since they never come into contact with the sea-bed.

Mussels are sorted by hand – not only here in Spain but also in Holland and on the east coast of America. Those that do not reach the required size are removed from the conveyor belt.

In New Zealand, the method is the same as in Spain but the approach is somewhat more modern. The calm, crystal-clear waters of the Marlborough Sound between the North and South Islands provides ideal conditions for this method of farming, with perfect tidal currents. So-called 'longlines' are stretched directly below the surface of the water and from these are suspended the long, vertical ropes on which the green New Zealand mussels are grown. They take about 18 months to reach their full size of around 10 cm (4 in).

OYSTERS
(*Ostreidae, Pteriidae, Malleidae*)

From the culinary viewpoint, the oyster is a prince among shellfish. The mere mention of these unprepossessing, unattractive, greyish-white or greyish-green, scaly bivalves makes the heart of any gourmet beat a little faster. Poets have sung the praises of this 'ornament of the ocean', festivals have been held in its honour. Casanova is said to have eaten at least fifty oysters every evening. The long-standing persistent rumour that eating oysters has highly stimulating side-effects has certainly added to its reputation. It is a fact that oysters are extremely nutritious. Although they are 83 per cent water, the remainder is made up of about 9 per cent protein, 4.8 per cent carbohydrate, 1.2 per cent fat, vitamins A, B_1, B_2, nicotinamide, biotin, folic acids and B_{12}, plus minerals – calcium, magnesium, zinc, iron, iodine and phosphorus. The calorie count is around 71.1 kcal per 100 g.

The history of the oyster goes back a long way. They were eaten as long ago as prehistoric times. The Chinese and the hedonistic Romans discovered their delights. These much-sought-after shellfish were imported, mainly from Gaul and Britain, in amphorae filled with seawater. It was also the Romans who, 2,000 years ago, began to farm oysters in sheltered bays. In France, the first attempts to cultivate oysters artificially began much later, with the first large farms being established in 1858.

With the introduction of the Bonamia virus in the early 1970s in imported Pacific Cupped Oysters (*Crassostrea gigas*) from Japan, the oyster beds on the French coast were almost totally destroyed. It was some time before the Bonamia virus was identified and by this time it had also found its way to Holland in cultivated oysters.

There are over 100 types of oyster distributed throughout the world's moderate and warm seas. Although they may differ in shape, size and colour, all have irregular, scaly shells and a single dorsal muscle. With the left, flatter valve they cement themselves to a hard surface. Their food consists of small plant and animal organisms (plankton) filtered out of the water as it passes through the gills (also known as the 'beard').

Unlike most bivalves, most oysters are hermaphrodites, with male and female sex cells which mature at different times. The food supply and water temperature determine when an oyster will reach the male or female stage. From the fertilized eggs (a European oyster produces between 600,000 and 3,000,000 eggs per year), larvae develop. These spend several weeks in the water as plankton before forming shells and attaching themselves to a hard surface. In suitable rocky spots, enormous beds containing millions of oysters can develop.

After about three years, the oysters are fully grown – sooner in areas particularly rich in plankton. Some types of oysters can live for up to thirty years.

Up to now we have been talking about the true oysters, the *Ostreidae*, but the term 'oyster' is used commercially to cover other bivalves, similar in appearance but totally unrelated to the true oyster. These include the wing oysters (*Pteriidae*) and hammer oysters (*Malleidae*). Since they are usually sold as oysters we have included them here in the oyster section.

Long, wearisome work: oyster farming

Oyster farming is a lengthy, labour-intensive occupation. It takes three to four years and thirty-five different processes to produce a marketable oyster.

First, the tiny larvae – which, after spawning (from June to August), spend some time free-swimming before starting to look for an anchorage – have to be caught. The oyster farmers help the larvae by providing a suitable site, known as a 'collector'. These can take the form of slates or roof tiles covered in calcium, mussel shells suspended on wires, or plastic rods or bricks.

After about eight months, the young oysters are picked off the collectors and transferred to so-called 'oyster parks'. These are enclosures – usually protected by low grilles against storms and the oyster's natural enemies (crabs, starfish, robber snails, squid) – laid out in tidal areas rich in plankton. The young oysters are laid out on the sea-bed or occasionally on low racks, either free in shallow wire cages, or in wide-meshed plastic sacks. Here they are left for two to three years to reach a marketable size. During this time, they have to be nursed and looked after. They must not be allowed to grow too close together and algae and mussels must be removed.

Now is the time for fattening and improving the oysters – a must with the French 'marennes' or 'fines de claires' – in so-called 'claires', shallow basins or converted salt-pans in which the water is extremely rich in plankton but less salty than that in the parks. Here the oysters take ten to twelve months to reach top quality and to take on their characteristic flavour, produced by the different water and food conditions in each 'claire'. The most famous claires are those in Marennes in France, which not only give the oysters a fine nutty flavour but also colour them a delicate shade of green. This colouring is produced by an alga which contains copper, on which the oysters mainly feed.

Finally, before the oysters can be sold, they spend a few days in clean basins, regulated by the authorities, where they expel sand and other impurities. In the Marennes basins, the oysters also have to 'learn' how to survive out of water. To this end, the basins are emptied at night and the oysters soon catch on to the fact that they must keep their shells hermetically sealed to retain water. This 'training' is impor-

Arcachon on the French Atlantic coast is an oyster centre steeped in tradition. Here there are extensive oyster parks, producing the flat, round oysters sold as 'Gravettes d'Arcachon'. Many Marenne oysters also come from Arcachon, where they grow to market size in the parks before being transferred to the claires at Marennes, where they are purified and take on their green colour.

tant if they are to survive transportation and storage, which with refrigeration can last up to two weeks.

In Europe, the traditional oyster season falls in the months that contain an 'r' – that is, from September to April. Of course, this varies in other parts of the world where different seasonal conditions prevail.

Nowadays, oyster farming takes place along the coasts of most industrialized countries. World leaders are the United States, Japan, France, Denmark, Holland, England, Ireland, Australia, New Zealand and Canada. Only 20 per cent of the American production is eaten raw, the rest being preserved by various methods. Oysters can be smoked, frozen or even air-dried, but most are bottled. In Europe, quite the reverse is true: a good 80 per cent are eaten fresh.

French 'huîtres creuses' – like these from Brittany – are always cupped oysters from the *Crassostrea* family, either the native 'Portugaises' or the Pacific 'Japonaises', introduced into Europe in the 1960s.

Common Oyster, Flat Oyster, Plate Oyster

(Ostrea edulis), Fr. Huître Plate, Ger. Europäsische Auster, Nor. Östers, Swed. Ostron, Dan. Europaeisk Østers, Dut. Oester, Span. Ostra, Ostion, Port. Ostra, Ital. Ostrica

Until the mid-1940s, this flat, almost circular oyster supplied almost all the requirements of restaurants and homes in Germany and northern Europe. Since then, oyster beds along the Atlantic and North Sea coasts have been decimated by the Bonamia virus. Few consumers have been aware of the shortage, since oyster farmers made up the shortfall with English and Irish oysters and by introducing into Europe the Pacific or Japanese oyster (*Crassostrea gigas*).

The Common Oyster grows to 5–12 cm (2–5 in) in diameter. It takes about three years to reach full size, longer than the other native European oyster, the Portuguese Cupped Oyster. There is a wide colour variation, from pale grey or green to sand-coloured. Colour, shape, size and flavour are greatly influenced by the oyster's environment. The mineral content of the water and the type of food available produce different characteristics, so oysters are often distinguished by their place of origin. The Common Oyster comes onto the market in a wide range of different varieties, whose names reflect their place of origin. In France there are Belons, Marennes or Gravettes d'Arcachon, in Belgium Ostendes, in Holland Imperialen, in Denmark Limfjords and in Ireland Rossmoie, Red Bank or Galway Oysters. In England there are Colchester, Helford, Pyefleet and Whitstable Oysters, known collectively as Native Oysters.

The mild-tasting Common Oyster is native to Brittany, although nowadays the oyster parks in this French region are better known for the stronger-flavoured Portuguese Cupped Oysters.

Portuguese Cupped Oyster

(Crassostrea angulata), Fr. Huître Creuse, Huître Portùgaise, Ger. Portugiesische Auster, Felsenauster, Dan. Portugisisk Østers, Dut. Portugese Oester, Ital. Ostrica di Portugal, Span. Ostra de Portugal

This, the second most important type of European oyster, is found to a large extent in the same areas as the Common Oyster, described

Clarifying basins are known in Holland as 'oesterpotten' or 'verwaterbassins'. Oysters ready for the market – such as the Imperial shown here – spend a few days in quarantine before they are sold. Here in Yerseke in Holland the basins are watered by the Oosterschelde. The basins also provide storage for up to six weeks.

above. There are, however, marked differences between the two, mainly in flavour, which is less delicate in the Portuguese Oyster.

The Portuguese Oyster is slate-grey to brown in colour. In shape it resembles a scaly, unpolished pebble with the division between the two valves often hardly distinguishable. While the flesh of the Common Oyster is beige or sand-coloured, in the Portuguese Cupped Oyster it is greyish-violet.

France is the country best known for the cultivation of Portuguese Oysters. In the oyster basins, or claires, around Marennes-Oléron a special kind of alga is grown to feed the oysters. It is this alga, with its high mineral content, that gives the oysters their green colour. These oysters, known as 'Fines de Claires' or 'Spéciales Claires' are considered the best of the Portuguese Cupped Oysters, and their name gives a good indication of the method of cultivation. Oysters cultivated in the usual way which come to the market direct from the parks without being fattened and refined in the claires, are known as 'Huîtres de Parc'. French oysters used to be known in Germany and northern Europe as 'Arcachons' but nowadays this name is reserved for Common Oysters.

Production of the Portuguese Cupped Oyster has declined considerably since the 1960s. In Europe, it has been replaced largely by the Pacific Cupped Oyster, although it is being cultivated increasingly in the United States.

Eastern or Atlantic Oyster, American Cupped Oyster
(Crassostrea virginica), Fr. Huître Creuse Américaine, Ger. Amerikanische Auster
Although in zoological terms this oyster belongs to the same family as the Portuguese Cupped Oyster, its round shape makes it much more like the Common Oyster. With its gondola-like shape it closely resembles the English Colchester.

Eastern Oysters are found along the entire Atlantic coast of the USA, from the Gulf of St Lawrence to Florida. They provide for around 85 per cent of oyster consumption in the eastern United States. In America, they are to be found under a variety of names, most of which show the precise place of origin: Blue Point, Cape Cod, Kent Island, Chincoteague, Apalachicola.

The flesh is similar in colour to that of the Common Oyster. While the weight of flesh per oyster is higher, it is inferior in quality to the Common Oyster.

Attempts to cultivate the Atlantic Oyster in Europe have proved unsuccessful, on the whole, because of the lower water temperature.

Pacific Cupped Oyster, Pacific King Oyster, Japanese Oyster
(Crassostrea gigas), Fr. Huître Creuse du Pacific, Ger. Pazifische Felsenauster, Japanische Auster, Chin. Mau Lai, Indon. & Malay. Tiram, Phil. Talaba, Jap. Ma-gaki
This type of oyster is native to the waters around Japan and the China Sea. Similar sub-species are found in the Indo-Pacific area and in South Sea coral reefs. Wholesale cultivation is carried out in Hong Kong, China, Japan and Korea. Because of their immense size – up to 30 cm (1 ft) in length – they are often called Giant Oysters. They are similar in shape to the Portuguese Cupped Oyster but are more highly domed and compact, not unlike a gondola in shape. Because of their size and richness, they are often cooked and served in hot dishes. In Asia they are often dried, especially those produced in Hong Kong.

In the early 1950s, a start was made on cultivating the Pacific oyster on the west coast of the United States. Since this oyster, unlike most others, does not change sex, a genetic sorting process is possible. Nowadays they are found all along the western seaboard from Alaska to California. In the early 1960s, when yields of Common Oysters fell off sharply, especially in Holland and France, Pacific oysters were tried here, too, and

Fine, round English oysters are often more popular with gourmets nowadays than the famous French Belons. For many, the Colchester (far left) with its 'incomparable flavour and just enough bite' is the king of oysters, while others swear by the mild-flavoured Whitstable (near left).

The robust 'Portugaise', *Crassostrea angulata* (far left), is another European oyster, slightly inferior to *Ostrea edulis*. Nevertheless, these 'Huîtres Creuses' include some culinary favourites, namely the green 'Fines de Claires' and 'Spéciales', produced from the claires at Marennes. Similar to the Portuguese is the Pacific Cupped Oyster, such as this 'Yearling' from the American Pacific coast (near left).

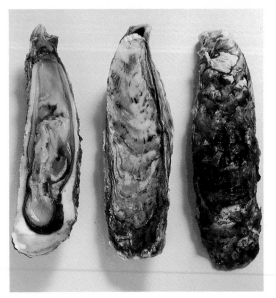

The resilient Pacific Cupped Oyster (*Crassostrea gigas*) is native to Japanese and Chinese waters, but was introduced into Europe and the United States to replace the decimated native varieties. Nowadays, it supplies most of the demand in both areas. Owing to their size and richness, Pacific oysters (far left, a particularly large American variety; near left, a 'Komimoto') are often served in cooked dishes.

proved resistant to the troublesome Bonamia virus. Like the Portuguese oyster, which they resemble, 'Japonaises' as they are known in France are also classified by the cultivation method. To some extent, it has also become usual practice to complete the classification with the name of the area of production.

Today the Pacific Cupped Oyster supplies most of the demand in the United States and Europe. It has recently become the main oyster cultivated in Europe. From the western Mediterranean to the Dalmatian coast, it is gradually replacing the native Portuguese oyster.

While European oyster farmers are increasingly introducing this rounded oyster, the flat North European oyster is growing in popularity in Canada and Japan, where it is farmed intensively and much appreciated for its fine flavour.

Western Oyster, Olympia Flat Oyster, Native Pacific Oyster
(Ostrea lurida), Fr. Huître Plate Indigène, Ger. Westamerikanische Auster, Span. Ostra
The oyster native to the American Pacific coast shows marked signs of relationship with the Common Oyster. It grows up to 5 cm (2 in) in diameter and has an extremely delicate flavour. Numbers have fallen considerably as a result of overfishing and water pollution but an effort is being made to improve the situation through cultivation, so that in future this oyster should regain its former importance.

Sydney Rock Oyster
(Crassostrea commercialis), Ger. Australische Auster, Sydney Felsenauster, Indon. Tiram, Malay. Tiram Batu, Phil. Talaba
A cupped oyster widespread on the southern coast of Australia. As early as 1870, cultivation of this wild oyster began on the coast of New South Wales between Wallis Lakes and the George River/Botany Bay.

This is another oyster which

Different as they may appear, these oysters are all the same type: six examples of *Crassostrea virginica*, all from different regions. As with the European oysters, the names of these American oysters point to the exact place of origin. Arranged on their bed of ice are (top, left to right) the spicy-tasting Blue Point from Long Island, the Chincoteague from Virginia, the small Apalachicola, named after the river in Florida and (bottom, left to right) a Chatam from the East Coast, a fine Belon from Maine and a Box Oyster from Long Island.

These oyster scales are used to sort the shellfish by weight for the market. Each oyster is placed individually in one of the scale pans, the scales begin to rotate and stop at the scale showing the correct weight. The oyster then falls through into the container below.

No cheaper by the dozen

Oysters are usually sold by the dozen or half-dozen and are eaten alive. The price is determined first by the type (and quality) and also by weight (i.e. size). The system of classification for the market is just as confusing as the names of the various types. Further confusion is added by the fact that this system has changed considerably over the years.

In Holland, the round flat oysters known as 'Imperials' (*Ostrea edulis*) are classified by a system of zeros, which at present covers the following minimum weights:

3/0 = 60 g (2 oz)
4/0 = 75 g (2½ oz)
5/0 = 90 g (3 oz)
6/0 = 105 g (4 oz)
6/0E = 120 g (4¼ oz)

In England, France and Ireland, on the other hand, *Ostrea edulis* is classified by

minimum weight as follows:

No.4 = 40 g (1½ oz)
No.3 = 50 g (1¾ oz)
No.2 = 60 g (2 oz)
No.1 = 75 g (2½ oz)
No.0 = 90 g (3 oz)
No.00 = 100 g (3½ oz)
No.000 = 110 g (4 oz)
No.0000 = 120 g (4¼ oz)
No.00000 = 150 g (5¼ oz)

For the cupped 'Portugaises' (*Crassostrea angulata*) and the Pacific Cupped Oysters or 'Japonaises' (*Crassostrea gigas*), the French have a different, simpler system, as follows:

—very large (TG), over 100 g (3½ oz) per oyster
—large (G), 75–99 g (2½–3½ oz)
—medium (M), 50–74 g (1¾ – 2½ oz)
—small (P), less than 50 g (1¾ oz)

The Americans have the simplest system of all, with only three sizes:
—large
—medium
—small

changes sex and is extremely fertile. In the space of three years, it grows to around 7 cm (3 in) and to a market weight of around 55 g (2 oz). Despite its fine flavour, this oyster has the drawback of being difficult to open.

Australia is one of the world's leading oyster producers. In the area mentioned above, there are about 400 oyster-farming businesses. Since 1983, there have been contacts between Australian producers and European importers, to explore the possibility of farming Australian oysters in European beds.

Oyster

(*Lopha frons*), Fr. Huître, Ger. Klammerauster
This small bivalve, found in coastal waters in the Caribbean and South Pacific, has an irregular oval shape with an extremely knobbly surface, deeply etched with irregular ribs. It lives on rocks or coral.

Wing Oyster, Pearl Oyster

(*Pinctada spp.*), Ger. Flügelauster, Perlauster, Vogelmuschel, Chin. Chun Chu Law, Malay. Sapanda, Togok, Indon. Tapis-tapis
Wing Oysters are a group of Pacific bivalves, of which the *Pteria* (formerly *Avicola*) and *Pinctada* (formerly *Melegrina*) families are the best known. The shell is more regular in shape than that of European or American oysters, is usually larger and has a long, wing-like extension on one side. The inside of the shell is mother-of-pearl. These oysters can reach 20 cm (8 in) in diameter. The flesh is a great delicacy in South-east Asia, but they are used mainly for producing mother-of-pearl and for making jewellery.

Hammer Oyster

(*Malleus malleus*), Fr. Marteau Commune, Ger. Schwarze Hammermuschel
The layered shell is shaped like a hammer or ice-pick. This species is between 10 and 20 cm (4–8 in) long and is found in the Indo-Pacific.

White Hammer Oyster

(*Malleus albus*), Fr. Marteau Blanc, Ger. Weiße Hammermuschel
The shell of this sand-burrowing bivalve can reach 20 cm (8 in) in length. Like the Hammer Oyster, it is a native of the Indo-Pacific.

ARK SHELLS
(*Arcidae*)

The family of ark shells is one of the oldest of all the bivalves. They go back as far as the Cambrian period, some 500,000,000 years ago. Both valves are identical in shape, either rectangular, trapezoid or oval, and are occasionally ribbed. Most of the 200 species are found in tropical waters. A remarkable feature of the ark shells is the hinge, made up of many apparently indentical teeth and almost as long as the shell. As in snails, the ark shell's foot is used for movement.

Noah's Ark

(*Arca noae*), Fr. Arche de Noé, Ger. Arche Noah, Ital. Arca di Noè, Span. Pepitona, Arca de Noe, Port. Castanholas, Grk. Cǎlognomi
This is the best known ark shell and of the greatest culinary importance. It is long and boatshaped, dark brown in colour with reddish zig-zags. Round the edge of the mantle are some 100 spots.

The Noah's Ark lives on a hard surface, often in niches in the rock, in the Mediterranean and east Atlantic. In Mediterranean countries the Noah's Ark, which grows to between 7 and 9 cm (3–3½ in) in length, is mainly eaten raw. In Italy, you will find it in any fish market.

West Indian Turkey Wing

(*Arca zebra*), Ger. Zebramuschel, Span. Pepitona (South America)
A bivalve similar in shape to the Noah's Ark. The shell is irregularly shaped, with white and brown stripes and ribs radiating outwards. It grows to 9 cm (3½ in) in length and is native to the southern Atlantic coast of the United States from North Caro-

lina via Bermuda and the Antilles to Brazil.

Giant Ark

(Anadara grandis), *Ger. Riesen-archenmuschel*, *Span. Sangara*
This bivalve grows to 15 cm (6 in) and has an extremely thick and heavy shell. It is similar in shape to a cockle. The white, heavily ribbed shell is covered on the outside with a thick, brown layer of chitin *(periostracum)*, which has usually flaked off around the vortex.

The Giant Ark lives on the west coast of Central America, from southern California to Peru, on tidal sandbanks. The local people collect them to use in soups, but they can also be boiled in their shells.

Mogai Clam

(Anadara subcrenata), *Fr. Clam Mogai*, *Ger. Japanische Archen-muschel*, *Span. Arca Japonesa*
This bivalve, with its pronounced radiating ribs and chitin covering *(periostracum)*, is widespread in China, Japan and Korea. In Japan, it is of considerable commercial importance. It grows to around 5 cm (2 in) in length.

Blood Cockle

(Anadara granosa), *Fr. Arche Grenue*, *Ger. Rotfleischige Archenmuschel*
This ark shell, 6–9 cm ($2\frac{1}{2}$–$3\frac{1}{2}$ in) in length, is widespread in the Indo-Pacific. It is similar in appearance to the Mogai Clam, except that the radiating ribs have distinct tubercles. The flesh is a striking blood-red. In some South-east Asian countries, they are bred commercially.

Eared Ark

(Anadora notabilis), *Ger. Schöne Arche*
The shell of this species is similar to that of the cockle, only wider. It is white to ivory in colour and has about twenty-five radiating ribs, crossed by fine concentric growth lines. It is native to the American Atlantic coast from Florida to Bermuda and Brazil.

A full-grown Giant Ark is a considerable weight, for its shell is thick and heavy. Seen from the side, it resembles the cockle. Characteristic of this shellfish is the thick brown chitin layer *(periostracum)*, which almost always flakes off at the vortex.

The round, thick-shelled Dog Cockle *(Glycymeris glycymeris)* is caught and sold all year round in the Mediterranean. It is not, however, popular with connoisseurs of shellfish, especially when full grown.

Ark Shell

(Senilia senilis, formerly Arca senilis), *Fr. Arche Large-côtes*, *Ger. Westafrikanische Archen-muschel*
This bivalve, with its thick, heavy shell and wide, flat, concentric ribs, is similar in shape to the cockle. It grows to 6–10 cm ($2\frac{1}{2}$–4 in) in diameter. It is found mainly on the West African coast, from the western Sahara to Angola.

DOG COCKLES
(Glycymeridae)

A family native to the tropics and warm to moderate waters, of which four species are known.

Dog Cockle, Bittersweet

(Glycymeris glycymeris, formerly Pectunculus glycymeris), *Fr. Amande de Mer*, *Ger. Samtmuschel*, *Ital. Piè d'Asino*, *Span. Excupiña, Inglesa, Pectuncolo*
The thick, flat, almost round shell, similar to that of the scallop, has distinct concentric stripes and is predominantly white with irregular brown mark-

ings and spots on the edge of the mantle. The Dog Cockle grows to 6–8 cm ($2\frac{1}{2}$–3 in) in diameter. It is found from Norway to Morocco and occasionally in the Mediterranean and lives buried in the seabed at depths of around 20 m (65 ft).

True Dog Cockle

(Glycymeris pilosa, formerly Pectunculus pilosa), *Fr. Amande de Mer*, *Ger. Echte Samtmuschel*
The True Dog Cockle is similar in shape and size to the species discussed above, but the shell is dark brown with fine concentric stripes. The white insides of the valves are strikingly flecked in brown.

Violet Bittersweet

(Glycymeris violacescens, formerly Pectunculus violacescens), *Fr. Pétoncle Violâtre*, *Ger. Violette Samtmuschel*, *Ital. Piè d'Asino*, *Span. Almejón, Perillo*
Unlike the previous two species, this dog cockle is irregular in shape. The top has fine, radiating ribs, slightly crimped at the edge. The shell is greyish-violet on the outside and pinkish-white with brownish-violet flecks inside. These bivalves grow to 4–8 cm ($1\frac{1}{2}$–3 in) in diameter and live on sand in shallow water to a depth of 60 cm (2 ft). Found along the Mediterranean and Atlantic coasts, from Portugal to Morocco.

The Giant Bittersweet *(Glycymeris gigantea)* has a striking brown zig-zag pattern. It is common for them to reach 10 cm (4 in) in diameter.

Giant Bittersweet

*(Glycymeris gigantea), Ger.
Große Pazifische Samtmuschel*
The shell is round and regular
with radiating ribs, white with
zig-zag markings. This species
grows to around 10 cm (4 in) in
diameter and is found in the Gulf
of California to Acapulco,
Mexico, at depths of 7–13 m
(23–43 ft).

FAN MUSSELS
(*Pinnidae*)

These large wedge- or fan-shaped
bivalves bury themselves point
first in the sand. When two-thirds
covered, they anchor themselves
in position with byssus threads.
At least one species of fan mussel
can be found in every sea and
ocean in the world.

Mediterranean Pen, Fan Mussel

*(Pinna nobilis), Fr. Jambon-
neau, Ger. Große Steckmuschel,
Edle Steckmuschel, Ital. Astura,
Ortura, Span. Alabarda, Ostra
Pena, Pina*
With shells up to 80 cm (30 in) in
length, the Mediterranean Pen is
the largest bivalve in European
waters. The shell is wide at the
top, tapering evenly to a point
and is reddish-brown in colour.
Particularly in the young, it is
closely covered with concentric
rings. The inside of the shell
gleams with a pinkish mother-of-
pearl. Fan Mussels like to live in
flat sand in up to 50 m (165 ft) of
water. They are often found near
stretches of grass-weed, where the
small mussel crab feeds on the
excretions and food of the
mussel. In recent years, numbers
of this mussel have been considerably depleted in shallow
water, largely by collectors and
amateur divers, for whom the
Mediterranean Pen is a great find.
In Italy, the strong outer byssus
threads are woven into cloth.

Stiff Pen

*(Atrina vexillum), Fr. Pinne
Pavillon, Ger. Schwarze
Schinkelmuschel*
The top half of this glossy, black
bivalve is semicircular, the lower
half sharply pointed. The shells,
which can exceed 30 cm (1 ft) in

diameter, are thin and fragile.
Unlike the *Pinna* types, the
Atrina family bury themselves
completely in sand, so that not
even the tip of the shell shows
above the surface.

SCALLOPS/
THORNY OYSTERS
(*Pectinidae, Spondylidae*)

According to Greek mythology,
Aphrodite, the goddess of love
and beauty, arose from the
waters of the Aegean and rode on
a scallop shell pulled by six sea
horses to the island of Cythara.

The famous Scallop is at its best between November and March – the
official fishing season in Europe. At this time of year, the orange-coloured
roe sac, the 'coral', is a delicacy in itself. The creamy-white flesh of the
hinge muscle is firm but tender to the bite. The 'beard' and all dark-
coloured parts should be removed before cooking.

Ever since, scallop shells have
been associated with beauty and
have been well represented in art
and architecture. Nowadays, the
scallop shell is best known as the
logo of the Shell oil company and
as a container for fish dishes.

The shells are covered right up
to the edge with radiating ribs. In
many species, they are irregular,
with the right valve round and the
left flat. On either side of the
hinge are the characteristic 'ears',
or wing-like extensions. These,
too, usually vary in size. Another
characteristic feature is the edge
of the mantle, with its distinctive
'eyes' and tentacles.

Scallops are not burrowing

creatures; with a few exceptions,
which are firmly fixed like oysters, they are able to swim. By
rapidly opening and closing their
valves, scallops move themselves
forwards in great bounds.

The flesh of the scallop is
tender and slightly sweet. Relative to the shell size, the scallop
has more flesh than the oyster.
The large red or orange roe sack
(coral), which is easily removed
once the shell is open, is in itself a
delicacy.

Worldwide, there are around
300 species of *Pectinidae*, but
only some two dozen of these are

of any commercial significance.
In Europe, the best scallops come
from the seas around Scotland,
Ireland, the Isle of Man and
France. They are collected in
trawl nets between November
and March. In European waters,
the fishing season is strictly
controlled. In the United States,
scallops are second only to oysters in popularity. There, as in
Canada, it is mainly the creamy-
white flesh of the hinge muscle
which is eaten. This is firm in
consistency but tender to the bite.
In scallops of average size, the
muscle is 1–3 cm ($\frac{1}{2}$–1 in) across
and weighs around 30 g (1 oz).
The best selling scallop is the Sea

Scallop (*Placopecten magellanicus*), which comes from the
east coast of the United States
and Canada, but for the con-
noisseur the Bay Scallop (*Pecten
irradiens*) is superior.

In Canada, too, the scallop is
well represented in fish markets.
Most of the catch is exported,
however, 75 per cent of it going to
the United States.

Scallop, Fan Shell

*(Pecten jacobaeus), Fr. Coquille
St-Jacques, Peigne de St-
Jacques, Vanne, Manteau, Ger.
Pilgermuschel, Jakobsmuschel,
Ital. Capa Santa, Conchiglia di
San Jacopo, Pellegrina, Span.
Rufina, Capa Santa, Pelegrina,
Port. Vieira, Penteola, Romeiro,
Dut. Grote Kamschelp*
The Scallop's name in many
languages commemorates the
apostle James, who met a
martyr's death in Palestine before
his bones were taken to Spain.
After the alleged discovery of his
tomb in Compostella in 820 AD,
the town became a place of
pilgrimage and James the patron
saint of Spaniards and of fishermen. The scallops caught nearby
served the pilgrims as food and
the beautiful shell soon became
the badge and symbol of all
pilgrims.

The shell of the Scallop is
almost pure white and reaches
10–13 cm (4–5 in) in diameter,
with 14 or 16 wide ribs, each
made up of four grooves. The
Scallop prefers a sandy or coral
habitat and is found mainly in the
Mediterranean.

The Great Scallop and Queen
Scallop are often sold as scallops.

Great Scallop, Common Scallop

*(Pecten maximus), Fr. Grande
Peigne, Grande Coquille St-
Jacques, Escallop, Ger. Große
Pilgermuschel, Ital. Ventaglio,
Span. Vieira, Concha de
Peregrino*
The shell of this scallop, which
measures 13–16 cm (5–6 in) in
diameter, is reddish to reddish-
brown with a violet lustre. Twelve
to thirteen round-topped ribs run
parallel to the top and continue
onto the ears, which are relatively
large.

The Great Scallop occurs on fine to coarse sand, both in shallow water and in depths of up to 200 m (650 ft). Its distribution is mainly in the Atlantic, from Norway and the British Isles to the coast of Africa. It is not, however, found in the Mediterranean.

Lion's Paw
(Nodipecten nodosus, formerly Chlamys nodosus), Fr. Peigne Coralline, Ger. Knotige Kammuschel
A reddish-brown scallop which is slightly irregular in shape. On the top are seven ridged ribs, dotted with tubercles. The ears are asymmetrical. The diameter of the shell is between 7 and 15 cm (3–6 in). The Lion's Paw is found along the southern coast of the United States, on the Brazilian coast and in the Caribbean.

Atlantic Deep-sea Scallop, Sea Scallop, Giant Scallop, Smooth Scallop
(Placopecten magellanicus), Fr. Pétoncle, Pecten d'Amérique, Ger. Atlantischer Tiefwasser-Scallop
This round scallop, with its symmetrical ears and numerous fine ribs on a light-brown shell, is the most common scallop on the east coast of the United States, as well as being the best-selling and most popular. It is caught mainly on the Maine coast but can be found from Labrador to North Carolina. The shell can reach 24 cm (9½ in) in diameter. It is caught in trawl nets at depths of up to 280 m (920 ft).

Iceland Scallop
(Chlamys islandicus), Fr. Pétoncle, Ger. Isländische Kammuschel
After the Atlantic Deep-sea Scallop, this is the second most important scallop of the North American Atlantic coast, where the main catch is from northern Newfoundland. The shell is around 10 cm (4 in) in diameter and a brownish-green in colour. The whole surface is covered in radiating ribs, roughened and whitish towards the edge. The ears are asymmetrical. This scal-

The Lion's Paw is aptly named, as it does look somewhat like the paw of a lion.

The Purple Scallop gets its name from the inside of the shell, with its wide, deep-purple border. The scallop shown here comes from Chile.

The Pacific Pink Scallop is found along the entire Pacific coast of the United States, from Alaska to California. The shell is almost perfectly circular.

The Noble Scallop is one of the most attractive. With its even ribs and rich colouring (violet, salmon and yellow tones), it is indeed a noble shell.

lop is found from Iceland and Greenland through the Arctic seas to the coast of Japan.

Variegated Scallop
(Chlamys varius, Pecten varius) Fr. Vanneau, Pétoncle, Peigne, Ger. Bunte Kammuschel, Ital. Pettine Vario, Canestrello, Span. Golondrina, Volandeira, Port. Leque, Penteola, Romeira, Dan. Jomfruøsters, Swed. Urskjell, Dut. Bonte Mantel
In a wide range of colour tones and with a pronouncedly domed shell up to 6 cm (2½ in) in diameter, the Variegated Scallop is found from Norway to West Africa and the western Mediterranean.

Purple Scallop
(Argopecten purpuratus, formerly Chlamys purpuratus), Fr. Peigne Pourpré, Ger. Purpurkammuschel, Span. Ostión del Norte, Concha de Abanico, Jap. Harategai
Like most members of its family, this scallop has asymmetrical ears. It also has around twenty-five ribs, of which seven are well formed and rounded. The ribs are flecked in white and red. The Purple Scallop is found on the coasts of Chile and Peru on sand and gravel, at depths of up to 90 m (300 ft).

Queen Scallop, Common Scallop
(Chlamys opercularis), Fr. Vanneau, Vanne, Pétoncle, Ger. Reisemantel, Kleine Pilgermuschel, Ital. Canestrello, Pettine Opercolare, Span. Golondrina, Zammoriña, Volondeira, Dut. Wijde Mantel
The reddish-brown shell of the Queen Scallop is similar in shape to that of the Great Scallop, but the surface is slightly marbled and the eighteen to twenty-two ribs less pronounced.

The Queen Scallop lives in the Mediterranean and eastern Atlantic, from Norway to the Canaries. The shell grows to around 8 cm (3 in) in diameter.

Pacific Pink Scallop
(Chlamys hastata hericia), Ger. Alaska-Kammuschel
The valves, which are almost round, have between ten and

twenty-one main ribs and several smaller ones in the spaces between. The colour varies from pink to pale yellow or white. This scallop prefers shallow water, up to 35 m (115 ft) deep, and is found on the Pacific coast from Alaska to California.

Noble Scallop, Old Scallop
(Chlamys nobilis), Fr. Peigne Sénateur, Ger. Königsmantel
A symmetrical scallop with about twenty ribs and ears of different sizes in striking violet, salmon and yellow tones. The shell is 8–15 cm (3–6 in) in diameter.

It is found in Japanese waters, from central Honshu to Kijushu, at depths up to 20 m (65 ft).

The similar-shaped but much smaller Senator Scallop (*Chlamys senatorius*), which grows to 3–6 cm (1–2½ in) and has from twenty-four to forty flat ribs, is found in the Indo-Pacific from East Africa to Tonga. It is a beautifully marked shell, mottled brown and violet.

Mantle Scallop
(Chlamys pallium), Ger. Herzogmantel
A common scallop of the Indo-Pacific, with an orange to purple shell. About fifteen prominent ribs are interspersed with three light-coloured strips. The inside edge of the shell has brownish-red stripes 5–10 mm (¼–½ in) wide.

Asian Moon Scallop
(Amusium japonicum), Ger. Japanische 'Sonne- und Mond'-Muschel, Japanische Fächermuschel
This amazingly symmetrical, small-eared scallop, found in Japanese waters, takes its name from the different colouring of the two valves. The left valve is reddish-brown, symbolizing to the Japanese the sun, while the right valve is light ivory like the moon. These scallops grow to between 10 and 12 cm (4–5 in) in diameter.

Atlantic Thorny Oyster
(Spondylus americanus), Fr. Spondyle d'Amérique, Ger. Atlantische Stachelauster
A round, flat relation of the scallop found in the waters

around Florida and the Caribbean. Like the oyster, it attaches itself to rocks. The shell is reddish with yellow spines.

Similar, but more spiny still, is the Regal Thorny Oyster (*Spondylus regius*) of South-east Asia, which grows to between 8 and 12 cm (3–5 in) in diameter.

Another related species, the Pacific Thorny Oyster (*Spondylus princeps*) – reddish in colour with wide, flattened spikes – is found on the west coast of South America, from Panama to Peru.

COCKLES (*Cardiidae*)

Known as heart clams in the United States, all members of this large family are heart-shaped when examined from the side, a shape formed by the closed, extremely convex valves. All cockles are virtually identical in shape and colour, circular or semicircular with pronounced ribs, sometimes with spines, scales or thorns. Yet there are cockles that have an almost smooth surface.

Characteristic of most cockles is the long, finger-shaped foot, by means of which they move forwards in short jumps. On a firm surface, cockles can fling themselves as far as 50 cm (20 in) in a single bound. With similar movements, they can burrow into the sea-bed when danger threatens.

Cockles take in food through two short siphons, the ends of which are often covered with fine tentacles, which take in and eject water.

Members of the *Cardiidae* family are found in every ocean, and the further south one goes the greater the number of species to be found. In Europe, they are eaten chiefly in France and Italy.

Common Edible Cockle, Heart Shell

(*Cerastoderma edule*), Fr. *Coque, Bucarde, Bigon, Rigadot,* Ger. *Eßbare Herzmuschel, Gemeine Herzmuschel,* Ital. *Capa Tonda, Capa Margarota, Cuore Edule,* Span. *Berberecho, Carneiro, Perdigone,* Port. *Berbigão, Nor/Dan. Hjertemuslinger,* Dut. *Gewone Hartschelp, Kokkel*

This cockle lives mainly on tidal sand or silt at depths up to 10 m (33 ft). It is found in the North Atlantic, Mediterranean, Black Sea, North Sea and the Baltic to the Gulf of Bothnia. The fact that it is so widespread points to its great adaptability, especially to varying salt levels.

The Common Cockle is fished commercially on the German North Sea coast and along the coasts of England, Holland, France, Spain and Portugal. In western Europe and the United States, the shells are used by oyster farmers as 'collectors'.

Shell colours range from ivory to brown and the ribs are well defined. They reach about 5 cm (2 in) in diameter.

Rough Cockle, Knotted Cockle

(*Acanthocardia tuberculata*), Fr. *Bucarde Tuberculée,* Ger. *Dickrippige Herzmuschel, Knotige Herzmuschel,* Ital. *Cuore Tuberculato,* Span. *Carneiro, Marolo,* Port. *Berbigão*
A larger cockle, which can grow to 5–9 cm (2–3½ in) in diameter. The thick shells are white to brown in colour. The pronounced ribs have wart-like tubercles. Found on the European Atlantic coast from southern England to the Canaries and in

the Mediterranean below low-water mark in depths of up to 100 m (330 ft).

Spiny Cockle

(*Acanthocardia aculeata*), Fr. *Coque Rouge Mediterranée, Coque Epineuse,* Ger. *Stachelige Herzmuschel,* Ital. *Cuore Spinoso,* Span. *Marolo, Concha,* Port. *Berbigão, Crica, Nor. Pigget Middelhavs Hjertemuslinger*
A species similar in shape and colour to the Rough Cockle, found from southern Norway to the North African coast and in the Mediterranean. Instead of warts, this cockle has sharp spines on the ribs. It grows to around 8–11 cm (3–4 in).

Prickly Cockle, Red-nosed Cockle

(*Acanthocardia echinata*), Fr. *Grande Coque, Coque Rouge,* Ger. *Dornige Herzmuschel,* Span. *Carneiro,* Port. *Berbigão,* Dut. *Gedoornde Hartschelp*
This cockle, which is especially popular in France, is deeply grooved and has curved spines around the rim. The ivory to off-white shells turn brownish-red towards the edge and can measure up to 8 cm (3 in) in diameter. They are found throughout the

Special boats like these are used by the Dutch to catch 'kokkels'. Water is pumped into the sea-bed under pressure through large pipes and the sand and cockles it contains are caught in baskets. On board, the sand is washed away. The shellfish are factory-bottled for export, mainly to France.

Atlantic and Mediterranean at depths of between 10 and 350 m (33–1,150 ft).

Heart Cockle

(*Corculum cardissa*), Ger. *Halbherzmuschel,* Jap. *Torigai*
In this white to ivory cockle, with its uniform ribs, the heart-shape is particularly well defined. The sides of the beak are lightly toothed. The Heart Cockle, which grows to between 6 and 9 cm (2½–3½ in), is found throughout the Indo-Pacific. In Japan, the flesh and the muscular foot are considered a great delicacy. The darker end of the flesh is shaped like a hen's beak and the flavour, too, is not unlike chicken. Hence the Japanese name, 'Torigai': *tori* means chicken, *gai* means shellfish.

GIANT CLAMS (*Tridacnidae*)

This bivalve family, native to the Indo-Pacific, includes the largest

The flesh content of the Common Cockle is small, being only around 15:85 in ratio to the shell. For several years, the Dutch have been trying to farm cockles but, despite the shellfish's great adaptability, the results have not proved very encouraging to date.

bivalve of all, the Giant Clam (*Tridacna gigas*). Giant clams have extremely thick, undulating shells. They lie in shallow water with the hinge side on the sea-bed and the valves, slightly open, pointing towards the surface. The young secure themselves with byssus threads, but later their weight is sufficient to anchor them to the sea-bed.

Giant Clam
(*Tridacna gigas*), *Fr. Tridacne Gigantesque, Ger. Riesenmuschel, Indon. Kimah, Malay. Kima, Gebang, Thai. Hoy Mu Sua, Dut. Reuzenmossel*
At 1.3 m (4¼ ft) in length, this is the largest bivalve anywhere in the world. A single clam of this size can weigh up to 500 kg (10 cwt). The shells, with their four to six smooth, distinctive ribs, can be up to 30 cm (1 ft) thick. The hinge muscle is extremely powerful and the shell, which is usually slightly open, can be snapped shut with lightning speed. There are many stories of divers who have caught a foot or an airpipe in a giant clam and have been unable to escape its sudden vice-like grip – but these are just stories.

The giant clam is found in the tropical area of the western Pacific, particularly in the South Sea coral reefs, where the natives eat its flesh.

Elongated Clam
(*Tridacna elongata*), *Fr. Tridacne Allongée, Ger. Kleine Gienmuschel, Arab. Arbinembus*
A smaller member of the giant clam family, found mostly in the Red Sea. These sand-burrowing clams are 12–20 cm (5–8 in) in length. They are found from the Red Sea to the Indian Ocean at depths of 5–15 cm (2–6 in). They are much loved by the Arabs.

VENUS SHELLS
(*Veneridae*)

With over 500 species, the venus shells are an extremely large family. They are represented in almost every sea and along every coast. They live in soft ground, preferably sand or gravel, into which they usually burrow. Their sturdy, porcelain-like, pale yellow shells often have brightly coloured markings. They have distinct concentric stripes and often radial ribs as well. Many venus shells have the same type of foot as the cockle, with which they are able to jump along.

Wart Venus, Baby Clam
(*Venus verrucosa*), *Fr. Praire, Coque Rayée, Ger. Rauhe Venusmuschel, Ital. Verrucosa, Tartufo, Capparozzolo, Span. Escupina Gravada, Almeja Vieja, Port. Pé de Burro, Dut. Wrattige Venusschelp*
This brownish-red, slightly oval, convex bivalve, 3–8 cm (1–3 in) in diameter, is one of the best known venus shells in Europe. Characteristic are the distinctive concentric stripes, some of which end in wart-like tubercles or are crossed by irregular, bumpy lines. The Wart Venus is found on sandy coasts in western Europe, the Mediterranean countries and West Africa to Cape Town, from shallow water to depths of up to 100 m (330 ft).

Striped Venus Clam
(*Chamelaea gallina*), *Fr. Clovisse, Petit Praire, Palourde, Venus Poule, Ger. Strahlige Venusmuschel, Ital. Vongola, Cappa Gallina, Beverazza, Poverazza, Span. Almeja, Port. Pé de Burrinho, Dut. Venusschelp*
This small, light-brown bivalve grows to 3–4 cm (1–1½ in). The shells have irregular rings and, usually, concentric stripes. The species lives on clean, coarse sand in shallow water and is found mainly in the Mediterranean, where it is much fished, especially in Italy.

Lamellate Venus
(*Venus lamellaris*), *Ger. Kleine Pazifische Venusmuschel*
A beige and violet bivalve with scaly rings, toned reddish on the inside, this species measures 4–5 cm (1½–2 in) in diameter and is found in the Indo-Pacific and West Pacific.

Giant Callista, Sunray Venus Clam
(*Callista gigantea, Macrocallista nimbosa*), *Ger. Riesenvenusmuschel*
The elongated shape of the Giant Callista is similar to that of the European Pond Mussel. The shells are smooth and thin with concentric rings. They can reach 15 cm (6 in) in length. This species is found from North Carolina to Florida and Texas.

Large Pacific Venus
(*Callista lilacina*), *Fr. Cythérée Lilacine, Ger. Große Pazifische Venusmuschel*
This ivory to brown venus shell is found throughout the tropical Pacific. The shell, with its regular, concentric rings is up to 8 cm (3 in) in diameter.

Smooth or Brown Venus Shell
(*Callista chione, Pitaria c., Meretrix c.*), *Fr. Cythère Vernie, Ger. Glatte Venusmuschel, Braune Venusmuschel, Ital. Issolon, Cappa Chione, Span. Concha, Saveriña*
This species has a thick, brown shell from 8 to 12 cm (3–5 in) in length, with wide concentric bands. The concentric growth rings, which are crossed by radiating white lines, are not well defined. The highly polished surface feels almost smooth. This shellfish is found from south-west England to the Canaries and in the Mediterranean. It is more common in the south than the north.

Grooved Carpet Shell
(*Venerupis decussata*, formerly *Tapes decussata*), *Fr. Palourde Croisée, Ger. Kreuzmuster Teppichmuschel, Ital. Vongola, Span. Almeja*
This bivalve has a large brown and yellow shell, which widens at the posterior end. It has longitudinal ribs with cross-stripes giving a lattice pattern and reaches 4–8 cm (1½–3 in) in length. It is found from Norway to Senegal, including the Mediterranean.

Pullet Carpet Shell
(*Venerupis pullastra*), *Fr. Clovisse, Palourde, Ger. Getupfte Teppichmuschel, Span. Almeja, Dut. Tapijtschelp*
This species, which grows to 6–7 cm (2½–3 in), is similar to the other venus shells in shape. The surface markings, with their lengthways and cross stripes, resemble woven cloth or the back of a carpet. It is found mainly on the European Atlantic coast,

The distinctive concentric stripes on the shell of the Wart Venus (*Venus verrucosa*) are wedge-shaped. This makes it easier for the creature to burrow into the sand. Venus shells, which are very popular in Europe, are often eaten raw but, like mussels, they can be cooked in a variety of ways.

The **Striped Venus Clam** (*Chamelaea gallina*) is popular and plentiful in the Mediterranean countries. In Italy, it is fished commercially as 'Vongola', 'Cappa Gallina' or 'Beverazza'. It is usually boiled before eating. It is exported in cans and is often served in Italian restaurants as the main ingredient of 'Spaghetti Vongole'.

The **Grooved Carpet Shell** (*Venerupis decussata*) is much sought after for its fine flavour. To the Bretons, the 'Palourde Croisée' is the best of the venus shells and its flavour is brought out superbly when cooked Breton-style – braised in wine, garlic, bay leaf and pepper. Alternatively, they are often just eaten raw.

from Norway to Senegal, and in the Mediterranean.

Lettered Venus

(*Venerupis* or *Tapes literatus*), Ger. *Pazifische Teppichmuschel*
This irregular, oval bivalve has on its shell weakly defined concentric rings, overlaid with a brown pattern which resembles writing. The shell reaches 9 cm (3½ in) in length. The Lettered Venus is found throughout the tropical Indo-Pacific.

Manila Clam, Baby Clam, Japanese Littleneck Clam

(*Tapes philippinarum*, formerly

Venerupis philippinarum), Fr. *Clam Japonaise*, Ger. *Japanische Teppichmuschel*, Jap. *Asari*
The attractive brown and white patterned shell is 4–5 cm (1½–2 in) long and similar in shape to that of the Grooved Carpet Shell, although the ribs are more pronounced and the Manila Clam is rather more pointed at the posterior end. This Japanese variety was introduced in the Puget Sound on the west coast of the United States in 1935 and today it is to be found from Puget Sound to northern California. It is fished commercially in Washington State and British Columbia.

Quahog, Hardshell Clam, Lord Clam

(*Mercenaria mercenaria*), Fr. *Praire, Clam, Ger. Ostamerikanische Venusmuschel, Quahog-Muschel*
This bivalve is found on the east coast of Canada and the United States (from the Gulf of St Lawrence to Florida) and in the Gulf of Mexico. The Algonquin Indians of the eastern United States made them into tubular white or purple beads, which were strung and used as money. They were also made into wide necklets and belts. Originally, the Algonquin tribe used these 'wampum' belts to record important events in pictorial form, using figures and symbols that only the initiated could interpret.

The name Quahog, by which this species is generally called in the United States, comes from the Algonquin word 'quahaug'. In fact, it is normally known as Bay Quahog to distinguish it from its relative, the Black Quahog, which is found only in the deep waters of the north Atlantic.

The shell of the Bay Quahog is oval, sand-coloured, thick and quite smooth, with irregular, thin concentric rings. It measures 4–13 cm (1½–5 in) in diameter.

Another relative, the Southern Quahog (*Mercenaria campechiensis*), is found further south between Virginia and Texas. It is larger, with a thicker shell. The quahog is also known in Europe, mainly on the French Atlantic coast and particularly in the mouth of the River Charente. It is also found on the English and French Channel coasts. It has been introduced for commercial purposes in both Europe and California.

WEDGE SHELLS (*Donacidae*)

These small, hard-shelled bivalves come in a variety of shapes – rounded, elongated or triangular, with concentric or radial stripes. They are found in moderate, warm or tropical seas, usually in sand near the shoreline. The family includes a great number of types and sub-types but we have space here to mention only the most important species.

White Sand Mussel, Giant South African Wedge Shell

(*Donax serra*), Ger. *Südafrikanische Dreiecksmuschel*
The shell is white or ivory to brownish-purple in colour, al-

The **Smooth or Brown Venus Shell** (*Callista chione*), one of the largest and tastiest of the venus shells. Their size makes them slightly tough but they are delicious stuffed.

The **Manila Clam** (*Tapes philippinarum*) is served raw 'on the half shell' in America.

most smooth with extremely fine cross and radial ribs, which form a fold or wedge at the posterior end. This helps the creature to burrow into the sand. The shell is 7–9 cm (3–3½ in) long and has a violet lustre on the inside. The White Sand Mussel lives in the surf of the South African coast.

Striped Wedge Shell

(Donax striatus), Ger. Gestreifte Koffermuschel, Span. Chipi-chipi (South America)
The brown shell is covered with fine, radiating ribs and wide concentric stripes. It is around 4 cm (1½ in) in length and is found in the Caribbean.

Coquina Shell, Pompano Shell, Wedge Shell

(Donax variabilis), Ger. Schmetterlingsmuschel
This small, triangular shell is only 1.5–2 cm (½–¾ in) long. It comes in a variety of colours and has attractive radial stripes. It is found on the American coast, from Virginia to Florida and Texas.

Wedge Clam

(Donax trunculus), Fr. Haricot de Mer, Donace, Ger.

Mittelmeer-Dreiecksmuschel, Ital. Calcinello Troncato, Trilatera, Span. Xarleta, Tellerina, Port. Cadelinha, Dut. Zaagje Muizetandje
A small shell with brown, concentric stripes, which grows to around 3 cm (1 in). The inside is deep purple. The edge of the lower shell has saw-like teeth.

The Wedge Clam lives in shallow coastal waters from the Bay of Biscay to Morocco and in the Mediterranean, often in large colonies. It prefers sand, in or below the surf-line.

Banded Wedge Shell

(Donax vittatus), Fr. Donace, Olive, Flion, Ger. Gebänderte Dreiecksmuschel, Sägezähnchen, Span. Chirla, Xarleta, Dut. Zaagje
This clam has fine teeth on the interior margin of the shell and a posterior end tapering to a point. The shell is about twice as long as it is wide, with the beak at the centre. The outside of the shell is white to yellowish-brown and the inside is usually violet. It has concentric rings crossed by irregular white stripes. This bivalve of 4–5 cm (1½–2 in) in length lives on the east Atlantic coast, from Norway to Morocco, and also in

the Mediterranean and the German Bight.

Carribean Coquina

(Donax denticulatus), Fr. Donace Denticulée, Ger. Karibisches Sägezähnchen, Span. Chipi-chipi (South America)
A small bivalve of only 2–2.5 cm (¾–1 in) in length, in a variety of colours, the Caribbean Coquina has a wedge-shaped, convex shell with attractive and well defined radial stripes, crossed by concentric rings. The shell has finely toothed margins. This species is found in the Caribbean and along the coast of Central America to northern Brazil.

RAZOR SHELLS, JACK-KNIFE CLAMS
(*Solenidae*)

Throughout this family, the shells are long and narrow, either straight or slightly curved, so as to resemble the sheath of a knife or sword. The two identical valves are smooth, slightly open and squared at the ends. The hinge is at one end. Using the foot and squirting out water, some types are able to escape their enemies in a series of jumps up to 50 cm (20 in) in length.

Wedge shells, like the common Mediterranean species *Donax trunculus,* are quite small and are therefore normally eaten raw. You can usually find plenty of their shells on Mediterranean beaches.

Razor and jack-knife clams like soft sand into which, because of their powerful foot and elongated shape, they are able to burrow at great speed. In the vertical holes they make, they are able to move up and down. Most types are found in the tropics but they are present in all seas except for the very coldest.

Jack-knife Clam, Grooved Razor Clam, Samquin Clam

(Solen marginatus), Fr. Couteau Gaine, Ger. Gemeine Scheidenmuschel, Messerschneide, Ital. Cannolicchio, Capalonga, Manicaio Fodero, Span.

Little Neck Clams are actually Quahogs (*Mercenaria mercenaria*). In the United States, quahogs have different names depending on size. The Little Neck is the smallest and is usually eaten raw.

The Cherrystone is the next quahog up in size and is named after Cherrystone Creek in Virginia. To qualify for this name, quahogs have to be around five years old and measure up to 7 cm (3 in).

All quahogs larger than Cherrystones are sold as Chowder or Steamer Clams, since they are now too big to be eaten raw and are usually made into chowders (fish soups).

Longueirón, Navaja, Mango de Cuchillo, Dut. Messerscheede
This tubular, white to yellowish-brown shell reaches 12–16 cm (5–6 in) in length. The two valves, each of which has a cardinal tooth at the hinge, are divided lengthways into two pointed triangles, produced by different colour tones and textures. The graining of each of the two areas runs into the other along the length of the shell. At the anterior end is the foot and at the other end the two siphons.

The Grooved Razor Clam can burrow to a depth of 1 m (3 ft). It is found in the warmer waters of the Atlantic from the English coast to Mauretania, throughout the Mediterranean and in the Black Sea. Winter is the main fishing season.

Rosy Jack-knife Clam

(Solen rosaceus), Ger. Rosa Scheidenmuschel
This razor shell, which reaches 7.5 cm (3 in) in length, is coloured green and pink, with the pink mainly in the concentric rings. It is found on the Pacific coast of southern California and Mexico.

A similar species, the Rose-spotted Solen (*Solen roseomaculatus*), lives in the Indo-Pacific, from Madagascar to Japan and New Guinea. It is slightly curved and is coloured in shades of pink with darker spots on both the outside and the inside of the shell.

Giant Japanese Solen

(Solen grandis), Ger. Große Japanische Scheidenmuschel
This species has a relatively wide shell, square at one end and rounded at the other, olive to light brown in colour with brown concentric growth rings. It grows up to 12 cm (5 in) long and is native to China and Japan.

Gould's Solen

(Solen strictus), Ger. Kleine Japanische Scheidenmuschel
Similar to the Giant Japanese Solen in colour and markings, but much narrower and square at both ends, Gould's Solen also reaches 12 cm (5 in) in length and is found in Japan and China.

Atlantic Jack-knife Clam, Atlantic Razor Clam

(Ensis directus), Fr. Couteau de l'Atlantique, Ger. Amerikanische Schwertmuschel, Dut. Americaanse Zwaardscheede
Its whitish colouring and shape are similar to those of the European razor shells but the shell is wider and slightly curved. Both ends are slightly rounded. It grows to a length of up to 17 cm (6½ in) and is found from Labrador to South Carolina. Recently introduced into the North Sea, it is now widespread in the German Bight.

Sabre Razor, Sword Razor

(Ensis ensis), Fr. Couteau Sabre, Couteau Courbe, Ger. Kleine Schwertmuschel, Span. Langueiron, Ital. Cappa di Deo, Cappa Lunga, Dut. Kleine Zwaardscheede, Span. Caravela, Navaja
Around 8–13 cm (3–5 in) long and gently curving like a sabre, the Sabre Razor has two cardinal teeth at the hinge on the left valve and one on the right valve. As in the Grooved Razor Clam, concentric stripes are so arranged as to form two pointed triangles. The light-yellow ground colour is crossed by reddish-brown stripes, parallel to the growth lines. This small razor shell lives in the Atlantic, from Norway to Morocco, in the Mediterranean and the Black Sea, and in the German Bight.

Pod Razor

(Ensis siliqua), Fr. Solen Silique, Ger. Große Schwertmuschel, Ital. Capalonga Nostrana, Span. Navaja, Longueiron, Mango de Cuchillo, Dut. Tafelmesheft
This large razor shell grows to 15–22 cm (6–9 in). The shell is slightly curved with squared ends and is yellowish-white in colour, with violet growth rings. It lives in fine sand in the Atlantic, from Norway through the British Isles to Galicia in northern Spain.

In the Mediterranean, off the Moroccan coast, lives a very similar sub-species, *Ensis siliqua minor*. Another species, *Ensis arcuatus*, differs from *Ensis sil-*

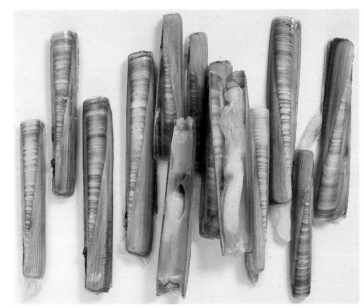

A sub-species of the Pod Razor is the smaller *Ensis siliqua minor* of the Mediterranean. The flesh is creamy-white and can be eaten raw or cooked. Braised in butter and garlic, it is a real delicacy. The razor shells, with their unusual shape and markings, are extremely difficult to catch and rarely appear on the market.

iqua through its lightly curved, narrower shape. This species grows to 17 cm (6½ in) and is found from Norway to Portugal, including the German Bight, but not the Mediterranean.

Chilean Razor

(Ensis macha), Ger. Chilenische Schwertmuschel, Span. Navaja del Mar, Navajuela, Huepos, Machi
This razor shell grows up to 20 cm (8 in) long and 4 cm (1½ in) wide. It lives on the coast of Chile, from Calera southwards to Tierra del Fuego and northwards up the Atlantic coast to Argentina (Golfo de San Martin). It is caught by hand and eaten fresh-boiled along the entire Chilean coast. It is also fished commercially.

TROUGH SHELLS
(Mactridae, Mesodesmatidae)

Trough shells are richly represented in all the seas of the world. The shells are usually equivalve and triangular, oval or elliptical in shape. The coloration is normally a chalky grey, and the shells range from thin and fragile to thick. The hinge is made up of V-shaped cardinal teeth.

Winged Surf Clam

(Mactra alata), Ger. Geflügelte Trogmuschel
The basic shape is like that of other trough shells, but extended into wings on both posterior sides. The almost silky shell has fine concentric rings. The Winged Surf Clam grows to 8 cm (3 in) and is found in the Caribbean.

Rayed Trough Shell, Surf Clam

(Mactra corallina, Mactra stultorum), Fr. Mactre Coralline, Ger. Gemeine Trogmuschel, Span. Escupiña Bestia, Huevo, Pechina Lisa, Dut. Groote Strandschelp
This white, round to triangular bivalve reaches 6 cm (2½ in). The fine concentric markings on the almost smooth surface are crossed at irregular intervals by radiating rays. The inside of the shell is often pale violet.

The Rayed Trough Shell prefers sand and is found in the Atlantic, from southern Norway to Morocco, as well as in the Mediterranean and Black Seas.

The **Thick Trough Shell** (*Spisula solida*) is one of the tastiest of all shellfish. It is widely distributed but is fished mainly by the French and English. From France it finds its way onto the German market, where it is frequently available. It is delicious braised.

Fragile Atlantic Mactra
(*Mactra fragilis*), Ger. *Zerbrechliche Atlantische Trogmuschel*
The shell is pale brown in colour and semicircular in shape, extending to a triangle at the hinge. It is found in the Atlantic, from North Carolina to Texas, and off the Antilles and grows to 6–8 cm (2½–3 in) in diameter.

Hians Surf Clam
(*Mactra hians*), Ger. *Gestreifte Pazifische Trogmuschel*
An egg-shaped shellfish, about 9 cm (3½ in) long, with wide, concentric, brown bands crossed by light-coloured rays. The inside of the shell is pale violet. This clam lives mainly in South-east Asia.

An important smaller species, *Mactra australis*, is found on the coast of Australia.

Striped Trough Shell
(*Mactra striatella*), Ger. *Gestreifte Trogmuschel*
Like the Rayed Trough Shell in shape and colour, but with close-set concentric rings of various tones, the Striped Trough Shell reaches a diameter of up to 10 cm (4 in). It is found on the tropical Atlantic coast.

Thick Trough Shell
(*Spisula solida*), Fr. *Mactre Solide*, Ger. *Dickschalige Trogmuschel*, Dut. *Stevige Strandschelp*
This trough shell has an extremely thick, white, oval shell with irregular concentric rings and grows to a length of 3–5 cm (1–2 in). The indentations of the hinge muscle are clearly defined.

This species is found along the entire eastern Atlantic coast to North Africa, as well as in the German Bight and west Baltic.

Atlantic Surf Clam, Bar Clam
(*Spisula solidissima*), Fr. *Fausse-praire, Mactre Solide, Palourde de Dune*, Ger. *Riesentrogmuschel*, Dut. *Reuzenstrandschelp*
A white, oval shellfish which grows to 20 cm (8 in), with a strongly defined hinge. The shell is marked with irregular, concentric growth rings. A popular culinary choice in the United States, the Atlantic Surf Clam is found – together with two subspecies – on the American Atlantic coast, from Nova Scotia to Florida and Texas.

Common Otter Shell
(*Lutraria lutraria*), Fr. *Lutraire*, Ger. *Lange Trogmuschel, Ottermuschel*, Span. *Arola, Cabra, Navallón*, Dut. *Ovale Slijkschelp, Otterschelp*
The striking elongated shell of this trough shell has rounded ends and becomes darker in tone towards the edge. It grows to 9–13 cm (3½–5 in) long and lives on gravel and coarse sand in depths of up to 55 m (180 ft). It is found from Norway to West Africa.

The *Lutraria* family is represented by a few similar-looking members in every ocean and sea, including the Mediterranean.

Smooth Duck Clam
(*Anatina anatina*), Ger. *Weiche Entenmuschel*
The shell of the Duck Clam is more convex than that of the European trough shells, as well as being more compact and extremely fragile. The light-grey colour becomes darker towards the edge. The faded-looking concentric growth rings are also visible on the inside of the shell.

This shellfish, which is found in the western Atlantic from North Carolina to Brazil, prefers soft mud.

In Germany and Holland, the *Lepadidae* – which belong to the crab family – are known by the same common name as Duck Clams, but the *Lepadidae* are not related to the bivalves described here.

Channelled Duck Clam
(*Raeta plicatella*), Ger. *Nordamerikanische Gefurchte Entenmuschel*
In the irridescent white Channelled Duck Clam, the growth rings are much more pronounced than in the Smooth Duck Clam. These strong concentric rings vary in depth. The shape is semicircular to triangular and the shell can measure up to 9 cm (3½ in). This clam lives on silty sand from South Carolina to the Caribbean.

Chilean Trough Shell
(*Mesodesma donacium*), Ger. *Chilenische Trogmuschel*
In contrast to the true trough shells, in *Mesodesmatidae* the anterior end is generally much longer than the shortened posterior. This popular shellfish grows to 7–9 cm (3–3½ in) long and lives on tidal sand from Peru to Chile. It is fished commercially in both countries and it is an important export in Chile.

In New Zealand, *Mesodesma ventricosum* and *Mesodesma subtriangulatum* are sold as 'Toheroa' and 'Tuatua' and both are popular for eating.

PEPPERY FURROW SHELLS
(*Scrobiculariidae*)

This small family contains only one species, *Scrobicularia*, which lives on silt in shallow water, mainly in European seas.

Peppery Furrow Shell
(*Scrobicularia plana*), Fr. *Scrobiculaire, Lavignon*, Ger. *Flache Pfeffermuschel*, Ital. *Caparozzolo*, Dut. *Platte Slijkgaper*
The shells of this bivalve are 4–6 cm (1½–2½ in) in length, ovoid to round, and slightly pointed at the posterior end. The whitish-grey shell is covered with thick, concentric growth lines. This shellfish lives on sediment on calm Mediterranean beaches and also in warm, silty areas of the Atlantic coast. The name derives from the peppery after-taste, which typifies all shellfish of the *Scrobicularia* family.

GAPERS, SOFT-SHELL CLAMS
(*Myidae*)

The oval, extended, somewhat asymmetrical shells of this family of shellfish gape slightly at the posterior end – hence the common name. Gapers burrow up to 30 cm (1 ft) deep into sand and silt. In order to breathe and feed, a tube is extended from the open end of the shell to the surface. This contains two siphons for taking in and expelling water. This siphon tube is an extension of the edge of the mantle. Gapers grow to 5–12 cm (2–5 in) in length but with the siphon extended they can measure up to 40 cm (16 in).

Sand Gaper, Soft-shell Clam, Long Neck, Empire Clam
(Mya arenaria), Fr. Mye, Clanque, Bec-de-jar, Ger. Große Sandklaffmuschel, Sandmuschel, Strandauster, Span. Leito Ama, Dut. Strandgaper
The best known of the gapers, this shellfish has an ovoid shell with close-set, concentric growth lines. The shell is 5–12 cm (2–5 in) long.

Sand Gapers are found chiefly in the North Atlantic, including the North Sea and Baltic. On the American Atlantic coast, they are found from Labrador to North Carolina (Cape Hatteras), with the largest colonies on the coast of New England and in Chesapeake Bay. The Sand Gaper has also been transferred from the Atlantic to the Pacific coast and its distribution now extends from Alaska to California, where it is fished mainly in San Francisco Bay.

In the United States, it is usually eaten boiled or fried or even deep-fried. It is also used in stews and other cooked dishes.

Blunt Gaper, Truncated Soft-shell Clam
(Mya truncata), Fr. Mye Trouquée, Ger. Gestutzte Klaffmuschel, Dut. Afgeknotte Gaper
A smaller version of the Sand Gaper. The shell of the Blunt Gaper is truncated at the posterior end and more open. The shell, which grows to a length of 3–9 cm (1–3½ in), has similar markings to that of the Sand Gaper.

The Blunt Gaper lives in deep water in the North Sea, German Bight, western Baltic and on the American Atlantic coast (Massachusetts), as well as in the Atlantic, from the Arctic to the Bay of Biscay, and the Pacific (Sakhalin).

The Sand Gaper (*Mya arenaria*) is extremely popular in the United States, where it is known as the Soft-shell Clam. Americans love them raw (with a wedge of lemon) or boiled. They are often fried or deep-fried, too, and many people prefer them stuffed.

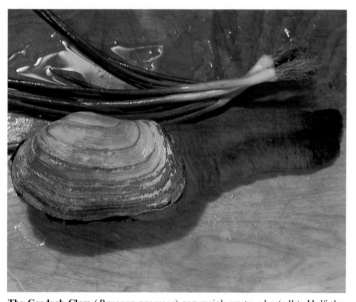

The Geoduck Clam (*Panopea generosa*) can weigh up to 4 kg (9 lb). Half the weight is made up by the characteristic siphon, which is usually sold separately. Sales of Geoduck Clams are rising in the United States and exports have recently begun, mainly to Japan and Hong Kong. It is often confused with the equally large Horse Clam (*Tresus nuttalli*), a trough shell which it resembles.

ROCK-BORERS (*Hiatellidae*)

The four species that make up this family live mainly in cold to very cold waters. Their shells all gape open to a greater or lesser degree and all of them burrow into sand or mud.

Geoduck Clam
(Panopea generosa), Ger. Geoduck
The largest shellfish of the American Pacific coast, with long siphons in a thick, fleshy tube which cannot be retracted into the shell. The siphons constitute

about half the weight of the shellfish, which can weigh up to 4 kg (9 lb). The siphons can be extended up to a length of 130 cm (51 in). Through them, the shellfish takes in and expels water. When the tide is out, Geoduck Clams can be located by the 'fountain' of water they send up. The shells, which can be up to 20 cm (8 in) long, are open at the posterior end.

On the American Pacific coast, Geoduck hunting is an established sport. It takes two people to lift the shellfish out of its burrow, where it may have burrowed to a depth of 120 cm (4 ft). The flesh is sliced and fried. The siphon tube, too, is skinned and chopped to use in soups and chowders.

SNAILS
(*Gastropoda*)

The second and largest group of molluscs are the snails, which are found throughout the world. They live in a wide variety of habitats, in the sea, fresh water and on land. Most have a spiral, univalve shell, but there are gastropods without shells and others with simple shells that, at first glance, look like the shell of a bivalve.

Zoologists refer to snails as gastropods. The most distinctive feature of all snails is the large foot. By contracting and extending the muscles in the sole of the foot, they move along at what has come to be known proverbially as 'a snail's pace'. Zoologists divide gastropods into three groups, according to the type and position of the breathing organs: those with anterior gills (*Prosobranchia*), posterior gills (*Opisthobranchia*) and lungs (*Pulmonata*).

In the *Prosobranchia*, which are found mainly in the sea, the gills are in front of the heart, while in the *Opisthobranchia* the single gill lies behind the heart. Many opisthobranchs have only a rudimentary shell and they are of no importance as human food. In the air-breathing snails, the gills have completely disappeared and the mantle cavity has become an air-breathing lung. Some types also breathe through the skin.

Snails have an easily recognizable head with one or two pairs of feelers, or tentacles used for feeling. On or at the base of the tentacles are the light-sensitive organs, often proper eyes with lenses. The mantle cavity and spiralling intestinal sac are found in the protective shell, to which the gastropod is joined by the spindle muscle. Most snails can withdraw completely into their shells and some can seal the shell with a horny or chalky lid attached to the back of the foot.

Characteristic of all snails is the *radula*, a rasp-like feeding tongue in the pharynx. This can be extended out of the mouth and used to remove growths, such as algae. It can also be used to chop up plants. Variations in the tongue provide for a wide variety of food sources. Snails include carrion-eaters, hunters and even some whose tongue has become a poison dart.

Most snails are found in the sea. Pulmonates live mainly on land but also in ponds, lakes or rivers, where they continually have to come up to the surface to breathe. Like bivalves, snails are either separately sexed or hermaphrodite. They are egg-laying. The marine species develop from free-swimming larvae, while the air-breathing snails emerge from the eggs as fully developed young.

Snails were eaten in Ancient Rome. In the last century BC, the Romans cultivated snails in breeding pens called *cochlearia* and these were later introduced into Gaul and Germania. In the heyday of the monasteries, snails were eaten on fast days. Sea snails were eaten as long ago as the Middle Stone Age.

The most attractive of all the snails are the marine species, with their varied, attractive shapes, colourings and markings. Land snails are, by contrast, dull in colour.

Snails range in size from a few millimetres up to around 60 cm (23 in). One of the largest is the Triton Shell. In Greek mythology, gods and centaurs used to blow them like bugels and the shells are still used today as a musical instrument in Buddhist monasteries. Helmet shells are used to make shell cameos. Abalone shells are much prized for their shimmering mother-of-pearl. Another famous shell is the cowrie, which was used as money in pre-Christian times.

Sea snails: anterior gilled (*Prosobranchia*)

ABALONES (*Haliotidae*)

To the untrained eye, these may look like mussels at first glance, yet abalones belong to the snail family. The scientific name, *Haliotis*, derives from the Greek and means 'sea-ear' – 'ear' because the shell resembles the human ear, with fine whorls at the beak widening towards the edge, so that the last whorl takes up the major part of the flat shell.

Abalones have a very strong, large clinging foot, the sole of which fills the entire shell opening. The foot is used to cling onto rocks and cliffs. The grip of the foot is so strong that it can withstand the most violent breakers, coping with strains up to 4,000 times its own weight. This makes abalones very difficult to remove from rocks by hand.

A characteristic of all abalones is a row of perforations along the edge of the shell, of which the last few are completely open. These openings are used to get rid of excrement, which would otherwise collect in the mantle cavity, and also for expelling water from respiration. Through the holes, tube filaments extend outside the shell.

Another feature of abalones is that the rasping tongue – which all snails have (the *radula*) – has, in addition to the central and side teeth, additional teeth along the edge arranged in a fan shape.

There are some 100 different species of abalone, some of which can reach 25 cm (10 in) in diameter. They live in surf and are completely vegetarian, feeding on algae. Abalones are found in all warm seas. They are prized not only as food but also for their beautiful shells, the inside of which is covered with an iridescent layer of mother-of-pearl. This can vary from green, turquoise, pink or black to white, depending on the species.

Since these shellfish are much sought after throughout the world, numbers have been considerably depleted. In the United States, in particular, this has made them a protected species. In California, for instance, it is against the law to bottle abalones, nor are they allowed to be exported either fresh or frozen, not even to another part of the United States. Any bottled abalones on the market are likely to be Japanese in origin.

Silver Paua

(*Haliotis australis*), Fr. *Haliotide Australe*, Ger. *Silbernes Meerohr*
The layer of mother-of-pearl on the inside of the shell, with its seven open perforations, shines bright silver. The outside of the shell may be white, olive or sand-coloured and has axial or radiating grooves.

This abalone, which grows to 7–9 cm (3–3½ in) long, is found in New Zealand but is less common than the larger *Haliotis iris*, which is fished commercially in the same area.

Pink or Corrugated Abalone

(*Haliotis corrugata*), Ger. *Rosafarbenes Meerohr*
The shell is relatively round, with two to four openings. The surface is striking, with its irregular corrugations, while the inside has a pink glow. The shell diameter is between 14 and 16 cm (5½–6 in). The Pink Abalone is found on the American Pacific coast, mainly off California down to the Mexican border, at depths of 5–40 m (15–130 ft).

Black Abalone

(*Haliotis cracherodi*), Ger. *Schwarze Abalone*
A smooth, oval shell, up to 15 cm (6 in) in length, with five to nine holes along the edge. This dark, almost black, abalone is found on the Pacific coast from southern Oregon to southern California, on the lower shore under stones and rocks.

Smooth Ear Shell, Green Lip Abalone

(*Haliotis laevigata*), Ger. *Glattes Seeohr*
The greenish-white shell of this abalone is 15–20 cm (6–8 in) long, oval, with evenly rounded edges and a relatively smooth surface. It has up to twelve small perforations. The Smooth Ear Shell lives on the bottoms or sides of rocks below the shore line. It is found in southern Australia between Victoria and Western Australia.

Southern Green Abalone

(*Haliotis fulgens*), Ger. *Grünes Meerohr*
This abalone ranges in colour from reddish-brown to greenish-opal, with brown speckles. The inside of the shell is a most striking dark-green to violet. The outside of the shell has thirty to forty relatively even whorls, with five to six small, open perforations, which are slightly raised. The Southern Green Abalone grows to 25 cm (10 in) long. It is found on the coast of California and Baja California, below the shore line at depths up to 8 m (25 ft).

Midas Abalone

(*Haliotis midae*), Fr. *Ormeau*, Ger. *Südafrikanisches Meerohr*, S. Afr. *Perlemoen*
This large, brownish-red to earth-coloured abalone has irregular spiral whorls on its shell and grows to 12–18 cm (5–7 in). Along the edge of the shell are nine raised, open perforations. The Midas Abalone feeds on seaweed and is found on the South African coast between Cape Town and Port Alfred.

Japanese Abalone, Kamchatka Abalone

(*Haliotis kamtschatkana*), Ger. *Kamtschatka-Seeohr*
An oval shell, 10–15 cm (4–6 in) long with a rough, irregular surface, comparatively high coils and four to five open perforations. This relatively small species

is found on the Pacific coast of the USA, from California to southern Alaska, above the surf-line. It is quite rare in California, but the further north one goes the more common it becomes. The Kamchatka Abalone is also found in Japan.

Roe's Abalone
(Haliotis roei), Ger. Roe-Abalone
The shell is a roundish oval, similar to that of the Southern Green Abalone, with distinct, spiralling, fibrous ribs. It is brownish-green in colour with seven open perforations. The shell is up to 12 cm (5 in) long. Roe's Abalone is found on the Australian coast, particularly in the south and south-west, including Tasmania, where it lives in moving, shallow water on calcareous rocks.

These Kamchatka Abalones (*Haliotis kamtschatkana*) were in fact photographed in California, although they are quite rare there. They are found in much larger numbers further north up the Pacific coast. California has introduced strict regulations to protect abalones, which prohibit them being exported from the state, either bottled or fresh.

Red Abalone
(Haliotis rufescens), Ger. Rotes Meerohr
With a shell up to 30 cm (1 ft) in diameter, this is one of the largest abalones and the largest found on the American Pacific coast. The white, sand-coloured or reddish-brown outside of the shell has scaly, concentric whorls crossed by radial ribs. The interior of the shell is white mother-of-pearl, while the flesh is black. This abalone is found on the coast of California, where it is extremely popular and (like other abalones) is protected against overfishing.

Ormer
(Haliotis tuberculata), Fr. Oreille de St-Pierre, Ger. See-ohr, Ital. Orecchia di San Pietro
An extremely flat shell, 8–10 cm (3–4 in) long, with spiral stripes, brown or pink speckles and slight marbling. Around the edge are six to eight open perforations. The mother-of-pearl layer on the interior is particularly fine. The Ormer, together with a smaller sub-species found in the Mediterranean (*Haliotis lamellosa*), is the only type of abalone found on the warmer coasts of the East Atlantic. Its distribution extends from southern England to Senegal.

Fresh abalones, like the three Smooth Ear Shells (*Haliotis laevigata*) from Australia shown here, rarely come onto the market in Europe. It requires considerable skill to separate the flesh from the shell. Before cooking, the intestinal sac (together with any dark-coloured parts) must be removed and only the white flesh used. They have to be cooked for quite a long time, unless beaten before braising or frying, since they are quite tough. Nevertheless, raw abalones are a popular ingredient of Japanese *sushi*.

LIMPETS (*Patellidae*)

Limpet shells are conical in shape, like a pointed hat. As with abalones, the shell is not unlike that of a bivalve. Many limpets are rather exotic in shape, structure and colour. Many shells have star-shaped radial ribs and coloured stripes. Others are circular, with beautiful colouring on the interior, resembling medallions. Some of the conical shells have a hole at the top, others are closed.

Limpets are found on rocky shores throughout the world, but most species are restricted to moderate and tropical waters. They live on the tide-line, where they cling to rocks and stones with their strong foot. As the tide recedes, they look for a permanent place to settle, preferably a small hole into which they just fit. Even the strongest breakers are unable to dislodge them. At night, limpets leave their hole to search for food, feeding on algae growing on rocks. In their search, they move in a circle of about 1 m (3 ft) diameter around their hole, to which they eventually creep back.

Most limpets are fairly small and not very fleshy, so that only a few of the larger types are of interest as human food.

Limpet

(Patella barbara), Fr. Patelle, Ger. Südafrikanische Napfschnecke
The shell of this clay-coloured, irregularly ribbed limpet has a markedly zig-zag edge. The interior is porcelain-coloured. This limpet grows to 10 cm (4 in) and is found chiefly on the southern African coast as far as Mozambique.

The same area is home to another, similar limpet, *Patella oculus*, the inside of which has a distinctive brown band at the edge. The outer shell, which reaches around 11 cm (4¼ in), is dark brown.

Mexican Limpet

(Patella mexicana), Ger. Mexikanische Napfschnecke
An off-white, thick-shelled limpet with well defined radial ribs and a horse-shoe-shaped muscle

The Common Limpet (*Patella vulgata*) is eaten in large numbers along the European Atlantic coast. It has a good flavour but the flesh is rather tough. You can often find their shells on the beach, washed white by the tide (left of photo).

marking on the interior of the shell. The flesh is black flecked with white. At 15–35 cm (6–13½ in) thick, this is the largest of the limpets, but its numbers have been decimated in recent years. It is found on the Pacific coasts of Mexico and Peru.

African Limpet

(Patella safiana), Ger. Afrikanische Napfschnecke
Similar to the Common (European) Limpet, but with radiating ribs in alternate groups of white and reddish-brown. These ribs are crossed by narrow, ring-shaped tubercles. The translucent shell, with its pearly interior, reaches 7 cm (3 in) in diameter. This limpet is found on the shoreline on the west coast of Africa, from Morocco to Angola.

Common Limpet

(Patella vulgata), Fr. Patelle Vulgaire, Bernique, Ger. Gemeine Napfschnecke, Span. Lapas, Ital. Patello
The orange-grey shell of this European limpet has alternating strong and weak ribs. The alternating colour forms rings. This limpet measures up to 6 cm (2½ in) and lives in coastal areas of the European Atlantic from the Lofotens, through England, to northern Spain.

In the Mediterranean is a related species, *Patella caerulea*. It is eaten by the local people in many coastal areas, although it is extremely tough.

Tortoiseshell Limpet

(Notoacmaea scutum), Ger. Shildkrötennapfschnecke
A slightly oval shell with wide, brown radial stripes on a reddish-brown background. The markings are like those of tortoiseshell. The interior, with a dark centre on a mother-of-pearl background, is like a medallion. This limpet, which measures 4 cm (1½ in) in diameter, is found on the Pacific coast from the Bering Strait to California.

Giant Owl Limpet

(Lottia gigantea), Ger. Große Eulennapfschnecke
The oval, greenish-brown shell has an interior like a medallion. The light-brown muscle mark on a pale-blue background, which resembles the shape of an owl, has a bluish-black outline. This limpet reaches 5–9 cm (2–3½ in) in diameter and lives on the southern Pacific coast of the USA and Baja California.

PERIWINKLES (*Littorinidae*)

Most periwinkles are very small, not more than 4 cm (1½ in) in diameter. With few exceptions, the shells are thick and wedge-shaped. In the periwinkle, the sexes are separate and both have gills with one or two rows of filaments. Many periwinkles live above the high-water mark, where they are splashed by the waves.

Periwinkles were eaten as early as prehistoric times. They are still widely eaten today and are prepared in a variety of ways. In some places on the French Atlantic coast, they are cultivated in 'winkle parks'.

Common Periwinkle

(Littorina litterea), Fr. Bigorneau, Ger. Gemeine Strandschnecke, Gemeine Uferschnecke
One of the commonest shellfish of the European coastline, the Common Periwinkle is found throughout the North Atlantic from 43° latitude and all along the German coast. Its wedge-shaped, sharply pointed shell is greyish-green with concentric stripes. It grows to around 4 cm (1½ in) in diameter.

Flat Winkle

(Littorina obtusata), Fr. Littorine Obtuse, Bigorneau Jaune, Ger. Stumpfe Strandschnecke
A small, almost round shellfish

The Common Periwinkle (*Littorina littorea*) is best known by its French name, Bigorneaux. One classic method of preparing them is simply to boil them in salted water (for not longer than 12 minutes) and serve them in a herb vinaigrette. The flesh is removed from the shell with a needle or a cocktail stick. It is essential to remove the lids with which the winkles close their shells, if these have not dissolved during boiling.

scarcely more than 1.5 cm ($\frac{3}{4}$ in) long, with a flat-ended shell with spiralling black and pale yellow stripes. The Flat Winkle lives in seaweed below the high-tide level, from Iceland to the Azores.

TOP SHELLS
(Trochidae)

A large family of shellfish of all sizes, whose shells resemble a child's top with their flat rather than convex spirals. Unlike in the *Turbinidae*, described below, the lid used to close the shell is thin and horny. The numerous species that make up this family live in moderately warm and tropical seas. Larger types in the Indo-Pacific are used for their mother-of-pearl.

West Indian Top Shell
(Cittarium pica), Fr. *Turbopie*, Ger. *Westindische Tigerschnecke*
This species has a thick shell with wide spirals, in black with light flecks. The conical shell grows to 6–10 cm ($2\frac{1}{2}$–4 in) in diameter. This shellfish is very popular in its native Caribbean, where it is eaten either cooked, in clam chowder, or raw as an aphrodisiac!

TURBAN SHELLS
(Turbinidae)

Comprising some 100 members, this large shellfish family is distributed throughout the world. The shell is similar to that of the periwinkles but is generally thicker. Most species have a thick, chalky lid with which the opening of the shell is sealed.

Turban Shell
(Astraea rugosa, formerly *Turbo rugosus)*, Fr. *Turbo Scabre*, Ger. *Turbanschnecke*, Ital. *Occhio di Santa Lucia*
The thick, greenish-brown, conical shell has seven rounded whorls, each edged with a row of small knobs. The oval lid is brown on the inside and orange outside. The Turban Shell, which grows to about 4 cm ($1\frac{1}{2}$ in), likes to attach itself to a hard surface at a minimum depth of 3 m (10 ft). It is found from the Basque coast to

the Canaries and Azores, as well as in the Mediterranean.

Green Turban
(Turbo marmoratus), Fr. *Turbo Marbré*, Ger. *Grüner Ölkrug*
The large, thick, pointed shell may measure anything from 15 to 20 cm (6–11 in) in diameter. The green surface is marked with brown and white or brownish rings. The wide opening is pink mother-of-pearl. The Green Turban is found from the Red Sea to the South Seas, at depths of 15–40 m (50–130 ft). Natives of the Pacific Islands not only eat the flesh, but make the shells into buttons and ornaments. As a result of overfishing, export is prohibited in some parts of the Pacific.

Horned Turban
(Turbo cornutus), Fr. *Turbo Cornu*, Ger. *Gehörnte Turbanschnecke*
The golden-brown, rather unprepossessing, asymmetrical, pointed shell grows to 7–10 cm (3–4 in) and often has two rows of knobs. In calm waters, the knobs are generally absent. A very popular shellfish, which is much fished, the Horned Turban is found at depths of 4–10 m (13–33 ft) off the coast of Korea and Japan, between southern Hokkaido and Kiushu. It occupies an important place in Japanese cooking.

CONCH SHELLS
(Strombidae)

On the coast of Florida, the native conch, one of the *Strombidae* family, is extremely popular. They are much eaten in the

Florida Keys, although stocks have been much depleted by overfishing. Columbus made the acquaintance of the conch when he came across the Arawak Indians in the Bahamas. They not only ate the flesh of this large shellfish but also fashioned the shells into tools and ritual objects. The shells are popular collectors' items today.

Queen Conch, Edible Pink Conch
(Strombus gigas), Ger. *Riesenflügelschnecke*
This conch, found from the coast of Florida to Trinidad, grows to around 30 cm (1 ft). The shell has five to seven blunt knobs.

The eating of this and other conches may occasionally cause vomiting. As a preventative measure, they are often boiled twice; that is, the water is changed part-way through cooking. The flesh is also quite difficult to remove from the thick shell.

In Florida, conch-eaters distinguish between 'thick-lipped' and 'thin-lipped' conches. Thin-lipped conches are young animals, whereas older ones have a thick growth around the mouth opening.

Fighting Conch
(Strombus pugilis), Ger. *Fechterschnecke*
This tropical shellfish is similar in shape to the Queen Conch but much smaller at only 8 cm (3 in). Like all conches, it has a claw-shaped foot with a sharp-edged lid, which it beats frantically to and fro when danger threatens – hence its name. The shell is pale

orange and is found at depths from 2–6 m ($6\frac{1}{2}$–20 ft).

MUREX SHELLS
(Muricidae)

A large family, native to tropical, subtropical and moderately warm seas. The highly decorative shells have three to twelve axial frills, known as varixes, covered with prickles. Murex shells are carnivorous, feeding on other shellfish by boring into their shells.

Both types of murex described here were once used for purple dye. A gland on the mantle produces a fluid which turns yellow, red and then purple when exposed to sunlight.

Purple Dye Murex
(Murex brandaris), Fr. *Murex Massue, Rocher Epineux*, Ger. *Mittelmeerschnecke, Herkuleskeule*, Ital. *Murice Comune, Garusolo, Cornetto di Mare*, Span. *Busano*, Port. *Búzio*
The shell is usually yellow and 6–10 cm ($2\frac{1}{2}$–4 in) in length. It is variable in shape and may have axial ribs only or may have prickles, too. A long siphonal canal resembles a tail.

This shellfish, found in the Mediterranean and the Algarve, prefers sand below the tide-line at depths of up to about 20 m (65 ft). It is usually caught in fishermen's trawl nets and sold in local markets.

Truncated Murex
(Murex trunculus), Fr. *Rocher à Pourpre, Biou Nègre, Cornet*, Ger. *Purpurschnecke*, Ital. *Murice, Scoglio Troncato*,

Only the muscle of the Queen Conch *(Strombus gigas)* is edible. The horny lid is removed and the muscle skinned. The meat is then beaten to tenderize it, or chopped.

In Italian fishmarkets, you will often come across the Purple Dye Murex *(Murex brandaris)*. It is usually caught accidentally by fishermen trawling for fish.

The Truncated Murex *(Murex trunculus)* is another Mediterranean shellfish. The flesh is none too tender, but it has an excellent flavour after boiling.

*Garusolo Femena, Span. Can-
ailla, Caracol de Roca, Bucios*
The truncated shell has ribs or
short prickles. The siphonal canal
is short and fat. The brownish
shell has two dark-brown stripes
on each whorl. The Truncated
Murex is found throughout the
Mediterranean on hard surfaces,
such as rocks or boulders, and is
often caught in fisherman's nets
and sold locally.

WHELKS
(*Buccinidae* and
Melongenidae)

Whelks have an important part
to play as the 'health inspectorate' of the ocean, for most
are scavengers. With their highly
developed sense of smell, they can
detect food at distances of up to
30 m (100 ft).

Other types of whelk bore into
the shells of other shellfish to get
at their flesh, including one which
is a real oyster specialist.

Their shells vary in shape from
oval, pear-shaped or round to
spiral.

Whelks are found from both
polar seas to the equator. Large
whelks, such as *Buccinum undatum* (described below), are of
culinary importance.

Common Whelk, Waved Whelk, Buckie
(*Buccinum undatum*), Fr. *Bulot,
Buccin, Ondé,* Ger. *Wellhornschnecke*
The Common Whelk is found
chiefly on soft sand, but also on
rock and pebbles, at depths of up
to 1,200 m (3,935 ft) from the
Arctic Ocean, through the North
Sea and western Baltic to the Bay
of Biscay.

The Spiral Babylon (*Babylonia
formosae*) is a native of the tropical
Pacific. Boiled, and served in a hot
sauce, these whelks are extremely
popular in South-east Asia.

The wedge-shaped, light-
brown to sand-coloured shell
grows to 11 cm (4¼ in). It has
typical fine, concentric, spiralling
ribs, crossed by lighter grooves.
The inside of the mouth is white
to pale pink, with a channel for
the siphon or breathing tube.

Despite their heavy shells,
Common Whelks can move fairly
quickly. On the beach, you may
occasionally come across round
clumps of something resembling
grapes. These are the egg capsules
of the whelk. Usually they will be
empty, with the young whelks
already away.

Common Whelks are a regular
feature of seaside fish markets
but are sometimes available from
fishmongers or delicatessens inland. The main consumers are
the French and French-speak-
ing Canadians, who sauté boiled
whelks or deep-fry them in batter.
Common Whelks can also be
used in clam chowder or similar
dishes.

Mediterranean Whelk
(*Buccinum humphreysianum*),
Ger. *Mittelländisches Tiefsee-
wellhorn*
Found in the Mediterranean and
the Atlantic between Norway
and Portugal at depths from 80 m
(260 ft), the Mediterranean
Whelk has a thin, slightly transparent shell up to 6 cm (2½ in) in
length. It is ivory-pink in colour
with irregular, light-brown flecks.

Horn Whelk
(*Euthria cornea,* formerly
Buccinulum corneum), Ger.
*Hornschnecke, Sardische
Wellhornschnecke*
The Horn Whelk has a yellow,
symmetrically spiralling shell of
about 7 cm (3 in) in length. It has
a thick, flared outer lip and an
inverted siphonal canal and lives
at depths up to 30 m (100 ft) in the
Mediterranean, especially off the
coasts of Sardinia.

Spiral Babylon
(*Babylonia formosae*), Ger.
Spirale von Babylon
This whelk has a thin, white shell
with several whorls covered with
almost rectangular brown markings and is up to 7 cm (3 in) in

These Whelks, of the species *Buccinum undatum*, can be bought alive in
Parisian markets. They are 4–8 cm (1½–3 in) long. They are very popular in
France, especially in Normandy, where they are used mainly in fish soups
or cooked dishes. You can also buy them ready-boiled or bottled in
vinegar.

length. It lives on fine sand at
depths of up to 20 m (65 ft) and is
found in the tropical Pacific, from
Taiwan to Vietnam and southwards to Malaysia.

Japanese Babylon
(*Babylonia japonica*), Ger.
Japanische Babylonschnecke
Similar in shape to the Spiral
Babylon but with the whorls,
with their irregular brown mark-
ings, more rounded, the Japanese
Babylon measures up to 8 cm
(3 in) long. It is found mainly in
Japanese waters, at depths of up
to 20 m (65 ft).

Signum Whelk
(*Siphonalia signum*), Ger.
*Gestreifte Japanische Wellhorn-
schnecke*
A small shellfish, up to 6 cm
(2½ in) in length, the Signum
Whelk is found in great numbers
in sand off central and southern
Japan. The whorls of the shell are
broken at intervals by fine edges.
One fine, brown stripe spirals up
to the point, against an ivory
background. The opening has a
rounded edge.

Hirase's Whelk
(*Japelion hirasei*), Ger. *Große*

Japanische Wellhornschnecke
A narrow, yellowish-brown shell,
about 12 cm (5 in) long, with flat
whorls. This whelk is found
mainly in the cold waters off
northern Japan.

Dilated Whelk
(*Penion maxima*), Ger.
*Südaustralische Wellhorn-
schnecke*
A whelk up to 25 cm (10 in) in
length, with a white and brownish shell, whose whorls resemble
the roof of a pagoda. The
opening is elongated at the base
by a channel for the siphonal
tube. The Dilated Whelk is found
on deep sandbanks between Australia and Tasmania.

Channelled Whelk, Pear Whelk
(*Busycon canaliculata*), Ger.
Gefurchte Birnenschnecke
A large, thin-shelled whelk, particularly common on the American
Atlantic coast between Boston
and the Gulf of Mexico. The shell
differs from that of most other
whelks so far described, in that its
whorls are so flat-topped that
they restrict the body to the lower
part of the shell. The surface of
the brownish shell is irregularly
channelled, and it grows to

15–18 cm (6–7 in) in length. This species lives on sand in shallow water.

Knobbed Whelk, Giant Whelk
(Busycon carica), Ger. *Knotige Birnenschnecke*
A whelk found on the East Coast of the United States, from Massachusetts to Florida, which grows up to 20 cm (8 in) in length. It is distinguished from the Channelled Whelk by a ring of knobs on the two largest whorls, disappearing towards the top. The opening of the grey shell is brick-red. The Knobbed Whelk is the largest univalve on the North American coast.

Whelks are caught in the same way as lobster and crayfish, mostly using baskets.

The main buyers of whelks in the United States are Italian fish merchants. The Channelled Whelks shown here (*Busycon canaliculata*) are market leaders, with Common Whelks (*Buccinum undatum*) and Knobbed Whelks (*Busycon carica*).

Land snails
(Pulmonata)

SPIRE SNAILS, GIANT SNAILS
(Achatinidae)

The spire snails, native to tropical Africa, are the largest living land snails. Their light-coloured, rounded shells, most of which are elongated into a spire, are covered with brown lines and stripes. A single snail can weigh up to 500 g (18 oz) without its shell. This has made the *Achatina* family of increasing economic importance.

The true Spire Snail (*Achatina achatina*) is found only in a small area of West Africa (Sierra Leone, Liberia and the Ivory Coast). Its shell can exceed 20 cm (8 in) in height and 10 cm (4 in) in width. It lives mainly in rain forests. In new plantations, its voracious appetite often causes great damage.

Agate-type Snail, Giant African Snail
(Achatina fulica), Fr. *Escargot Achatine*, Ger. *Gemeine Achatschnecke*
Originally native to the East African coast and Madagascar, this species has now been introduced throughout Asia and into America. The first examples in California were discovered after the Second World War. They are thought to have been introduced by the Japanese, who love them.

Their flesh makes an excellent substitute for Bourgogne Snail, which it closely resembles, and is becoming increasingly important

Bourgogne Snails are seldom sold fresh; more usually, they are sold pre-cooked in cans. They can also be bought frozen in the shell, often complete with the savoury butter for making Escargots à la Bourguignonne.

in Europe. These snails are cultivated in various parts of South-east Asia and exported to Europe in tins.

TYPICAL SNAILS
(Helicidae)

The large *Helicidae* family, which has representatives worldwide, belongs to the *Pulmonata*, or air-breathing group. They have no gills but a mantle cavity developed into lungs. Nevertheless, a few types live in fresh or brackish water. All typical snails are hermaphrodite. In inclement weather, the rounded shells can be sealed with a lid to protect against cold or drought. They are vegetarians and so are often regarded as pests, as in the case of the Garden Snail (*Cepaea hortensis*). The largest central European species is the Bourgogne Snail, which is an important food.

Bourgogne Snail
(Helix pomatia), Fr. *Escargot de Bourgogne*, Ger. *Weinbergschnecke*
This land snail, found throughout the moderate European zone, used to do great damage in vineyards, where it loved to eat the young vine shoots. Nowadays, it has been eradicated from the wine-growing areas. It can be found in gardens, parks and hedgerows, and on the edges of fields, meadows and woodland. It prefers not too dry, chalky soil with shade.

With the onset of winter, Bourgogne Snails burrow up to 30 cm (1 ft) into the ground and seal the shell with a calcarous lid. The spring sunshine brings them out once more. As soon as they have made up the water lost during hibernation, they begin mating. After about six to eight weeks, they lay eggs of about 3 mm ($\frac{1}{8}$ in) in diameter, twenty-five to twenty-eight days later, tiny snails with delicate, transparent shells crawl out of the eggs. One snail can lay up to fifty-five eggs per year.

Bourgogne Snails eat by means of a curved, coarse rasping tongue, the *radula*. In the areas

where they are bred, you can hear them eating on calm summer evenings.

Nowadays, the Bourgogne Snail is a great delicacy, whereas at one time it was a popular food for the lower classes. Although fewer snails are eaten nowadays, nature can no longer supply the demand. Snails are bred and fattened in farms. At one time, most winter snails were exported, since they kept better and were quite plump, thanks to their winter reserves. Nowadays, the emerging spring snails are preferred. Summer snails are not so good for eating, since they contain a lot of chalk at this time of year.

Most Bourgogne Snails come onto the market frozen or pre-cooked and canned or bottled.

Bourgogne-type Snail
(Helix aspersa), Fr. *Escargot Petit Gris*, Ger. *Gesprenkelte Weinbergschnecke*
A slightly smaller, southern European snail with white and yellow flecks on the shell.

The same area also produces other close relatives of the Bourgogne Snail; for example, the small *Theba pisana* from the Venice region or the *Helix secernenda* of Croatia and Albania. Another type, *Helix naticoides*, is found in southern Italy where, except for the damp winter, it lives under the ground almost all the year round. Another similar snail is *Helix ligata*, found in central and southern Italy to Calabria. The larger *Helix lucorum* is found in Italy east of the Appennines, in the Balkan peninsula and in Asia Minor. These species are being increasingly imported into western Europe to replace the Bourgogne Snail (*Helix pomatia*), which is becoming scarce.

CUTTLEFISH/SQUID/ OCTOPUSES
(*Cephalopoda*)

The cephalopods, which include cuttlefish, calamary, octopuses and nautilus, are the most highly developed of the molluscs. They are thorough-going sea creatures. Among them are found the largest of the ocean's invertebrates. In the depths of the sea live squid of the genus *Architeuthis*, whose bodies can measure 6 m (20 ft) in length and whose extended arms give an overall length of around 17 m (55 ft). Evidence of suckers has been found in the stomachs of sperm whales that indicates creatures up to 21 m (70 ft) long. They are also the fastest of the marine creatures.

The cephalopods, which are closer to the snails than to fish, have highly developed sensory organs and an equally highly developed nervous system. They have three-dimensional vision, can distinguish colours and are capable of 'learning' and 'remembering'. The head, with its large lensed eyes, is clearly distinguishable from the body. In the mouth, together with the rasping tongue (*radula*) – which we have already met in the snail, and which here is no more than a rough tongue which makes swallowing food easier – there are two jaws, similar to a parrot's beak. These are used to tear up the prey – mainly shellfish, crabs and fish.

The mouth is surrounded by extremely mobile tentacles, often with suckers, which are used to seize prey as well as for feeling and crawling. On the stomach side of the sack-shaped body is a roomy mantle cavity, containing the gut and urinatory and sex organs as well as the gills. Through a front opening in the mantle cavity, water for respiration floods in and is passed out through a narrow tube. Expelling water through the tube provides an efficient method of backwards jet propulsion, used to escape an enemy. For slower movement, most species also have fins on the side of the body.

Almost all cephalopods have a bag of pigment, the ink sack. When an attacker approaches, a gland which opens into the mantle cavity produces a brownish-black fluid, which is emitted at the front as the animal projects backwards. The fluid spreads in a cloud around the cephalopod and hides it from its enemy (be it a dolphin, sperm whale, tuna fish or cod). Often, the cloud of ink takes on the shape of the threatened creature, so that the attacker snaps at the empty cloud.

The skin of most cephalopods contains moveable colour cells, which enable the animal to change colour. In some species, this is used as a mating display but for those that live on the sea-bed, such as the octopuses, it also serves as camouflage.

All cephalopods are separately sexed. They lay eggs from which the young emerge fully developed. Most cephalopods living today do not have the external shell of the bivalves and snails. One of the few shelled types still extant is the Nautilus of the South Seas. Fossil finds indicate, however, that there were once many more cephalopods with similar four-chambered, spiral shells. Most modern cephalopods do in fact have a shell, but it is inside the body. Only a very few have no shell at all.

This calcium shell, known as cuttle-bone, is usually an elongated oval and slightly domed. Tiny, gas-filled chambers make it porous and extremely light. These shells can often be found on the beach. Pet shops sell them as whetstones for caged birds and jewellers use them as moulds.

Cephalopods are divided into those with four and those with two gills. The Nautilus is the sole surviving representative of the four-gilled cephalopods; all the other species alive today are two-gilled. In South-east Asia, the Nautilus is still caught in large quantities, especially in Burma, for both its flesh and its handsome shell.

The two-gilled cephalopods are again sub-divided according to the number of their tentacles. Some have eight (*Octobrachia*)

In Mediterranean countries, squid and octopus form part of the everyday diet and they are really delicious when they are properly prepared. The people of Galicia, for instance, serve a number of delicacies made with octopus. Even in America, these creatures are gaining in popularity – especially on the West Coast, thanks to cooks from Italy, Spain and Greece.

and some ten (*Decobrachia*), with two longer catching arms in addition to the eight usual tentacles.

Cephalopods are richly represented in all the world's seas and have been an important source of food for coastal dwellers since time immemorial. Thanks to canning and freezing techniques, cuttlefish, squid and octopus now have an important market and are available almost everywhere. Their importance as human food is bound to increase in the future, as they are widespread and their stocks – so far – are much less depleted than those of most sea creatures.

Cephalopods with ten tentacles
(*Decabrachia*)

CUTTLEFISH (*Sepioidea*)

Of the families that make up the *Sepioidea*, the main ones of interest here are the *Sepiidae* families, which include the Common Sepia amongst their eighty species, and the *Sepiolidae*, which include the Large Ross-cuttle (*Rossia macrosoma*) of the Mediterranean and north Atlantic.

Common Sepia, Cuttlefish
(*Sepia officinalis*), Fr. Seiche, Ger. Sepia, Gemeiner Tintenfisch, Ital. Seppia Commune, Seppia Officinale, Span. Luda, Sipia, Port. Choco, Dut. Gewone Inktvis

As in all members of the *Sepia* family, the body of the Common Sepia is a flattened oval to round, extending into thin fins at the sides. Typified by black and white zebra stripes on the back and light colouring on the underside. The two catching tentacles are long, with four rows of suckers, but are usually kept rolled up and hidden in openings on either side of the mouth. When likely prey approaches, the Common Sepia can extend these tentacles with lightning speed.

Normally, the Common Sepia will be found near the sea-bed, raking up loose sand with its fins to act as camouflage. Larger specimens can reach 65 cm (25 in) in length, almost half of this made up by the catching tentacles. The

The Common Sepia or Cuttlefish (*Sepia officinalis*) is the best known cuttlefish of all, and is rarely referred to as 'sepia'. Recipes for dishes 'en su tinta' are mostly Spanish in origin and are so called because the ink itself is used in the dish. This makes the cooking liquid almost black. Squid, too, are sometimes cooked in their own ink.

The Common Octopus (*Octopus vulgaris*) is extremely plentiful and popular in the Mediterranean. It can be identified by its eight tentacles, each with two rows of suckers. As for all inkfish, the important thing when preparing it is to cook it for long enough. Octopus needs to cook longer than cuttlefish and squid, and with larger octopuses it is a good idea to tenderize it by beating before cooking.

body will measure, on average, 25–30 cm (10–12 in). The Common Sepia is found throughout the Atlantic, from Norway to South Africa, but there is a representative of the *Sepia* family in every ocean.

Ross-cuttle
(*Rossia sp.*), *Fr. Rossie, Ger. Rossie, Ital. Seppiola Grossa, Span. Rosia*
As far as the markets are concerned, the most important member of the *Rossia* family is the Large Ross-cuttle (*Rossia macrosoma*), which is found in the Atlantic north of the Equator and in the western Mediterranean. While *Rossia* vaguely resemble the sepias, they have two rounded, wing-like side fins, while the internal shell has almost completely disappeared. The sack-like, brown body is more truncated than that of the sepia. The tentacles are webbed with skin where they join the body.

Members of the *Rossia* family have eyes that produce a shiny film, which is expelled through the funnel when the creature is

disturbed. The Deep-sea Ross-cuttle (*Rossia mastigophora*), found in the Indian Ocean, has developed this feature more than most and can actually 'dazzle' its pursuers.

Little Cuttle
(*Sepiola spp.*), *Fr. Sépiole, Ger. Sepiole, Kleine Sprutte, Span. Globitos, Sepiola, Ital. Seppiola, Port. Pota, Zula, Dut. Dwerg-inktvis*
This cuttlefish, which is found mainly in the Mediterranean, is very small and is sometimes referred to as the Dwarf Cuttle. They grow to only 3–6 cm (1–2½ in) in length and the interior shell is practically non-existent. They swim by means of fins on the rump, which they beat like the wings of a bird.

Deep-water *Sepiola* have eyes similar to those of the ross-cuttles, with which they can dazzle and throw off their pursuers, while those that live nearer the coast evade their enemies by burrowing or with a cloud of ink.

SQUID (*Teuthoidea*)

In contrast to the *Sepioidea*, squid or *Teuthoidea* have a long, slender, torpedo-like body, ending in a rhombus-shaped tail fin. The head with the tentacles is also elongated. The mouth tentacles are relatively short, with two rows of suckers. The two catching arms have two or four rows of suckers. Unlike those of the *Sepioidea*, these catching tentacles can be only partially drawn in. Squid are excellent swimmers. Since they can change the angle of the funnel through which they expel water, they can swim in any direction, either backwards or forwards. They are active hunters, mainly of fish.

The most important squid in commercial terms belong to the *Loliginidae* family. There is quite a large market for squid in the United States and they are also appreciated as a nutritious and tasty food by the peoples of the Middle and Far East and the Mediterranean. Squid is usually eaten fresh but is also frozen, pickled and canned.

Squid are divided into two super-families, lidless and lidded squids. One of the lidless squid is *Lycoteuthis diadema*, which is semi-transparent and has twenty-two light-sensitive organs. Another member of this group is the Giant Squid of the *Architeuthidae* family, which weighs several tons and grows to 17 m (55 ft) in length. Giant Squid have long been a source of fishermen's stories and doubtless will long continue to be so.

Calamary, Long-finned Squid
(*Loligo vulgaris*), *Fr. Calmar, Encornet, Ger. Gemeine Kalmar, Ital. Calamàro Comune, Span. Calamar, Port. Lula, Calamar, Dut. Pijlinktvis*
The *Loligo* group, part of the *Loliginidae* family, is well represented in the fish markets of Europe.

The Calamary grows to between 30 and 50 cm (12–20 in) in length and can weigh up to 2 kg (4½ lb). The skin is smooth, and sandy to brown and red.

In North America, *Loligo pealei*, the North American

The Calamary (*Loligo vulgaris*) is widely available in European fish markets. It provides 80 per cent edible flesh which is firm, lean and rich in protein – and not at all tough. It becomes tough only if it is wrongly prepared. It should be cooked for 30–45 minutes, depending on size, and if it is to be fried it is best to beat it first to tenderize it. Small Calamarys are excellent for boiling whole. The sack-like body is ideal for stuffing, and many recipes include the finely chopped tentacles in the stuffing. In the Mediterranean countries, you will find Calamary in every fish soup and it is often eaten boiled. We are more used to finding it in Italian restaurants cut into pieces and fried or made into a salad. It is a pity that it is often like chewing on a rubber band.

Squid, is the species most widely sold. They swim in large groups in the formation of migrating birds, a formation which is kept with every change of direction. The inner shell has been reduced to a horny pen.

From the culinary viewpoint, it is *Loligo opalescens*, caught in large numbers in California, which takes pride of place. Members of the *Loliginidae* family prefer shallow coastal waters but can be found at depths of up to 200 m (650 ft).

Atlantic Squid

(Illex spp.), Ger. Kurzflossenkalmar
Members of the *Illex* family are found mainly in the Atlantic – right across to the American coast – and in the Mediterranean. They are excellent swimmers and usually live in large shoals. They hunt for fish, herrings being a particular favourite. The heart-shaped fins are not used for swimming, which is by means of backwards propulsion achieved by expelling water through the funnel.

Squid

(Ommastrephes spp.), Fr. Encornet, Ger. Pfeilkalmar
In this squid, the fins are diamond-shaped. These bluish-violet creatures can grow to 150 cm (5 ft) in length and 15 kg (33 lb) in weight. They are found in large quantities in the North Atlantic, as far as Norway, and are much fished.

Cephalopods with eight tentacles
(Octobrachia)

OCTOPUSES (*Octopodidae*)

While the cephalopods discussed so far have an interior shell, the cuttlebone, *Octopodidae* have no shell at all, nor do they have the two elongated catching tentacles. Unlike cuttlefish and squid, they are not swimmers, but spend their time on the sea-bed. They have no fins at all. They are able to swim by backwards propulsion but this is restricted to short distances when they have to escape an enemy. They spend most of their time in clefts and hollows in the rock, whose entrances they block with stones and shellfish and which they defend against other octopuses.

The truncated body runs directly into the tentacles, which are all of equal length with one or two rows of suckers. The *Octobrachia* order includes five other large families besides the *Octopodidae* described here, which is the most important from a culinary and economic viewpoint, especially in the Mediterranean and Japan.

Giant Squid are often wrongly referred to as octopuses, while octopuses are frequently termed polyps, which is equally wrong, since polyps belong to the jellyfish family.

Octopuses are found in every ocean, with the largest species having tentacles 5 m (16 ft) long.

Common Octopus, Sucker, Poulp (USA)

(Octopus vulgaris), Fr. Pieuvre, Poulpe, Ger. Gemeine Krake, Ital. Polpo Comune, Span. Pulpo Comun, Port. Polvo, Dut. Achtarm
The Common Octopus is found mainly on rocky Atlantic coasts and in the Mediterranean. On the sack-like body are staring, lidded eyes. The smooth tentacles each have two rows of suckers. These octopuses are also found in the North Sea, where they reach a total length of around 70 cm (27 in). In the Mediterranean and other warmer seas they can reach 3 m (10 ft) in length.

Like other cephalopods, the Common Octopus hunts by night, feeding mainly on crabs, shrimps and shellfish. The powerful tentacles can even overcome a full-grown lobster.

Octopuses live singly except at mating times, when there are often fierce fights between males seeking a mate. In males, one tentacle is used for mating; it is inserted into the female's mantle cavity. A female octopus can lay up to 100,000 eggs. The eggs, with their transparent protective capsules, are attached in clumps to solid objects like rocks. From them emerge fully formed tiny octopuses, which swim freely for about two months. The mother usually dies after laying her eggs.

The octopus is an important ingredient in Far Eastern cooking, especially in Japan and Korea. It is often sold ready-boiled and bottled in brine, like the large octopus in the foreground. Smaller ones, like those shown at the back, are often marinated in herbs and spices. The octopus, or 'Tako' as it is called in Japan, is a common ingredient of *sushi*, for which the tentacles are usually used. Boiled and sliced, they are arranged on a bed of sticky sushi rice.

Curled Octopus
(*Ozaena cirrhosa*), *Fr. Eledone, Pourpre Blanc, Ger. Zirren-krake, Ital. Polpo Bianco, Span. Pulpo de Alto, Port. Polvo do Alto*

This octopus, with only one row of suckers on each tentacle, is also found in the Mediterranean and Atlantic. At around 40 cm (16 in) in length, they are smaller than the Common Octopus. The tentacles are linked by skin where they join the body, to form a sort of umbrella.

Very similar in both shape and size is *Ozaena moschata*, which is usually found on sand or mud in the Mediterranean. Like most other octopuses, it is able to alter its skin colour to blend in with its surroundings.

The Curled Octopus is less sought-after than the Common Octopus.

Other Seafood

Two large zoological groups dominate the edible seafood market, both described above – crabs and molluscs. There are, however, a number of other sea creatures without which this book would be incomplete. The various groups to which they belong are just as important in zoological terms and just as large as the crustaceans and molluscs but, for the most part, they are of minor importance in terms of food and need not long detain us. They are all included in the following pages.

MEDUSAE/JELLYFISH
(*Scyphozoa*)

The *Cnidaria* family, which includes sea anemones and corals as well as jellyfish, has some 7,700 different species. Medusas or jellyfish are amongst the most familiar marine creatures. The umbrella is mushroom- or bell-shaped, with tentacles hanging from it. Jellyfish are found in the deep waters of every sea and ocean. In Europe, jellyfish are almost unheard of as a source of food, but some species are edible. They are eaten mainly in Asia.

The Chinese are particularly fond of them, for they are 'tender, crisp and elastic', a combination of qualities brought out in cooking. The jellyfish are first dried and sliced before they reach the shops. These slices are then steeped in water and cut into strips and then repeatedly scalded with hot water, which makes them curl up. The strips are served in a sauce of sesame oil, soy sauce, vinegar and sugar.

In Japan, you can buy whole, dried jellyfish. A traditional method of preparation is to mix the soaked and sliced jellyfish with sea urchins. This is a very popular nibble with rice wine.

Jellyfish
(*Rhizostoma pulmo*), *Fr. Rhizostome, Ger. Wurzelmund-qualle, Jap. Kurage, Turk. Deniz Anasi, Ital. Botte di Mare, Span. Aguamar*

This edible jellyfish has an extremely stable umbrella, which can grow to 50–80 cm (20–30 in) in diameter. It is cream to pale yellow in colour and cobalt blue at the rim.

From the Black Sea, where it is numerous, large numbers make their way through the Bosphorus to the Sea of Marmara. Here, the Turks have recently begun to fish them, to bottle them in brine and then export them, after much washing, to Japan. Current annual production is around 15 tonnes ($14\frac{3}{4}$ tons).

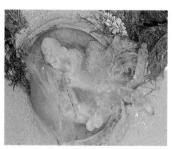

Jellyfish (*Rhizostoma pulmo*) are also found in the North Sea, but these are not used as a food source. This one was washed up on the North Sea island of Wangerooge.

Edible Jellyfish
(*Rhopilema esculenta*), *Ger. Pazifische Wurzelmundqualle, Jap. Kurage, Morasaki Zuken, Viet. Sua, Chin. Hoy Cheek*

A large jellyfish found in the warm western Pacific and eaten mainly in China, Japan, Thailand and Indonesia, this species can reach 45 cm (18 in) in diameter. Sold either dried or in brine, the annual turnover is estimated at around US $1,000,000.

HORSESHOE CRABS
(*Xiphosura*)

The strange-looking horseshoe crabs are zoologically related to the spiders (*Arachnida*), for both are members of the large group of *Chelicerata*. Fossil finds reveal that they have changed little in 500,000,000 years.

These worm- and mollusc-eaters rake through the mud in shallow, coastal water. They usually walk but are also capable of swimming. Unlike insects and crustaceans, the first pair of limbs do not take the form of antennae, but of gripping, tearing pincers. Horseshoe crabs have compound eyes, like insects, whereas all other *Arachnidae* have simple eyes.

The main area of distribution lies along the coasts of the southern Indo-Pacific and the American Atlantic, where they can be found in large numbers.

Horseshoe Crab
(*Limulus polyphemus*), *Fr. Xiphosure, Ger. Schwert-schwanz*

The Horseshoe Crab is found from the shallow Atlantic coast of the southern states of America into the Caribbean. Beneath the smooth head and body section are five pairs of walking legs, the first four of which have pincers and the fifth, fan-like fins. The compound eyes sit on the sides of the shell and are inset for protection. There are also a pair of simple middle eyes. The anterior shell ends in downward-pointing spikes. Hinged to this front shell is a domed, irregular rear shell, covering the lower body and edged with a row of sharp spikes.

This ends in a tail, which is almost as long as the two segments of shell together and gives a total length of around 50 cm (20 in).

The Horseshoe Crab is of very minor importance for human consumption in the Americas, where only the liver and eggs are eaten, although it is popular as a food in East Asia.

Beetle Crab, Horseshoe Crab

(Tachypleus spp.), Fr. Xiphosure, Ger. Pfeilenschwanzkrebs, Molukkenkrebs, Indon. Mimi, Ikan Mimi, Malay. Keroncho, Belangkas

The Indo-Pacific has two families of horseshoe crab, each with four different species. In appearance and behaviour, they scarcely differ from the Atlantic horse-shoe crabs; the only difference is that the females do not lay their eggs in sand but carry them around with them until the larvae hatch.

The Beetle Crab is found from Japan to Indonesia. The liver and, especially, the eggs are great delicacies. The flesh is sometimes used, too, mainly in soup.

Carcinoscorpius rotundicauda is another species from the same area, which should on no account be eaten as it is poisonous, and is reputed to be deadly.

SEA URCHINS
(Echinoidea)

For holidaymakers on Mediterranean beaches or further afield, sea urchins may have unpleasant connotations. The sharp prickles can make a painful wound if trodden on. Nevertheless, many of these creatures, which are similar in size to a plum or apple, are edible.

Sea urchins belong to the 6,000-strong group of *Echinodermata*, which also includes the sea cucumbers described below, starfish, feather-stars and sea-lilies. Of the 860 species of sea urchin, only a few are suitable for human consumption and of these it is only the ovaries of the female or gonads of the male that are recommended for eating and which gourmets consider a great delicacy.

Horseshoe crab – at first glance this creature (here, *Tachypleus gigas*), which belongs to the *Chelicerata*, is very like a horseshoe. In South-east Asia, the eggs and liver are considered great delicacies but the meat is rarely eaten. Horseshoe crabs have little economic importance, although they are often sold in local fish markets – for example, in Thailand.

The body of the sea urchin is enclosed in a round or slightly flattened calcarous shell, formed in the subcutaneous connective tissue and consisting of many separate connected plates. Over this skeleton lies the skin, which also covers the prickles. Muscles, together with a kind of ball joint on the plates of the shell, cause the prickles to move, but they can also be held rigid. The prickles vary in size and shape depending on the species. Between the prickles are biting, cleaning and poisonous pincers, as well as tube-feet with suckers and a hydraulic system by which they are extended.

The jaw is of a particularly complicated construction. Five teeth protrude from the mouth on the underside, which together with fifteen other small bones form a sort of pyramid, held together by tendons and muscles. This perfect chewing device was noted as early as the time of Pliny (23–79 AD).

Sea urchins live in all the world's seas. Some are carnivorous but most live on seaweed and algae. Some camouflage themselves with shells, seaweed or small pebbles. The females are slightly larger than the males and different in colour.

Edible Sea Urchin

(Echinus esculentus) Fr. Oursin, Ger. Essbare Seeigel, Ital. Riccio di Mare

The Edible Sea Urchin, which is found throughout the North Atlantic from Iceland and Norway to Portugal, is bluish, violet or reddish-green in colour. The prickles are symmetrically rayed, as is clearly evident from the dried skeleton. Sea urchins like to live on rocks overgrown with algae below tide level, from the shallows to depths of 40 m (130 ft). They can grow to around 16 cm (6 in) in diameter and live up to eight years.

Common Sea Urchin

(Paracentrotus lividus), Fr. Chataine, Châteigne de Mer, Oursin Mediterrané, Ger. Steinseeigel, Ital. Riccio Marino

Comune, Span. Erizo de Mar, Ikinua, Port. Ourico do Mar, Dut. Zee-egel

This deep-violet, brownish-green or occasionally golden-brown or black sea urchin, which measures up to 7 cm (3 in), is the most common in Europe. It lives in the warmer areas of the European Atlantic, from Ireland and Scotland to the Canaries and western Sahara, as well as in the Mediterranean, at depths of up to 80 m (260 ft). On rocky shores you will often find them in their hundreds and thousands, eating the algae off the rocks. On coasts with strong breakers, they will bore into the rock – on English and Irish chalk coastlines, for instance. This sea urchin is the one most often eaten in the Mediterranean region.

Black Sea Urchin

(Arbacia lixula), Ger. Schwarzer Seeigel, Ital. Riccio di Mare

This blue-black sea urchin has irregular, very long spines – longer, in fact, than the body diameter. It is found on rocks near the coasts of the northern and western Mediterranean and on the North African coast.

Short-spined Purple Sea Urchin

(Arbacia punctulata), Ger. Kurzstacheliger Purpurseeigel

This violet-greenish sea urchin reaches 5–9 cm (2–3½ in) in diameter and has short spines. It is found mostly in the warm, coastal waters of the American Atlantic and Caribbean.

Green Sea Urchin

(Strongylocentrotus spp.), Ger. Grüner Seeigel

Another short-spined sea urchin, of an attractive green, with the spines symmetrically arranged. It lives in the cold zones of the northern Atlantic and Pacific.

Long-spined Purple Sea Urchin

(Strongylocentrotus purpuratus), Ger. Langstacheliger Purpurseeigel

This large, purple sea urchin can reach 25 cm (10 in) in diameter. The deep purple spines vary in length, the longest ones having

light-coloured tips. This sea urchin is found on the coast of
California and throughout the
tropical Pacific.

SEA CUCUMBERS
(Holothurioidea)

Sea cucumbers, or sea slugs, are –
like sea urchins – a class of
echinodermates. The few edible
types, like those listed below,
mostly belong to the *Holo-
thuriidae, Stichopodidae* and *Cucumariidae.*

These elongated slug- or
cucumber-like animals have
either a leathery, velvety or slimy
skin, partly covered with cross-

In Agrigento market in Sicily, fresh-
caught sea urchins are sold or even
eaten on the spot. All you need is a
pair of pincers to crack the shell.

**These sea urchins from the
Caribbean** are eaten in quite large
numbers by local people. They are
an essential ingredient of 'Blaff', a
tasty and popular fish dish from the
French Antilles, which has become
something of a national dish.

grooves. The skeleton is limited
to small spicules in the skin and a
bony ring around the gullet. The
mouth at the front end is usually
surrounded by ten to twenty
tentacles, arranged around it like
the petals of a flower. An unusual
feature are the thin grub- or
prickle-like feet on the underside,
which sometimes extend onto the
back, with which the creatures
drag themselves along.

It is mainly in East Asia that
sea cucumbers are used for food.
In China, particularly, but also in
Japan, they are considered a
great delicacy, which may have
something to do with the fact that
they are considered to be an
aphrodisiac. The natives of Polynesia, Micronesia, New Guinea
and the Malay archipelago once
made their living supplying the
great demand. They caught sea
cucumbers, dried them and exported them as 'Trepang'. Demand in China is now met mainly
by the Caribbean islands, which
export dried sea cucumbers.

The best types of sea cucumbers for drying are those with flat
or shield-shape feelers. Once
caught, they are kept in large vats
of seawater and then boiled. The
shrivelled, boiled cucumbers are
dried in the sun between two or

This sea urchin *(Paracentrotus
lividus)* is the most common in
Europe, the one most often eaten
and also the best. Only the ovaries
or gonads are suitable for eating,
however.

It is difficult for Europeans to understand the popularity of sea cucumbers in South-east Asia and particularly in China – but the various processes involved in turning them into an edible substance are so lengthy and time-consuming that there must be something about this remarkable marine creature to make it worthwhile. They are sold dried as 'Trepang' (left) and after soaking (right) are cooked in a variety of ways.

three steamings in fresh water. Finally, they are smoked for several months. After this lengthy process, the sea cucumbers are sorted (for some types sell better than others) and then sold. Before cooking, they need to be steeped in water and gutted.

Another method of dealing with sea cucumbers is to cut them open, gut them, press them, rub them inside and out with chalk and then dry them in the sun and smoke them, but those prepared in this way are generally considered inferior.

Spotted Fish, Tiger Fish
(Holothuria argus, H. scabra, Bohadschia argus), Ger. Indopazifische Seegurke, Jap. Ayami-shikiri, Indon. Tripang, Teripang, Malay. Trepang
A sea cucumber with a flat belly and widely domed back, light- or chestnut-brown broken by red or orange patches, black specks and pockmark-like white spots. The Spotted Fish, which grows to 40 cm (16 in) in length, lives – as its German names implies –

throughout the Indo-Pacific. They are caught in large numbers and prepared to make 'Trepang'.

Teat Fish, Mamma-teat
(Holothuria nobilis, Microthele nobilis), Ger. Brustwarzen-seegurke
A large, elliptical sea cucumber with a dark back with yellow flecks. On the back are five or six flat, wide growths with conical, nipple-like protuberances (*papillae*). It is found in the Indo-Pacific, from Suez to Samoa.

Sea Cucumber, Sea Slug
(Holothuria tubulosa), Fr. Bêche de Mer, Biche de Mer, Balate, Ger. Röhrenholothurie
This sea cucumber, native to European waters, is about 30 cm (1 ft) long and 6 cm (2½ in) in diameter. It is brown to light-brown and has many prickles of various lengths or papilla-type feet along the back. The underside is usually lighter in colour. It lives on sand or sandy mud, as well as in vegetation on rocks, from shallow water to depths of

up to 40 m (130 ft). This sea cucumber is common in the Mediterranean but not in the Atlantic or Indo-Pacific.

Brown Sea Cucumber
(Leucospilota spp.), Ger. Braune Seegurke, Phil. Hea Sim, Indon. Tripang Talengko
This medium-length sea cucumber has a brown back and lighter stomach and feet. It is the kind most frequently available in Indonesia.

Slender Sea Cucumber
(Holothuria vitiensis), Ger. Schlanke Indopazifische Seegurke
The Slender Sea Cucumber is like a long worm. The top is yellow to brown with very small, dark spots. The feet are surrounded by irregular, reddish-brown rings. This sea cucumber, which grows to 40 cm (16 in) long but only 6–8 cm (2½–3 in) in diameter, lives in the seas around Indonesia, the Philippines and Polynesia.

Japanese Sea Cucumber
(Stichopus japonicus), Ger. Japanische Seegurke, Jap. Namako
Like all members of the *Stichopodidae* family, this short, truncated sea cucumber is dotted with sharp, pointed tubercles. On the underside are tiny feet. This rock-dweller comes in a variety of colours, from brown to dark-green. It is found chiefly in the seas around Japan.

Sea Slug
(Parastichopus californicus), Ger. Kalifornische Seegurke
The posterior half of this red or yellowish-brown sea cucumber tapers into a tail. On the back are thick, thorn-like nipples. Around the mouth opening, the tentacles form a wide 'flowerhead'. This species grows to 25–40 cm (10–16 in) in length and is found on the Pacific coast of Canada, the United States and northern South America.

Northern Sea Cucumber
(Cucumaria sp.), Ger. Nord-amerikanische Seegurke
The Northern Sea Cucumber,

which is a member of the *Cucumariidae* family, has numerous tiny feet and long rows of papillae on its back. The tentacles around the mouth are thickly branched. This species is found in both the northern Atlantic and Pacific, off the United States and Canada.

SEA SQUIRTS
(Ascidiacea)

Some sea squirts are similar in shape to sea cucumbers but they belong to another order entirely, the Tunicates. This is a group of some 1,000 different species, all of which live in the sea. The tunicates are closely related to the vertebrates, which makes them a highly developed group.

Sea squirts are the least popular of all seafoods. They live singly or in colonies, are white, red or brown in colour. Their bodies are cylindrical, tuber-shaped or flat with a thick gelatinous or leathery covering. Most tunicates anchor themselves to the sea-bed and blend well into their surroundings, often being covered with moss-like animals. Sea squirts are eaten raw, like oysters.

Sea Squirt
(Microcosmus sulcatus), Fr. Violet, Bijou de Mer, Figue de Mer, Ger. Grosse Meerscheide, Ital. Ovo di Mare
From the plump, bag-shaped body, 8–10 cm (3–4 in) in diameter, emerge two tubes. These are carmine-red on the inside, although they are usually closed once the creature has been caught. These are used to take in and expel the water from which the Sea Squirt filters its food. This species lives in the Mediterranean, near the coast on sand or broken shells.

The inside of the Sea Squirt usually smells strongly of iodine, which is unpleasant if inhaled. As filterers, Sea Squirts also accumulate dangerous or poisonous substances, so they should not be eaten if there is any possibility that they come from polluted waters.

COOKING TECHNIQUES

'Good cooking is the source of true happiness.'

It would be difficult to find a more fitting introduction for the second section of this book – on cooking and cooking techniques – than the words of the world-famous chef, Auguste Escoffier (1846–1935). For cooking seafood is synonymous with good cooking: show me the person who has once eaten a Lobster Thermidor or a 'mere' Spanish Zarzuela, who would not describe the experience as the greatest 'true' happiness!

Good cooking means, above all, a good grasp of the basic techniques and fresh, top quality products – both of which are essential with seafood. Nowadays, good cooking does not mean elaborate confections and complicated creations (such as those that made the reputations of international chefs as recently as ten years ago), but recipes that are easy to put together and cooking methods which bring out the natural flavour of the food. Ignorance of how to deal with shellfish and crustaceans deters many people – including professional chefs – from cooking them. They are content to leave this to high-class restaurants or to the local restaurants of Mediterranean resorts. This book therefore concentrates on the practical aspects of dealing with seafood, with three main considerations. Firstly, all the recipes are easy to follow and include, where necessary, step-by-step photographs to illustrate the main steps. Secondly, the recipes are by no means restricted to gourmet dishes but concentrate on simple dishes, which you can prepare at home. Thirdly, all the recipes allow scope for imagination and creativity.

There is one more practical aspect that has had to be taken into account – the use of canned or frozen products. In spite of modern methods of refrigeration and storage and improvements in transportation, it is still often impossible to get hold of fresh seafood. We believe that frozen foods, provided they are of top quality, can provide an acceptable alternative.

So now it is up to you to leaf through the following section and then to try out the recipes, assured of success.

Note: unless otherwise stated, each of the recipes serves 4.

SAUCES, STOCKS AND SOUPS

The bases of good seafood cooking

In dealing with sauces and soups, we must look first of all at the basic ingredient, the stock. With seafood, this may consist of either a concentrated extract of crab, lobster or prawns – particularly from the shells, which have the most concentrated flavour – or a concentrated stock, made by boiling the shellfish.

The art of making sauces is to find the ideal combination of flavours between the dish and its sauce. Soups, too, are based on a concentrated stock that helps to bring out the full flavour of the main ingredient.

Seawater, the best stock for crustaceans

Court-bouillon is the name that French chefs give to fish stock. Since it has been fathered by a host of famous chefs, its ingredients can vary and are usually chosen to complement whatever is to be cooked in it – fish, crustaceans or molluscs. But the great original of all fish stocks is the sea – with its slight salt content and water tasting of oxygen and a fresh breeze. This is still the best stock for crustaceans, bringing out their basic flavour and reflecting their origins. No wonder, for the sea is their natural element (if we disregard freshwater crabs, for the time being). Very few of us, however, have the sea on our doorsteps to provide us with seawater – and even if we had, we would be none too keen to use this water to cook expensive fish, for European seas are no longer what they were.

The easiest way is to cook crustaceans is in salted water with a little caraway and dill. Many people prefer a stronger flavour, however, so it is customary to cook crustaceans in a reduced fish stock known as *Fumet de poisson*. This is an excellent way of cooking lobster, crab and crayfish to be eaten plain, for the stock adds extra flavour.

Flavour is also added by the classic court-bouillons, or various types of fish stock. Three are included here, all of which can be used for crustaceans and shellfish. The chapter on crustaceans includes two further examples, which can also be used for freshwater crabs. In each case, three basic rules apply:

● Court-bouillon with vegetables should be boiled for 40 minutes, to allow the full flavour to permeate the stock.
● If wine is used, it should be added halfway through the cooking time. This will allow the stock to absorb the full flavour of the vegetables, without losing any of the flavour of the wine.
● Coarsely crushed peppercorns are best added just before the end of the cooking time, to prevent their flavour from dominating the stock.

The first example (top right) is a stock made with water, vinegar, vegetables, herbs and seasoning. The second (centre right) has more onions and wine. The third (bottom right) is another vinegar stock, with bouquet garni, caraway and onions. The first two are best for lobster and crayfish, the third for any kind of crab.

Parsley and carrots give the court-bouillon a light, aromatic flavour. Boil 3 litres/5¼ pints water, 6 tablespoons vinegar, 45 g/1¾ oz salt, 350 g/12 oz sliced carrot, 230 g/8 oz onion rings, 50 g/2 oz parsley and 1 bay leaf for 40 minutes. Finally, add 1 tablespoon crushed peppercorns and remove from the heat.

Here, white wine is used. Bring 2 litres/3½ pints water to the boil with 20 g/¾ oz salt. Add 230 g/8 oz sliced onion, 1 sprig each parsley and thyme and 1 bay leaf. Simmer for 40 minutes. After 20 minutes, add 700 ml/24 fl oz dry white wine. Add ½ teaspoon coarse pepper towards the end of the cooking time.

Red wine vinegar is the basis for this highly flavoured court-bouillon. Bring 3 litres/5¼ pints water, 6 tablespoons red wine vinegar and 45 g/1¾ oz salt to the boil. Add 1 bouquet garni, 1 tablespoon caraway seeds and 350 g/12 oz thickly sliced onion. Cook for 40 minutes over a low heat.

Boiling lobster

Gourmets may well enjoy this delicious crustacean without knowing what happened to it before it reached their plate. But there is no escaping the fact that these creatures, which are alive when we buy them, have to be killed. Only by buying live crustaceans can we guarantee top quality.

In some countries, it is the practice to kill lobsters with a stab to the head. British research has shown, however, that this is not a humane way to kill a lobster. Although crabs can be swiftly killed by piercing their two main nerve centres (beneath the vent and in the shallow depression above the mouth) with an awl, lobsters have numerous nerve centres in a chain down the mid-line of the body.

The British Universities Federation for Animal Welfare has discovered that lobsters can be humanely killed by putting them in a plastic bag in the deep freeze (at a temperature at least as low as − 10 C) for two hours. The lobster will gradually lose consciousness and die. It can then be plunged into boiling water.

If a deep freeze is not available, make sure that there is at least 1 gallon of water per lobster, that there is a very hot flame under the pot and that the water is boiling fast.

Then plunge the lobster in, head first, and ensure that it is totally immersed. Hold it under the water with tongs or wooden spoons for at least two minutes. The lobster should die within 15 seconds. If the recipe calls for uncooked lobster, remove it after two minutes, to prevent over-cooking.

Fish stock

Fumet de poisson

It is impossible to get far in cooking seafood without Fish stock, or Fumet de poisson, for it is an essential ingredient of many prawn, crab, lobster or crayfish dishes and for many deliciously creamy sauces and soups. We must, therefore, give it the attention it so richly deserves.

It takes time to make real fish stock but it is time well spent. If you are fond of seafood, it will be worthwhile to keep some in store, and fish stock freezes well.

It is made from the bones of white fish, a bouquet garni, shallots, garlic, peppercorns, juniper berries, cloves, water, white wine and a dash of vermouth. All these, boiled together and strained, form the basis for fish sauces and soups that surpass the range of everyday cooking – the very best, in fact.

In addition, it is the basis for the best consommés and aspics. These are produced by clarifying the stock to a crystal-clear, amber-coloured consommé. When cold, this forms a jelly which is an essential ingredient of cold fish dishes such as mousses or terrines.

A short summary of where to use fish stock will be useful. Stock is an important ingredient of White butter sauce and absolutely essential in White wine sauce, both of which are ideal with seafood dishes. For a red wine sauce, a proper stock is again essential (unless you plan to serve it with crab or lobster, in which case you may prefer a stock made with the shellfish themselves).

1 kg/2¼ lb bones and skin of white fish, such as sole, turbot, burbot, haddock or cod
1 bouquet garni containing:
150 g/5 oz leeks (white leaves)
20 g/¾ oz celery
1 bay leaf
1 sprig thyme

60 g/2 oz shallots
1 clove garlic
20 white peppercorns
3 crushed juniper berries
1 clove
750 ml/1¼ pints water
250 ml/8 fl oz dry white wine
3 tablespoons dry vermouth

Ingredients continued overleaf.

To clarify stock

125 g/4½ oz shin of beef, boned
125 g/4½ oz white fish fillet
1 leek
1 stick celery
1 carrot
1 tomato
1 onion
1 clove garlic, unpeeled
1 sprig thyme
¼ bay leaf
3 juniper berries
dash of dry vermouth
4 egg whites
6 ice cubes
1.25 litre/2¼ pints cold fish stock
salt
pepper

3 **Strain the stock**. Line a conical sieve with a linen or muslin cloth and pour the hot stock through the cloth into a pan. Squeeze the stock out of the solid ingredients by pressing gently with the back of a ladle. This stock is the best possible basis for practically all fish sauces and soups.

6 **Add 250 ml/8 fl oz cold fish stock to the clarifying ingredients and stir well**. Then gradually pour in the remaining fish stock (1 litre/1¾ pints) and again stir very thoroughly. Place the pan on the hob and heat, stirring continuously with a flat-bladed wooden spatula.

1 **Prepare the ingredients**. Soak the fish carcasses in water for about 30 minutes for a fresher stock. Tie the leek and celery – washed and trimmed – with the bay leaf and thyme to make the bouquet garni. Get the shallots, garlic, seasonings, wine and vermouth ready.

4 **For consommé or aspic, prepare the ingredients for clarifying**. Coarsely mince the shin of beef and white fish fillet. Trim the vegetables. Cut the leek into rings and the celery into chunks. Dice the carrot. Quarter the tomato, halve the peeled onion and prepare the garlic, thyme, bay leaf and juniper berries.

7 **Stir until boiling**. Run a spatula over the base of the pan, for the egg white can easily stick to it. If this should happen, pour the mixture immediately into another pan. Stop stirring once the mixture has boiled and the clarifying ingredients have risen to the top. Simmer for 20 minutes.

2 **Bring the ingredients to the boil**. First, place the carcasses and bouquet garni in the pan. Then add the finely chopped shallots, the garlic clove, seasonings, water, wine and vermouth. Simmer gently for 20 minutes, skimming often.

5 **Place all the clarifying ingredients in a pan**. First the meat, then the fish, vegetables, garlic (with the inner skin but with the husk removed) and seasonings. Cover with the vermouth, lightly whisked egg whites and ice cubes.

8 **Strain the stock**. Line a sieve with a muslin cloth and pour in the stock and the solid ingredients. Leave to drain. Do not squeeze out the solids this time, for the fish consommé must be crystal-clear. Season to taste. Use immediately or leave to cool and then freeze.

98

White butter sauce

Beurre blanc

This is a sauce of the most delicate consistency and the most excellent flavour. It goes extremely well with fresh-cooked seafood, underlining rather than masking its fine flavour.

1 shallot
10 g/⅓ oz butter
3 tablespoons white wine
dash of good quality vinegar
dash of vermouth (optional)
250 ml/8 fl oz fish stock
salt
150 g/5 oz fresh, chilled butter,
cut into pieces

The chopped shallot should not be allowed to colour in the slightest in the butter, for this would spoil the flavour of the sauce. After the white wine, add the highly aromatic vinegar. A few drops of slow-matured vinegar, made with highly concentrated grape juice, is sufficient to give the required flavour. If you like the taste of vermouth, include a dash of this too. After adding the fish stock, salt, and reducing to a quarter of the original volume, strain the sauce carefully. To complete the sauce, add the freshest possible butter – this will make your sauce a great culinary experience.

2 **Melt the butter with the wine mixture**. Add the fish stock, reduce the liquid to a quarter and then strain. Reheat the sauce in the pan and gradually melt in it the pieces of ice-cold butter, tipping the pan to distribute the butter evenly.

3 **Whisk with an electric mixer**. Once all the butter is in the pan, it should be whisked until frothy. Season lightly with a few drops of vinegar and a very little salt. This fine sauce has so much natural flavour that too much seasoning would spoil it. Serve at once.

1 **Add the white wine to the shallots**, which are first finely diced and stirred in butter over a low heat, without browning. Then add a dash of vinegar and a dash of vermouth, if liked. Reduce so that the shallots are just moist.

Every seafood cook needs to have stocks and consommés in stock – for it is impossible to make any fine sauce or soup without them – so it is fortunate that stocks and consommés can be made in advance and frozen in suitable quantities.

Crayfish stock

Fumet d'écrevisse

400 g/14 oz crayfish shells
3 tablespoons olive oil
2 tablespoons cognac
250 g/8¾ oz carrots
50 g/2 oz celery
50 g/2 oz leeks
50 g/2 oz shallots
2 medium garlic cloves
2 tomatoes
1 bay leaf
1 clove
3 juniper berries, crushed
sprig of tarragon (or generous pinch of dried tarragon)

sprig of thyme (or generous pinch of dried thyme)
2 tablespoons vegetable oil
50 g/2 oz tomato purée
salt
pepper

When making a stock to use in cream sauces, it is best to cook the vegetables in 20 g/¾ oz heated butter. For consommé, oil is better. It is important to remember that crayfish shells should, in general, be cleaned very thoroughly and washed several times if the stock is to taste fresh. Then they are quick-fried in hot oil, making sure however that they are not allowed to become too brown or to burn, for this would ruin the stock. Add the cognac and set the mixture aside.

Vegetables, seasonings and herbs are cooked in a separate pan, in hot vegetable oil, over a low heat. The tomato purée is added and the vegetable mixture is then stirred into the crayfish shells. The ingredients are then covered with water and stirred until the water boils. Simmer for 45 minutes, removing the scum frequently, and finally strain the stock.

If you substitute lobster or crawfish shells for crayfish, the same method will give lobster or crawfish stock.

1 **Fry the shells in olive oil**. They should first be carefully cleaned and washed and any remains of tissue removed. After frying, add the cognac.

2 **Place the other ingredients in a pan**. Slice the trimmed vegetables and cook in hot oil with the tomato quarters and herbs for 5 minutes. Leave to stand for 2 minutes before adding the vegetable mixture to the shells. Cover with cold water and bring to the boil, skimming often. Simmer for 40 to 45 minutes.

3 **Strain the stock**. Line a conical sieve with a cloth, folded double, and place it over a pan. Gradually ladle the cooked stock into the sieve and allow the liquid to drain off before adding the next ladleful. Do not press the ingredients against the sieve with the ladle or the stock will be cloudy.

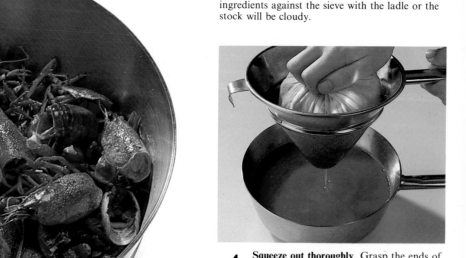

4 **Squeeze out thoroughly**. Grasp the ends of the cloth and twist, so that the ingredients are contained in a kind of bag. Now press down quite firmly to get out all the juices into the tasty stock.

You can use the crayfish stock as it is for sauces and soups, to which it will give an excellent flavour. When clarified, it can be used as consommé.

Crayfish consommé

Consommé d'écrevisse

250 g/8¾ oz burbot, cod or other
white fish fillet (not oily fish)
50 g/2 oz leeks (whites only)
40 g/1½ oz celery
1 tomato
2 shallots
1 garlic clove
1 clove
½ bay leaf
3 juniper berries, crushed
sprig of thyme
salt
3 egg whites, well chilled
3–4 ice cubes
1.25 litre/2¼ pints Crayfish stock
(see opposite)

Making a consommé with seafood – or fish, for that matter – is fairly difficult and several factors govern its success; for example, the amount of protein in the clarifying mixture. Sometimes, even after the greatest care and attention, the consommé is still cloudy, for seafood is a natural product, which can react differently at different times.

The essential thing is that the fish used for clarifying must be fat-free. It should be minced (using the largest blade) and mixed in a bowl with the prepared vegetables, herbs and seasonings. Then whisk the egg whites and work them into the mixture with the ice cubes. Transfer the mixture to a flat-bottomed pan.

Add the crayfish stock and whisk. Now, as the mixture is brought to the boil over a high heat, scrape the bottom of the pan continuously, using a wooden spatula, to prevent the egg white from sticking. If it does stick, tip the mixture into another pan immediately.

Reduce the heat and stop stirring when the clarifying ingredients rise to the surface. Now simmer for 45 minutes, to allow the clarifying ingredients to absorb all impurities. Then strain the consommé through a conical sieve, lined with a cloth. Allow all the liquid to run through but do not squeeze it through. This will give a crystal-clear, amber-coloured consommé to use in fine soups and jellies.

If you serve it as a soup, you can add fresh herbs, finely diced tomato with a touch of basil, chopped omelette, julienned vegetables or almost any seafood.

> To get the full flavour out of the carcasses, you can reboil the shells in the stock with sufficient water to cover them. Simmer for 30 minutes and then strain.

3 **Transfer to a saucepan and add the cold crayfish stock.** Mix it into the clarifying ingredients and ice cubes. It is a good idea to use a smooth-bottomed pan, for the egg white can stick extremely easily. Keep scraping the bottom of the pan thoroughly as the mixture comes to the boil.

4 **The clarifying mixture rises to the surface.** Stir the mixture continuously with a spatula until it boils, at which point the clarifying mixture will rise to the top in a thick scum. Reduce the heat, stop stirring and leave to simmer over a very low heat for 45 minutes, to allow the clarifiers to do their work.

1 **Mince the fish.** Prepare the remaining ingredients. Slice the leeks, dice the celery, shallots and garlic and cut the tomato into quarters. Set the clove, bay leaf, crushed juniper berries, thyme and salt ready to hand.

2 **Mix the clarifying ingredients with the egg whites.** The egg whites must be cold if they are to clarify successfully. Lightly whisk them and pour them over the other ingredients, including the herbs and a little salt. Stir in gently with the ice cubes.

5 **Strain the crayfish consommé.** Line a conical sieve with a muslin cloth, folded over three times. Ladle the consommé into the sieve and allow to drain into a bowl. This clarified consommé is now ready to serve as soup, but can also be used for sauces and jellies.

Lobster sauce

Sauce homard

Using exactly the same method as for the Crayfish stock (page 100), you can make a lobster stock which, after straining, can be used in a number of ways.

If you cook the vegetables in fresh butter, then proceed as in the recipe but add the double cream just before straining. You can use this recipe for a cream of lobster soup as well as a lobster sauce.

shell of 1 (600 g/21 oz) boiled lobster
2 tablespoons olive oil
2 tablespoons cognac
250 g/8¾ oz carrots
50 g/2 oz celery
50 g/2 oz leeks
50 g/2 oz shallots
2 fresh tomatoes
2 medium garlic cloves
20 g/¾ oz fresh butter
1 bay leaf
1 clove
3 juniper berries, crushed
generous pinch of dried (or sprig of fresh) tarragon
sprig of thyme
50 g/2 oz tomato purée
250 ml/8 fl oz double cream
salt

Before the lobster shell is cut up, it must be carefully cleaned to remove all the scraps of chitin and tissue, which could affect the flavour of the sauce. Fry the crushed shell in batches in the hot oil, so that it can fry evenly all over and develop its full flavour. Remove the shell from the heat, pour on the cognac and set aside.

Fry the vegetables in the butter with the herbs and seasonings. Then add the tomato purée. Mix the vegetables with the shell, cover with water, stir as it comes to the boil and simmer, removing the scum frequently. After 45 minutes, add the double cream, season with salt to taste and strain.

Whether you serve this recipe as a soup or a sauce, 2 tablespoons whipped cream per portion will make it even better (or, if you prefer, use crème fraîche).

2 **Two halves and two claws.** The lobster is now open. At the top end near the head you will see the liver, which can be worked into butter (in a ratio of 1:2) to make Lobster butter. The tail contains most of the tender meat, pale pink and extremely tasty.

1 **Halve the fresh-boiled lobster.** Hold the lobster firmly on a board. Twist off the claws at the first joint and reserve. Using a sharp knife, cut along the centre of the body, starting from the head and cutting right through to the board.

3 **Hold the lobster halves firmly by the tail.** With the other hand, remove the stomach sac, after first taking out the liver and setting it aside (top left of picture) for lobster butter. Take care to remove the stomach sac in one piece, so as not to contaminate the flesh.

4 **Remove the gut**. Start at the head and pull it gently down towards the tail, where it is attached. Cut it off with a knife. Then take out the meat. Crack the claws and remove the meat. (Use the meat for a separate dish – or use some of it in the soup.)

7 **Fry the shells in smoking-hot olive oil**, in batches, for 5 minutes per batch, until evenly fried. Pour on the cognac; this will add extra flavour to the sauce. A wok (Chinese frying pan) is excellent for frying the shells, as it distributes heat evenly.

10 **Reduce the mixture**. Simmer over a low heat, stirring occasionally, to reduce the mixture. The liquid content will be made up later when you add the double cream. The stock needs to simmer for 40 to 45 minutes, over the lowest possible heat.

5 **Remove the cream-coloured chitin**. Clean the carcass thoroughly. Remove any bits of meat that remain, and then wash the shell, the claw shells and the legs thoroughly under running water. Drain the pieces before proceeding.

8 **Fry the vegetables in butter**. Clean and slice the vegetables and quarter the tomatoes. Stir into the fresh butter with the herbs and seasonings, over a low heat. Add the tomato purée. Remove from the heat and leave to stand for 2 minutes.

11 **Add the double cream and stir it in well**. Bring to the boil, then remove from the heat and leave to stand on the side of the stove for 10 minutes. You can add a sprinkling of fresh tarragon or basil, depending on what you are going to use the sauce for.

6 **Crush the pieces of shell in a mortar**, as finely as you can. If you have strong wrists, you can break the shell into pieces first; otherwise, use a chopper. You will certainly need to use the chopper on the hard claw shells, unless you are superhuman!

9 **Add the vegetables to the shells**. Add sufficient cold water to cover and bring to the boil, stirring occasionally with a wooden spoon. Remove any scum as its forms – if you leave it, it will spoil both the flavour and look of the stock.

12 **Strain the sauce through a conical sieve**, in batches. Bang the handle of the sieve every now and again to shake through every last drop of sauce. The strained liquid should be light-brown and of a creamy consistency.

Prawn butter

Beurre de crevettes

Crab, lobster or prawn shells – cooked in butter with vegetables, onions, garlic and tomato purée – are all equally suitable for making a savoury butter, which can be used for up to four months.

The quantites given in this recipe are sufficient to allow you to pack and freeze the butter in portions. One portion will be sufficient to give soups and sauces, stews and all kinds of seafood dishes an incomparable flavour.

We have chosen Prawn butter to demonstrate the method. For crab or lobster butter, you will need the same quantity of crab or lobster shells as that given here for prawn shells.

Prawn butter will keep in the freezer for up to four months, provided that it is tightly wrapped in heavy-duty aluminium foil.

750 g/26 oz prawn shells
2 tablespoons olive oil
100 g/4 oz carrots
50 g/2 oz celery
50 g/2 oz leeks
50 g/2 oz shallots
2 medium garlic cloves
1 tablespoon tomato purée
750 g/26 oz butter
250 ml/8 fl oz water

2 **Add the prepared vegetables**. Trim, wash, peel and chop the carrots, celery, leeks and shallots. Remove the husk from the garlic but do not peel it. Fry the vegetables and garlic with the shells and then stir in the tomato purée.

1 **Fry the prawn shells in the olive oil**. First clean the shells and wash them thoroughly under running water, then tip them onto absorbent kitchen paper and drain thoroughly. The shells must be completely dry before they go into the hot oil. Fry them evenly all over, stirring continuously with a fish slice. The best pan to use is a wok, a Chinese cooking pan similar to a frying pan, which can go directly on the heat. The advantage of this type of pan is that it needs very little oil and the heat is evenly distributed over the whole pan, which speeds up the frying process.

3 **Add some of the butter, cut into pieces**. Stir with the fish slice until the butter has melted. Frying the shells in the butter allows it to absorb their flavour and produces highly flavoured cooking juices that also have the most wonderful aroma.

4 **Stir in the water**. Bring the mixture to the boil and then gradually melt the remaining butter in the pan. Remove from the heat and leave for 1 hour on the edge of the hob or cook slowly over the lowest possible heat, to allow the juices to absorb all the flavour. Strain through a sieve into a pan.

Coral butter

Beurre de corail

Although the gourmet loves the tender, white flesh of cooked lobster, with its beautiful red tinge, better than any other shellfish, the lobster offers an even greater delicacy. This is the coral – the roe of the female – a fabulous flavouring agent. In its raw state it is greenish-black, becoming as red as coral after cooking. Since lobster coral is usually mixed with butter to make coral butter, you can give any dish this delicious, pale pink colouring.

Alternatively, both the liver and coral can be worked together into butter and used to flavour sauces. This mixture is often used to make the sauce for Homard à l'Américaine, as it gives a really smooth sauce of superior flavour. You can also make lobster butter with the liver alone. In each case, the ratio is 1:2, twice as much soft butter as the weight of the coral.

It is no easy matter to obtain the uncooked coral or raw liver, for both have to be taken from a freshly killed, uncooked lobster. The method is as follows: Heat a deep pan of water over a high heat until it is boiling vigorously. Slide the live lobster – always head first – into the boiling water. It is a good idea to boil a little extra water separately and add it at this stage, to maintain the temperature. Cover the pan and boil vigorously for about 1–2 minutes. Transfer the lobster immediately to iced water and leave to cool.

Cut open the lobster beginning at the head, down to the start of the tail (as shown in the photograph on page 102). Spoon out the liver and coral, using a teaspoon. Work them into soft butter, either separately or together. To make Coral butter, you will obviously use only the roe. Wrap the flavoured butter in aluminium foil and refrigerate.

Coral butter (or butter with uncooked lobster liver) should be used only in dishes that are to be cooked. It is basically a flavouring and is not suitable for melting over fried fish or seafood. This is because the coral, or roe, is still raw and needs to be cooked.

5 **When cool, remove the prawn butter in pieces**. Refrigerate the mixture overnight in a covered bowl. The flavoured butter will set to form a solid layer on the top. You can cut this into portions with a knife and lift them off the bowl using a fish slice.

6 **Strain the liquid prawn butter**. Melt the savoury butter in a pan over the lowest possible heat. Strain the melted butter through a hair sieve into a square tin. Press it down gently, using a spoon. Leave to cool, then cover and refrigerate until set.

7 **Turn the prawn butter out onto a board**. Use a sharp knife to cut the butter into portions of the required size. If you plan to use some of it immediately, put this to one side. Wrap the remaining portions in extra-strong aluminium foil, taking care to expel all the air.

1 **Carefully remove the coral**. First, use a sharp knife to cut the shell of the freshly killed lobster in half and open it out (see page 102). Remove the greyish-green liver. This can be mixed with butter if you like. Using a teaspoon, carefully lift out the coral from the lobster.

2 **Mix the coral with soft butter**. Work the coral in gently, using a fork. You will need about 60 g/2¼ oz fresh, soft butter to give a ratio of 1:2: weigh the coral and then use double the weight of butter for a perfect consistency and flavour. A silver fork is the ideal tool for working in the coral.

3 **Wrap the Coral butter in foil**. Using a piece of aluminium foil to help you, shape the coral butter into a roll. Then pack the roll loosely, but without air pockets, in the foil and refrigerate until set. Cut slices whenever you need them to flavour cooked lobster dishes.

White wine sauce

Sauce au vin blanc

White wine sauce is the ideal sauce for seafood, for it harmonizes perfectly with their fine, delicate flavour. It is flavoured with a high-quality vermouth (such as Noilly Prat), white wine, double cream, whipped cream and a few grains of salt. It is based on the fish stock already described.

30 g/1¼ oz butter
3 shallots
3 tablespoons good quality vermouth
5 tablespoons dry white wine
500 ml/17 fl oz Fish stock (page 97)
200 ml/7 fl oz double cream
2 tablespoons whipped cream
salt (optional)

3 **Add the Fish stock.** Stir well and then reduce over a moderate heat to one-third of the original quantity. By reducing the liquid in two separate stages, the flavours of the butter, shallots, vermouth, white wine and stock are blended beautifully together.

1 **Pour the vermouth over the shallots.** First, heat the butter in a pan. Add the peeled, finely chopped shallots and fry for about 5 minutes, stirring until golden. Add the vermouth and stir gently with a wooden spoon, to blend.

4 **Stir in the double cream.** This makes the sauce creamy and gives a slightly sour flavour. At this stage, leave the sauce to simmer gently over a low heat for 5 minutes. This brings out the flavour of the sauce and helps to thicken it.

2 **Add the white wine.** But first reduce the vermouth until the shallots are just moist. This will take about 10 minutes on a moderate heat. Stir gently from time to time, as the liquid reduces to prevent the delicate sauce from overheating.

5 **Strain the sauce.** Line a conical sieve with a muslin cloth. Place the sieve over a pan and strain the sauce, a little at a time, pressing each batch gently with a ladle. To complete the sauce, lightly fold in the whipped cream and season sparingly.

Red wine sauce

Sauce au vin rouge

1 carrot
25 g/1 oz celery
25 g/1 oz leeks
1 small shallot
2 tablespoons oil
1 tablespoon tomato purée
1 tablespoon red wine
375 ml/13 fl oz Fish, Lobster or Crayfish stock (pages 97, 100)
375 ml/13 fl oz red wine
30 g/1¼ oz butter
salt
cayenne

Fry the finely diced vegetables (mirepoix) in the oil, without allowing them to colour. Add the tomato purée and heat through, stirring continuously. Stir in 1 tablespoon red wine. Mix the stock with the remaining red wine and add. Bring to the boil, stirring, scoop off any scum and lower the heat. Simmer for 30 minute, strain, reheat and reduce to the required quantity. Bind with the butter and season sparingly with a little salt and cayenne.

Scallops in basil sauce

Coquilles St-Jacques au basilic

2 small shallots
12 scallops
40 g/1½ oz butter
4 tablespoons dry white wine
3 tablespoons good quality vermouth
4 tablespoons Fish stock (page 97)
400 ml/14 fl oz White wine sauce
salt
dash of champagne or
1 drop good quality vinegar
8 small basil leaves, finely chopped
4 tablespoons whipped cream

Peel and finely dice the shallots. Remove the scallops from their shells and separate the flesh and roes. Cut the larger scallops in half horizontally. Wipe the flesh dry with kitchen paper. Heat the butter in a pan until frothy and fry the shallots until they are light-golden. Toss the scallops in the butter. Add the white wine, vermouth and Fish stock and bring the mixture to the boil. Remove the scallops from the pan and keep them hot.

Reduce the stock until there is only a little liquid left. Add the White wine sauce, bring

to the boil and strain. Season with salt and champagne or vinegar.

Return the scallops to the sauce and add the chopped basil. Fold in the cream. Serve with saffron rice.

To make the rice, fry finely chopped shallots in butter. Add short-grain rice and fry until the rice is transparent. Cover with chicken stock, season with salt and saffron and cook for 20 minutes.

Scallops should be cooked for only a short time if they are to remain soft and tender. In a velvety basil sauce on a bed of saffron rice, they make a delicious starter.

Preparing Velouté. Heat the butter in a pan over a moderate heat until frothy. Fry the diced onion until transparent. Stir in the flour, using a wooden spoon, and cook for 10–15 minutes. The mixture should remain a pale gold in colour. Now add the cold, defatted stock a ladle at a time and whisk in. Bring to the boil, stirring the bottom of the pan continuously to prevent the sauce from sticking and forming lumps. Simmer gently over a low heat for 30 minutes, stirring from time to time and removing any scum. Reduce by half and stir well. Simmer for a further 15 minutes, then strain through a cloth, lifting the corners of the cloth and twisting to squeeze the sauce through. Season the finished Velouté with salt and freshly milled pepper. The French word *velouté* means 'velvety' and is a very fitting name for this sauce.

Basic white sauce

Velouté

Makes 600 ml / 1 pint

20 g / ¾ oz butter
20 g / ¾ oz onion, finely chopped
35 g / 1½ oz flour
750 ml / 1¼ pints cold, defatted fish,
veal, chicken or vegetable stock
250 ml / 8 fl oz cream
salt
white pepper

Velouté has not been very popular for some time, perhaps because it tends to remind us of grandmother's rather heavy white sauce. Nowadays, however, so little flour is used that this sauce – when made by an expert – can compete with any of our more exotic sauces. Made with fish stock, it can even be served with scallops.

Crayfish consommé with green asparagus and peeled prawns

Consommé d'écrevisse aux asperges

250 g/8¾ oz fillet of burbot or other white fish (not oily fish)
50 g/2 oz leeks
½ head of celery
1 tomato
2 shallots
1 garlic clove
1 clove
½ bay leaf
3 juniper berries, crushed
sprig of thyme
salt
3 egg whites, chilled
3–4 ice cubes
600 ml/1 pint Crayfish stock (page 100)
12 fresh, green asparagus tips
12 cooked, peeled prawns

Trim, wash and coarsely mince the fish fillet. Trim, wash and finely chop the leek, celery and tomato. Dice the peeled shallots. Halve the garlic and remove the green germ. In a smooth-bottomed pan, mix all these ingredients with the clove, crumbled bay leaf, crushed juniper berries, thyme, salt and lightly whisked egg whites. Stir in the ice cubes.

Whisk in the cold Crayfish stock. Bring the mixture to the boil over a high heat, stirring continuously with a spatula to prevent the egg white from sticking to the base of the pan. Reduce the heat, or move the pan to the edge of the hob. Simmer very gently for 1¼ hours, stirring from time to time. Strain through a sieve lined with a cloth, and season. The Crayfish consommé is ready.

Trim and wash the asparagus tips and blanch them in boiling salted water for 2–3 minutes. Then plunge them immediately into cold water. Heat the asparagus through with the prawns in the consommé and pour the garnished soup into soup plates to serve.

Crayfish consommé – clear and amber-coloured, with green asparagus and prawns – is in the foreground. Behind it is the Cream of oyster soup and, in the cup, Lobster bisque.

Tender scallops, topped with caviare and served in fish consommé, are a real delicacy.

Cream of oyster soup

Crème aux huîtres

500 ml/17 fl oz White wine sauce
(page 106)
2 small shallots
10 g/⅓ oz butter
5 tablespoons Fish stock (page 97)
12 fresh oysters
250 ml/8 fl oz champagne
4 tablespoons whipped cream
salt
pepper

Prepare the White wine sauce. Finely dice the peeled shallots. Heat the butter in a pan until frothy, add the shallots and fry until the shallots are pale gold. Add the Fish stock and bring to the boil. Open the oysters and tip the flesh into the stock mixture, along with the juice. Cook until the oysters are firm and then remove the pan from the heat immediately, so that the oysters are just cooked. Bring the White wine sauce to the boil and strain the stock into it, preferably through a fine tea-strainer. Add the champagne and reheat, without allowing the soup to boil. Lightly fold in the whipped cream and season to taste.

Place the poached oysters in soup plates and pour the Cream of oyster soup over them. Serve at once.

Lobster bisque

Bisque d'homard

shell of 1 boiled lobster
2 tablespoons olive oil
2½ tablespoons cognac
100 g/4 oz carrots
50 g/2 oz celery
50 g/2 oz leeks
50 g/2 oz shallots
2 medium garlic cloves
2 tomatoes
20 g/¾ oz fresh butter
1 bay leaf
1 clove
3 juniper berries, crushed
generous pinch of dried
(or sprig of fresh) tarragon
sprig of thyme
50 g/2 oz tomato purée
250 ml/8 fl oz double cream,
plus 4 tablespoons whipped cream
250 ml/8 fl oz Lobster stock (page 100)
4 tablespoons lobster meat, from the legs
and claws
salt (optional)
2 sprigs of fresh tarragon, chopped
(optional)

Wash and thoroughly clean the lobster shell. Heat the olive oil in a pan until very hot and fry the shell for 5 minutes. Pour on 2 tablespoons cognac.

Trim or peel and finely slice the carrots, celery, leeks and shallots. Halve the garlic cloves and remove the green germ. Quarter the washed tomatoes. In a separate pan, toss the vegetables and garlic in melted butter, with the crumbled bay leaf, clove, crushed juniper berries, tarragon and thyme for 10 minutes over a low heat.

Stir in the tomato purée. Cook gently on

the side of the hob or over the lowest possible heat for 2 minutes, and then mix the vegetables and herbs into the shell. Add enough cold water to cover. Simmer for 40–45 minutes over a low heat, spooning off any scum as necessary.

Stir in the double cream and simmer for a further 10 minutes. Line a sieve with a cloth and strain the lobster soup.

Measure off 750 ml/1¼ pints and reheat with the Lobster stock and lobster meat, and then remove from the heat. Fold in the whipped cream. Season with a few drops of cognac and, sparingly, with salt. You won't need pepper, as the soup has a natural slightly peppery flavour. If you wish, you can chop 2 more sprigs of tarragon and sprinkle them into the soup.

Clear fish soup with scallops

*Consommé de poisson aux
coquilles St-Jacques*

1 litre/1¾ pints Fish consommé (page 98)
4 scallops
5 tablespoons Fish stock (page 97)
4 teaspoons caviare
4 sprigs dill

In a pan, bring the Fish consommé to the boil. Meanwhile, open the scallops. Remove the coral for use in another dish. Using a sharp knife, halve the scallops horizontally. Bring the Fish stock to the boil and poach the scallop halves for 30 seconds.

Pour the Fish consommé into four soup cups. Place two scallop halves in each cup. Top each with ½ teaspoon caviare and garnish with the sprigs of dill.

Fine mussel soup

Soupe aux moules

This method can also be used to make a delicious crab, lobster, crayfish or prawn soup. The more daring may, however, like to have a try with mussels. This is a delicious soup that will grace any country-style menu. Mussels may be inexpensive but those who love shellfish will always give them the respect they deserve.

1 kg/2¼ lb mussels
1 small shallot
1 small onion (20 g/¾ oz)
5 parsley sprigs
3 sprigs dill
¼ bay leaf
200 ml/7 fl oz dry white wine
50 g/2 oz carrots
50 g/2 oz celery
20 g/¾ oz butter
mussel stock (from boiling mussels)
500 ml/17 fl oz Fish stock (page 97)
350 ml/12 fl oz cream
1 egg yolk
salt
curry powder or white pepper
1 tablespoon chopped parsley (optional)

Scrub the mussels under running water and remove the beards. Throw away any mussels that are open. Then proceed as shown in the step-by-step illustrations.

2 **The cooked mussels have opened**, and it is essential that they do so. When the mussels have come to the boil, cook gently on the edge of the hob or on a low heat for 5 minutes and then remove immediately from the heat. *NB:* any mussels that are open before cooking are bad, and should be thrown away.

3 **The cooked mussel in the open shell**, from which the cooked flesh is easily removed using either your fingers or an empty shell, held and used in the same way as tweezers, to scoop it out. Discard any mussels that fail to open during cooking, as these are also not fresh. Shellfish that are not fresh can be poisonous.

5 **Fry the vegetables lightly in butter**. Cut the carrots and celery into thin julienne sticks and fry over a low heat in butter, without allowing them to colour. You will have to keep stirring to prevent them browning. If you allow the vegetables to brown they will spoil the delicate flavour of the soup.

6 **Add the mussel stock and Fish stock**. First, strain the hot mussel liquid through a cloth. Mix with the cold Fish stock and pour both onto the julienned vegetables. Reduce, if you like, but leave 1 litre/1¾ pints soup – otherwise the finished soup will be too heavy and the mussels may be overcooked.

1 **Pour on the white wine**. Place the carefully washed, scrubbed and debearded – that is, with the byssus threads removed – mussels in a pan with the finely chopped shallot and onion and the parsley, dill and bay leaf. Cover the pan and bring to the boil.

4 **'Debeard' the mussels once more**. This must be done if the mussels are not to be eaten as they come but served in a soup, as here. 'Debearding' is not really the correct term, for it is the slightly tough edge of the mantle that you are removing here.

7 **Add the cream**. Reserve a few spoonsful for later. Stir the soup over a moderate heat until it reaches simmering point and simmer for a few minutes, to give it a creamy consistency. Stir the mussel soup all the time that you are bringing it to the required temperature.

8 **Warm the mussels** through in the soup. After removing the mantle-edge, add the freshly cooked mussels to the soup and reheat – but do not boil, for this would make the mussels tough and rubbery. They taste good only when they are tender, so treat them gently – it is worth taking care at this stage.

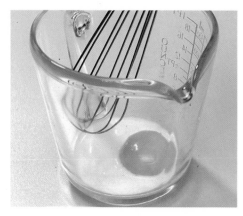

9 **Beat the egg yolk with the remaining cream.** Lightly beat with a hand whisk and stir into the soup to thicken it. On no account should the soup boil from this point, or the egg will curdle. Remove the soup from the stove and season with salt and pepper or curry powder.

10 **A ladleful of delicious mussel soup.** This is what it should look like – light, creamy, an appetising yellow in colour with the orange of the carrots and the delicious·mussels. To add a little more fresh colour and flavour, sprinkle in a little chopped parsley.

Seafood to serve in soup

If you are making a soup in which to serve seafood – a really delicious idea – it is best to make it with a fish stock base. Practically any seafood can be served in soup, be it lobster or crayfish, prawns or cockles or even whelks.

Potato and cress soup with lobster

Potage cressonnière à l'homard

2 medium potatoes
2 small potatoes
salted water for cooking
2 small onions
20 g/¾ oz butter
bunch of watercress
750 ml/1¼ pints Fish stock (page 97)
60 g/2¼ oz butter
16 slices fresh cooked lobster
salt
pepper
4 tablespoons whipped cream
4 teaspoons finely chopped watercress

Peel and wash the potatoes. Bring the medium potatoes to the boil in a little salted water and cook for 15–20 minutes. While still hot, press through a fine-mesh sieve. Cut the small potatoes into equal cubes and blanch in a little salted water for about 2 minutes, then drain.

Meanwhile, slice the peeled onions very finely and fry them in the hot butter for 1–2 minutes. Strip the watercress leaves from the stems, wash and thoroughly drain them before adding them to the onions and frying for a few minutes. Add the Fish stock and cook for about 4 minutes, until the watercress leaves are soft. Then blend in a liquidizer or food processor.

Stir the sieved potato carefully into the soup and then add the potato cubes. Melt the butter in the soup. Then add the lobster and heat gently. Season to taste and fold in the whipped cream. Bring the soup back to the boil and then remove it immediately from the heat. Pour into four serving cups and garnish with cress.

CRUSTACEANS

Warm ways with crustaceans

'A true gourmet chooses wisely, insists that food be prepared lovingly and carefully, eats with understanding and interest and rejoices over every good dish.' Golden words from the great gastronome Brillat-Savarin. He was also convinced that a true epicure lives longer – reason enough for us to follow in the footsteps of this famous Frenchman and to use the following pages to present modern-day gourmets with a number of culinary delicacies, all made with crustaceans. They are all hot dishes and many of them are far from expensive, which goes to show that pleasure does not always come dear. We hope to convince you that it need not always be lobster – a meal of less expensive crustaceans can be mouth-watering if turned into a 'good dish' in Brillat-Savarin's sense of the phrase. We should mention here that we have purposely not included a section on first courses, since it is merely a question of quantity whether a hot crustacean dish is served to open the meal or as a main course. The need for quality, of course, goes without saying in either case.

Boiled crayfish

Ecrevisses à la nage

Thanks to world-wide trade and modern air-freight methods, freshwater crayfish are now universally available. While not exactly cheap, they are well worth the outlay for most are of top quality. There is a Norwegian proverb which says, 'Fall in love while eating crayfish and you'll be unhappy' – and no wonder, for eating crayfish absorbs all the senses so exclusively that there is no room for love.

Crayfish can be cooked in a number of different stocks. If you plan to eat them plain-boiled, cook them in Fish stock (see page 97) seasoned with a little salt, dill, tarragon, basil and fresh coriander. The important thing here is to have enough vigorously boiling stock to cover the crayfish completely, as soon as they go into the pan. This is the only way to ensure that they are killed immediately, unless you have already killed them by placing them in the deep-freeze (see page 97).

It is a well known fact that all crayfish become 'lobster pink' when boiled. This is because only the red pigments in the shell

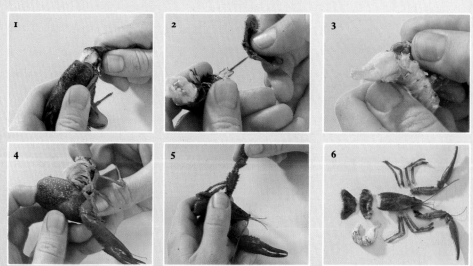

Shelling boiled crayfish. 1. Hold the crayfish between your finger and thumb and loosen the tail from the body by twisting it off with your right hand. **2.** Holding the tail covering between your thumb and index finger, twist it away from the body and gently pull the gut, which is attached to it, off the tail flesh. **3.** Carefully peel the tail. Hold each side of the shell between thumb and index finger and prise apart, until the thin underside breaks open and the flesh falls out. **4.** Hold the breast shell (carapace) in your left hand. With your right index finger, remove the whole underside with the gills and innards, without detaching the breastplate from the claws. **5.** Hold the breastplate in your left hand. Hold the claws between your right thumb and index finger and twist them gently off the breastplate. **6.** Now the small crayfish is in pieces. Only the meat in the foreground, and possibly the claw meat, is eaten. The breastplate – often with the claws attached – is a popular garnish for any kind of seafood dish. When cleaned, the shells (tail section, breastplate, legs and claws) can be used to make a crayfish stock and the delicious consommé which can be made from it. *NB:* large crayfish, such as marrons, are cut up in the same way as lobster.

are heat-resistant, and so retain their colour where others are lost.

If you can't get hold of the tasty Australian freshwater crayfish (marrons) used in our recipe (they are not yet imported in bulk), replace them with the same weight of lobster or another freshwater crayfish. If you use crayfish, you will need 12 per person, each 50–60 g/approx 2 oz in weight and 2 litres/3½ pints stock. Here is a stock suitable for all freshwater crayfish:

1 litre/1¾ pints water
1 litre/1¾ pints dry white wine
2 carrots
2 onions
2 sprigs each dill, tarragon and
fresh coriander
4 small basil leaves
about 3 tablespoons salt

In a large pan, bring the water, wine, sliced carrots and onions, whole washed herbs and salt to the boil. With this stock boiling vigorously, drop the prepared crayfish into the pan 12 at a time. Cover the pan. Boil for 3–4 minutes at the most, if you are going to use the crayfish in a cooked dish. Lift them out of the pan, using a serrated spoon, and cool in a pan of cold water.

If you plan to eat them immediately, boil them for 4–6 minutes and leave each batch to cool in the stock.

Keep the shelled crayfish in the refrigerator, covered with a damp tea-towel.

Crayfish with sweetbreads in puff pastry

Croustade d'écrevisses

about 1 litre/1¾ pints lukewarm water
salt
dash of vinegar
dash of white wine
1 carrot
1 leek (about 100 g/4 oz)
1 celery stick (about 100 g/4 oz)
1 onion
1 bay leaf
1 clove
1 garlic clove
2 juniper berries
1 sweetbread

1 **Whisk the Coral butter into the White wine sauce.** As it cooks, the grey-black coral butter – like the shells of crayfish or lobsters – turns coral pink. When stirred into a sauce, it makes the whole sauce a beautiful, appetising pink colour.

2 **Stirring with a spatula, fry the crayfish and sweetbread in butter** with the diced onion. Place the sweetbread in the pan first and heat it, without allowing it to colour, then add the crayfish with the cognac and the remaining butter.

3 **Strain the sauce into the pan.** To make it really smooth, strain the sauce through a fine-mesh sieve. Heat it through, without allowing it to boil. Season sparingly with salt and lemon juice, stir in the coriander and cream and sandwich between puff pastry leaves.

For the pastry:
120 g/4½ oz home-made puff pastry (or 2
sheets frozen puff pastry)
flour, for rolling out
1 egg yolk
For the filling:
250 ml/8 fl oz White wine sauce (page 106)
4 slices lobster or crayfish Coral butter
(page 105)
1 onion, diced
25 g/1 oz butter
40 g/1½ oz cooked crayfish meat
3 tablespoons cognac
salt
lemon juice
2 teaspoons chopped, fresh coriander,
plus sprigs to garnish
4 tablespoons whipped cream

Pour the water into a pan and add the salt. Add the vinegar, white wine, carrot, leek and celery (trimmed), together with the halved onion stuck with the bay leaf and clove, the peeled garlic, the juniper berries and the whole sweetbread.

Bring to the boil, then cook over a low heat for 15 minutes and leave the sweetbread to cool in the stock.

When cool, remove the segments of sweetbread from the skin. On a floured board, roll out the puff pastry to 5 mm/¼ in thick and cut into four rectangles 4 × 8 cm/1½ × 3 in. Cover and refrigerate for 30 minutes.

Brush the pastry with the beaten egg yolk. Prick a diagonal pattern into the top with a fork. Place on a baking sheet rinsed in cold water and bake in a preheated hot oven (230 C, 450 F, gas 8) for 12–15 minutes.

Bring the White wine sauce to the boil. Whisk in the lobster or crayfish Coral butter and reserve. In a saucepan, fry the diced onion in 20 g/¾ oz hot butter with the pieces of sweetbread. Add the cooked crayfish meat. Stir well. Add the cognac, with the remaining butter. Strain the lobster or crayfish sauce through a fine-mesh sieve into the pan. Stir in and season with salt and lemon juice. Fold in the coriander and whipped cream.

Halve the sheets of puff pastry horizontally and sandwich them together with the crayfish and sweetbread filling. Serve garnished with fresh coriander and crayfish shells.

Crayfish and sole fillets with green noodles

Ecrevisses et filets de sole avec nouilles vertes

12 sole fillets
150 g/5 oz green noodles
salted water
400 ml/14 fl oz Fish stock (page 97)
200 ml/7 fl oz dry white wine
1 piece buttered greaseproof paper
24 fresh-boiled crayfish, shelled
400 ml/14 fl oz Lobster sauce (page 102)
4 tablespoons whipped cream

Trim the sole fillets and cut off the skin along the long sides. Cut a slit 1.5 cm/½ in long at the wider end and thread the pointed end through it.

Cook the noodles in salted water, without allowing them to become too soft, drain well and keep hot.

Bring the Fish stock and white wine to the boil and add the sole fillets. Reduce the heat, cover with the buttered paper and simmer for 3–4 minutes.

Heat the crayfish in the Lobster sauce and stir in the cream. Arrange the noodles on 4 plates, surround with the sole fillets and crayfish and pour on the lobster sauce.

Crayfish in cream sauce on a bed of spinach

Ecrevisses à la crème et aux épinards

500 g/18 oz tender leaf spinach
250 ml/8 fl oz double cream
500 ml/17 fl oz Crayfish stock (page 100, but with vegetables cooked in 20 g/¾ oz fresh butter instead of oil)
50 g/2 oz butter, melted
salt
grated nutmeg
48 fresh-boiled crayfish, shelled
4 tablespoons whipped cream

Sort and wash the spinach and leave it in the colander. Stir the double cream into the Crayfish stock when it has been simmering for 40–45 minutes. Over a low heat, reduce the mixture to about 400 ml/14 fl oz and then strain.

Blanch the spinach in boiling, salted water. Cool in iced water and squeeze out lightly. Before serving, toss in melted butter and season with salt and nutmeg.

Half-cover four heated plates with spinach leaves, or chop the leaves and arrange on the plates.

Heat the crayfish in the cream sauce, without allowing it to boil. Stir in the whipped cream. Season sparingly with salt (home-made crayfish sauce is naturally highly flavoured). Spoon onto the plates and serve immediately.

Crayfish in dill stock with Chablis

Ecrevisses au Chablis

250 ml/8 fl oz Crayfish stock (page 100)
160 ml/5½ fl oz Chablis
4 small young carrots
1 small leek
salt
80 g/3 oz butter
48 fresh-boiled crayfish, shelled
4 sprigs dill, plus extra for garnish (optional)

In a pan, stir together the Crayfish stock and Chablis. Bring to the boil, stirring occasionally, and reduce over a low heat. Peel the carrots with a zig-zag knife, then thinly slice and blanch in the wine stock.

Trim and wash the leek and blanch the pale centre leaves in salted water, then plunge them into iced water. This not only helps retain the colour but also stops the leeks from cooking more than required. Cut the leek into even, slanting slices. Use only the centre of each slice.

Beat the butter vigorously into the reduced stock. Warm the crayfish and leek through in the stock but do not boil. Add the dill. Arrange on heated plates. You can also use sprigs of dill to garnish.

Crayfish gratin with cucumber and dill

Ecrevisses au gratin

32 boiled crayfish of about 60 g/2¼ oz
each
3 shallots
30 g/1¼ oz fresh butter
5 tablespoons dry white wine
3 tablespoons good-quality vermouth
500 ml/17 fl oz Fish stock (page 97)
200 ml/7 fl oz fresh cream
salt
¼ cucumber, sliced into julienne strips
2 teaspoons chopped fresh dill
150 ml/¼ pint whipped cream

Break open the crayfish tails and remove the gut (see page 114). Remove the shells. Cover the meat and keep hot.

Evenly dice, wash and dry the peeled shallots and fry in the heated butter. Add the white wine and vermouth. Reduce the liquid until the shallots are just moist. Add the Fish stock, reduce and then add the cream. Simmer for about 5 minutes over a low heat until you have a scant 500 ml/17 fl oz sauce. Strain through a fine sieve and season to taste.

Arrange the crayfish in four gratin dishes, with fine strips of cucumber and the dill to garnish. Stir the whipped cream into the sauce, bring to the boil and pour over the crayfish. Brown under a preheated grill for 2–3 minutes until golden-brown.

Marron in red wine sauce with broccoli

Ecrevisses au vin rouge

4 marrons of about 225 g/8 oz or
2 lobsters of 500 g/18 oz
6 tablespoons olive oil
1 carrot
25 g/1 oz celery
25 g/1 oz leek
1 small shallot
1 tablespoon tomato purée
375 ml/13 fl oz red wine,
plus 2 tablespoons
375 ml/13 fl oz Crayfish stock (page 100)
or light chicken stock
30 g/1¼ oz butter
12 florets broccoli

Wash and scrub the marrons or lobsters. Bring a large pan of water to the boil and add salt. Boil the marrons or lobster for 2–3 minutes to kill them. Transfer to cold water, then drain and halve lengthways. (Remove the corals, mix 1:2 with butter, wrap in foil and refrigerate to use in another dish.) Remove the lobster or marron meat from the body shell and claws.

Pound the shells in a mortar, then fry the pieces in 4 tablespoons hot olive oil, stirring occasionally. Add the cleaned, chopped vegetables (mirepoix) with the tomato purée. Heat through, stirring continuously. Add 2 tablespoons red wine. Add the

Crayfish or chicken stock. Bring to the boil and remove the scum. Simmer over a low heat for 30 minutes. Add the remaining red wine, strain and reduce until the sauce has sufficient flavour. Bind with the butter and adjust the seasoning. Blanch the broccoli in salted water until just firm. Cook the marron or lobster meat in 2 tablespoons olive oil for 3–4 minutes.

Serve in four portions, with the broccoli and red wine sauce.

Marron with cockle stew

Ecrevisses au ragoût de bucardes

2 marrons or lobsters of about
400 g/14 oz each
For the ragout:
120 g/4¼ oz cockles
salt
4 small onions
generous pinch of chopped garlic
40 g/1½ oz butter
600 ml/1 pint Fish stock (page 97)
4 tomatoes
2 teaspoons chopped fresh coriander
For the vegetable butter:
4 small shallots
4 small carrots
1 thin leek
40 g/1½ oz butter
400 ml/14 fl oz Fish stock (page 97)
salt
40 g/1½ oz butter, for the crayfish

Bring a large pan of water to the boil. Add the prepared marrons or lobsters, one at a time, and boil each for 3–4 minutes. Leave to cool in the water.

To make the stew, add the washed cockles to fast-boiling, salted water. Boil for 2 minutes. Rinse the cockles in cold water and then shell them. Cut off the grey parts and clean the cut edges.

Finely chop the onions. Fry with the chopped garlic in the butter. Pour on the Fish stock. Reduce until nice and thick. Add the peeled, deseeded, chopped tomatoes and the cockles and heat through. Add the chopped coriander.

To make the vegetable butter, peel the shallots and trim the carrots and leek. Finely dice all the vegetables. Fry in the heated butter. Add the Fish stock and reduce to the required consistency. Season sparingly with salt.

Meanwhile, halve the marrons or lobsters lengthways. Break off the claws and crack the shell. Fry the claws with the shell in the butter.

Spoon the vegetable butter into four shallow bowls. Place a lobster or marron half and 1 claw in each bowl. Fill the space in the shells with the cockle stew, and serve.

Marron in papaya sauce – a combination which any gourmet will enjoy. The flavour of the Australian crayfish is perfect for this dish, but other types of crayfish can be almost as delicious.

Crayfish in papaya sauce

Ecrevisses à la sauce papaye

A good example of how well sweet tropical fruit and hot chillies go with the delicate flavour of crayfish. It does not matter whether you use marrons, another sort of crayfish, or lobster – all are delicious in this sauce. Instead of the papayas, you can use a ripe honeydew melon. Serve with buttered rice or toast.

4 marrons or other crayfish of around
400 g/14 oz each, or 24 small crayfish
2 (350 g/12 oz) ripe papayas
30 g/1¼ oz butter
60 g/2¼ oz shallots, chopped
1 garlic clove, chopped
250 ml/8 fl oz Crayfish or Fish stock
(pages 100, 97)

250 ml/8 fl oz dry white wine
2 fresh, hot chillies
salt
6 tablespoons cream, lightly whipped
40 g/1½ oz butter, for frying
1 teaspoon chopped fresh basil

Drop the scrubbed crayfish into fast-boiling water and boil for 3 minutes. Remove from the pan and cool in cold water. Shell the tail and claws.

Halve the papayas and spoon out the seeds. Cut 16 balls of fruit, with a melon-baller, and reserve. Remove the remaining fruit from the skins and chop.

Melt the butter in a saucepan and lightly fry the finely chopped shallots and garlic.

Add the chopped papaya, with the stock and white wine. Wash, halve, deseed and finely chop the chillies and add to the pan. Reduce to about 250 ml/8 fl oz. Strain through a fine sieve. Reduce again to the required consistency (or to around 6 tablespoons). Season with salt and stir in the lightly whipped cream.

Meanwhile, halve the crayfish lengthways. Remove the gut. Fry the tail and claw meat in the hot butter for about 4 minutes, stirring frequently. Add the papaya balls and warm through. Transfer to four serving plates, pour on the sauce and sprinkle with chopped basil. Garnish with the claws.

119

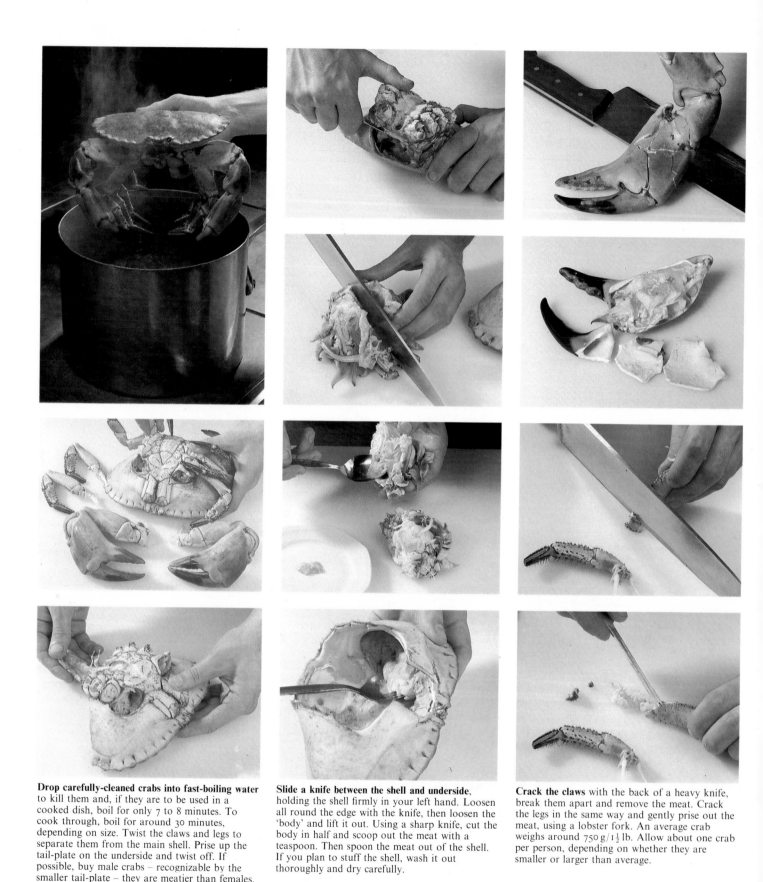

Drop carefully-cleaned crabs into fast-boiling water
to kill them and, if they are to be used in a
cooked dish, boil for only 7 to 8 minutes. To
cook through, boil for around 30 minutes,
depending on size. Twist the claws and legs to
separate them from the main shell. Prise up the
tail-plate on the underside and twist off. If
possible, buy male crabs – recognizable by the
smaller tail-plate – they are meatier than females.

Slide a knife between the shell and underside,
holding the shell firmly in your left hand. Loosen
all round the edge with the knife, then loosen the
'body' and lift it out. Using a sharp knife, cut the
body in half and scoop out the meat with a
teaspoon. Then spoon the meat out of the shell.
If you plan to stuff the shell, wash it out
thoroughly and dry carefully.

Crack the claws with the back of a heavy knife,
break them apart and remove the meat. Crack
the legs in the same way and gently prise out the
meat, using a lobster fork. An average crab
weighs around 750 g/1½ lb. Allow about one crab
per person, depending on whether they are
smaller or larger than average.

Crab meat differs surprisingly in consistency: top right are the large claw pieces and below the fine-textured meat from the shell. Bottom left is the darker body meat, which includes the delicately flavoured liver, and top left the leg meat.

On the underside of the beautifully shaped shell is a seam, going all the way round. You can cut around this with scissors and break the shell away cleanly at the seam. Now the shell is ready for stuffing.

Fill with a fine mixture of onions, leek and carrot, braised in butter, with fish stock added and then reduced. The crabmeat is then warmed through in the vegetable stock, seasoned and spooned into the shell to serve hot.

Stuffed crab

Crabe tourteau farci

4 (775 g/1¾ lb) crabs,
boiled for 7–8 minutes
4 small onions
pale green leaves of 1 leek
4 small carrots
80 g/3 oz butter
600 ml/1 pint Fish stock (page 97)
salt
500 ml/17 fl oz Lobster sauce (page 102)
4 tablespoons whipped cream
salt
cayenne

A 775 g/1¾ lb crab contains 120–150 g/4–5 oz meat, sufficient for a starter or light evening snack.

Remove the meat from the shells. Break the underside of the shells away at the seam. Wash and thoroughly dry the shells. Finely dice the peeled onions, the leek leaves and the trimmed carrots. Heat the butter in a saucepan until frothy and lightly fry the vegetables for 5 minutes. Add the Fish stock, bring to the boil and simmer, uncovered, for 5 minutes, until the vegetables are cooked but still firm. The liquid will have reduced until the vegetables are just moist. Heat the crabmeat with the vegetables and season sparingly with salt.

Heat the Lobster sauce, stir in the whipped cream and season with a little salt and cayenne. Stuff the shells with the crab mixture and serve with the lobster cream sauce.

Stuffed crab makes a delicious meal, to be savoured by anyone who loves fine food, especially if served with a lobster sauce rich in fresh cream, as here. This dish is equally good as a starter, savoury or special evening snack. It is best served with fresh-baked white bread and fresh butter.

Fresh soft-shell crabs should be cleaned before cooking and all the inedible parts removed. First, lift up the sides of the upper shell and remove the gills (centre right). Then, using sharp scissors (or a sharp knife with the crab on a board), cut off the head directly behind the eyes. Through this opening, you can scrape out the innards using a round-ended knife or teaspoon handle. Rinse the opening under running water. Finally, open out the turned-under tail, known as the 'apron', and cut it off with scissors (centre far right). Once prepared in this way (as they are when frozen, bottom right), the crabs are ready for the frying pan.

Soft-shell crabs

These are not a separate species but are crabs of various types caught immediately after changing their shell. They are considered a special delicacy throughout the world.

Like lobsters and crayfish, crabs outgrow their shells at intervals and discard them. At this stage, they are completely soft and excellent to eat. They can be eaten 'whole', so to speak, with no need to remove the meat from the shell. The pure white, tender meat tastes completely different from that of hard-shelled crabs.

In markets all along the coastline of Europe, you will occasionally find soft-shell crabs in the summer. If you do see them, seize the opportunity to buy them, for they are quite rare. They are extremely popular in the United States; the east-coast Blue Crab (*Callinectes sapidus*) makes a delicious soft-shell crab. In America, fishermen no longer rely on finding a few soft-shell crabs in their nets but catch them before they lose their shells and keep them in seawater enclosures, ready to take them out of the

water at exactly the right moment, directly after they lose their shells. Experienced fishermen can anticipate when this will happen by looking at a line above the rear legs. This changes colour from white to pink and then red at intervals of two weeks, one week and then a couple of days before the shell is discarded. Then every hour – even every minute – is important for, while in the water, the skin under the old shell begins to harden. It is only a matter of three hours before soft-shell crabs turn into paper-shells, or buckrams, as the skin begins to take on a leathery consistency. The meat tastes just as good but the skin is no longer edible at this stage. With paper-shells, only the top shell needs to be removed, as this hardens quicker than the underside.

It is only a matter of time before American soft-shell crabs are available on the European market (the first attempt, in Germany, proved a failure), for they are a delicacy that is just as good frozen as fresh.

Fried soft-shells

This is the ideal way of cooking these crabs, for frying in fresh salted butter is the only way to bring out the full flavour of the tender, white meat. The crabs should be dried and lightly seasoned with freshly ground pepper and, if you are using unsalted butter, a little salt. Dip both sides in flour and then shake until only the thinnest covering of flour remains.

Melt the butter in a frying pan and fry the top of the crabs first, over a high heat, for 2–3 minutes. Turn the crabs and fry for the same length of time on the underside and then – vital for the full flavour – serve immediately, so that the crabs are nice and crisp outside and soft and tender inside. You can serve fried crabs with a sauce and side-dishes of your choice.

Soft-shell crabs in lobster sauce

Chancre nageron à la sauce d'homard

1 green pepper
salt
20 g/¾ oz fresh butter
120 g/4 oz noodles
salted water, to cook noodles
8 soft-shell crabs
freshly milled pepper
flour for coating
80 g/3 oz fresh butter
6 tablespoons Lobster sauce (page 102)

Cut the green pepper into very thin strips, season with salt and fry in the butter until soft. Cook the noodles in the salted water until 'al dente'. Fry the crabs as described above and serve with the Lobster sauce, noodles and peppers.

Soft-shell crabs with vegetable sauce

Chancre nageron avec légumes fins

2 tablespoons oil
1 tablespoon finely chopped shallots
1 garlic clove, chopped
120 g/4 oz courgettes, diced
120 g/4 oz tomatoes, diced
3½ tablespoons dry white wine
1 tablespoon chopped herbs
salt
pepper
4 soft-shell crabs
flour, for coating
butter, for frying

Heat the oil in a frying pan and lightly fry the shallots and garlic. Add the courgette and tomato and then the white wine and herbs. Simmer for 6–8 minutes and season to taste. Fry the crabs as described above and serve with the vegetable sauce and freshly boiled potatoes.

123

Prawns – small but delicious

Live prawns are extremely rare away from the coast, so that many of the delicious ways of cooking them (for instance, the highly flavoured stock produced by boiling) are possible only for those who live on the coast. This is because the amino acid, glycin, (which forms part of the protein in prawn meat), makes them go bad very quickly. It is the chemical change produced in this acid by bacteria that produces the 'fishy' flavour of prawns kept for longer than two days at 7 c/55 f. To be on the safe side, prawns are usually cooked on board ship as soon as they are caught. This means that anyone living inland will have to rely on cooked prawns – either fresh, frozen or canned. Luckily, even these are delicious in fillings, salads and fish dishes.

Prawns in cider

Crevettes au cidre

500 ml/17 fl oz dry cider
500 ml/17 fl oz water
salt
white pepper
1 bouquet garni (sprig each of parsley and tarragon, 1 piece white leek, 1 piece carrot, ½ bay leaf)
500 g/18 oz fresh, peeled prawns

Pour the cider and water into a pan and season well with salt and pepper. Wash and trim the ingredients for the bouquet garni and tie into a bundle. Add the bouquet garni to the liquid in the pan, bring to the boil and simmer, over a moderate heat, for 10 minutes. Add the prawns and cook for 5 minutes. Drain and serve with bread, butter and cider.

Sole and prawn gratin

Filets de sole aux crevettes

4 small sole fillets
400 ml/14 fl oz Fish stock (page 97)
40 peeled prawns
20 g/¾ oz butter
salt
80 g/3 oz carrots, cut into thin strips
8 tablespoons whipped cream
scant 250 ml/8 fl oz White wine sauce (page 106)
4 sprigs tarragon, chopped

Carefully skin the sole fillets. Bring the Fish stock to the boil in a saucepan. Add the fillets, skin-side first, and twist them into prawn shapes. Poach for 3–4 minutes and then remove from the pan.

Warm the peeled prawns through in the fish stock. Grease four plates with butter and sprinkle sparingly with salt where you are going to place the fillets. Place the fillets on the plates and salt sparingly. Surround with the prawns and sprinkle with the raw carrot.

Gently fold the whipped cream into the warmed White wine sauce. Spoon onto the plates, sprinkle with chopped tarragon and grill until golden brown.

Prawn tartlets

Tartelettes aux crevettes

Whether served as a starter or as a nibble with wine or champagne, prawn tartlets are really appetising. For the filling, it is best to use small prawns or shrimps. The size of the tartlets will depend on how you plan to serve them. The following recipe is for eight 10-cm/4-in tartlets.

For the pastry:
270 g/9½ oz flour
125 g/4½ oz butter
1 egg, beaten
¼ teaspoon salt
1–2 tablespoons water
For the filling:
250 ml/8 fl oz Fish stock (page 97)
30 g/1¼ oz butter
2 shallots, chopped
200 g/7 oz fresh mushrooms
salt
white pepper
3 eggs, beaten
6 tablespoons fresh cream
400 g/14 oz peeled prawns
1 tablespoon chopped parsley

Sift the flour onto a pastry board. Make a well in the centre. Tip the butter, egg, salt and water into the well and work quickly together into a smooth shortcrust pastry. Wrap in foil and refrigerate for 2 hours.

On a floured surface, roll out the pastry to 2–3 mm/$\frac{1}{8}$ in thick. Cut out eight rounds of 13–14 cm/5–5$\frac{1}{2}$ in diameter. Use the rounds to line tartlet tins, making sure that the pastry does not tear. Press the edges firmly to the tin and trim off any excess.

Bake the tart cases blind; that is, without the filling. To prevent the sides collapsing fill the tarts with dried pulses. To do this, cover the bottom of the cases with rounds of greaseproof paper or aluminium foil and fill with dried peas, lentils or ceramic baking beans. Set the oven at moderately hot (200 C, 400 F, gas 6). When the oven is hot, bake the cases for 15 minutes, until slightly coloured. Tip out the pulses (keep them to use again) and remove the paper or foil.

To make the filling, reduce the Fish stock over a very low heat to 6 tablespoons, then leave to cool. In a large frying pan, melt the butter and lightly fry the finely chopped shallots. Peel and finely chop the mushrooms and braise them in the pan with the shallots for 4–5 minutes. Add the reduced stock and then remove the pan from the heat. Season sparingly with salt and pepper. Stir in the eggs and cream, then the peeled prawns and parsley.

Spoon the filling into the pre-baked tart cases. Set the oven at hot (220 C, 425 F, gas 7) and bake for 10 minutes, until golden-brown.

To check whether the tarts are done, move them gently in the oven. If there is any sign of liquid, bake for a few minutes more until the filling has completely set. Serve hot. Sprinkle with chopped parsley, if you wish.

Crawfish tartlets

Tartelettes à la langouste

For 8 tartlets:
pastry, as for prawn tartlets
For the filling:
250 ml/8 fl oz Fish stock (page 97)
50 g/2 oz butter
3 shallots, chopped
100 g/4 oz mushrooms, peeled and chopped
salt
white pepper
3 eggs, beaten
6 tablespoons cream
300 g/11 oz crawfish meat, boiled for a maximum of 3–4 minutes
20 g/$\frac{3}{4}$ oz truffles

Make and pre-bake the tart cases, as in the preceding recipe. To make the filling, reduce the Fish stock, over a low heat, to 6 tablespoons and leave to cool.

Heat the butter in a frying pan and lightly fry the finely chopped shallots. Add the peeled, chopped mushrooms and cook together for 4–5 minutes. Add the reduced fish stock and remove the pan from the heat. Season sparingly with salt and pepper. Stir in the eggs and cream and the crawfish, cut into even pieces. Then spoon the filling into the tarlet cases. Cut the trufles into the thinnest possible slices and sprinkle on the top. Set the oven at hot (220 C, 425 F, gas 7) and bake for 10 minutes, until golden-brown.

Delicious scampi

The many names given to scampi through-out the world are enough to confuse even the best travelled and the most knowledge-able gourmet. They are often confused with the larger types of prawn and what is described as crawfish often proves to be scampi. Nevertheless, it is generally agreed that this creature is one of the choicest of the crustaceans.

The exquisite meat of the langoustine (as the scampi or Norway lobster is known in classic French cuisine) is in the tail and it is usually just the scampi tails which are sold. These are normally boiled but are also available fresh or frozen. Occasionally, whole scampi are sold fresh or boiled. Like prawns, scampi soon go off. If they are really fresh, the meat will not disintegrate during cooking but will remain firm to the bite. This is also true of the mantis shrimps, whose fine flesh almost rivals the scampi and which are, in fact, often wrongly sold as 'scampi'.

Shelling scampi: 1. Hold the scampi by the head and tail and twist the tail off the body. **2.** Crack the thick shell, by squeezing it between your thumbs and index fingers. **3.** Holding the lower edge of the shell in both hands, break it open and take out the meat. **4.** Using a small, sharp knife, cut along – but not through – the back of the scampi and open out the meat to reveal the gut. **5.** Hold the gut between thumb and index finger and pull gently to remove it. **6.** The scampi meat is now ready to use in a variety of ways.

Sautéed scampi with herbs

Langoustines aux fines herbes

20 fresh scampi tails, in the shell
4 tablespoons oil
40 g/1½ oz fresh butter
2 tablespoons cognac
600 ml/1 pint Lobster or Fish stock
(page 97)
4 teaspoons chopped herbs, including
tarragon
80 g/3 oz fresh butter
salt
freshly ground white pepper

Wash the scampi, wipe dry and halve lengthways. Remove the gut. Heat the oil and butter in a frying pan until frothy. Fry the scampi halves, flesh side down, for about 2 minutes, until they begin to brown. Turn and fry on the shell side for about 1 minute. Remove from the pan and keep hot. Pour off the fat from the pan juices and stir the cognac into the sediment in the pan. Add the stock, and reduce. Stir in the herbs and thicken with the butter. Reduce to give a thick sauce. Stir the scampi into the sauce, season to taste and serve.

Flambéed scampi in cream sauce

Langoustines flambées à la crème

500 ml/17 fl oz Fish stock (page 97)
600 g/21 oz shelled scampi
salt
paprika
white pepper
150 g/5 oz butter
2 shallots
2 tablespoons pastis
5 tablespoons dry white wine
250 ml/8 fl oz cream
sprig of tarragon, chopped
100 g/4 oz butter, to thicken

Simmer the Fish stock for 30 minutes. Rinse the scampi and pat dry. Mix together the salt, paprika and pepper and sprinkle on the scampi. Heat the butter in a frying pan and lightly fry the scampi, without allowing them to colour. Add the finely diced shallots and fry lightly. Pour off the butter. Flame the scampi in the pastis then add the wine. Add the hot, reduced fish stock and simmer for 3 minutes. Remove the scampi from the pan and keep hot. Reduce the sauce by half, then add the cream and tarragon and cook until creamy. Beat in the butter. Serve the scampi covered with the sauce.

Scampi in the shell, whether sautéed, fried or grilled, are especially delicious, for during cooking the shell gives the meat extra flavour.

An appetising contrast: the lightly sautéed, pale slipper lobster and the pale yellow noodles on a black sauce made with cuttlefish ink and butter.

lobster meat, add the tomatoes, sprinkle with coriander and stir. Season to taste.

Pour the sauce onto four warmed serving plates. Top with the noodles and then the lobster and the diced tomato.

Black and white slipper lobster

Cigale à la sauce noire

If you ever see slipper lobsters for sale in Europe, you should buy them at once, for they are relatively rare here compared with Asia or Australia. The meat of the slipper lobster is delicious and compares favourably with lobster or crawfish. Any slipper lobster dish is equally good made with lobster, crayfish or other crustaceans.

4 slipper lobsters
2 litres/3½ pints court-bouillon
2 shallots
140 g/5 oz butter
3 tablespoons good-quality vermouth
800 ml/28 fl oz Fish stock (page 97)
120 g/4½ oz butter
ink from 4 small cuttlefish
salt
white pepper
200 g/7 oz fresh noodles
4 tablespoons vegetable oil
4 tomatoes, peeled and diced
4 tablespoons chopped fresh coriander

Cook the prepared slipper lobsters, one after the other, in the fast-boiling court-bouillon for 3–4 minutes. Break the cooked lobsters open and remove the tail meat. Finely dice the shallots and fry them in 20 g/1 oz butter, then add the vermouth. Add the Fish stock and reduce to one quarter of the original quantity. Beat in the remaining butter, a few pieces at a time, to thicken the sauce. Colour with the ink. Season to taste and keep hot.

Cook the noodles in salted water, until 'al dente'. Heat the oil in a frying pan. Seal the

Slipper lobster in pastry pockets

Cigale en pochettes

2 litres/3½ pints court-bouillon
4 long, green leek leaves
salt
200 g/7 oz leek hearts
40 g/1½ oz butter, plus butter for greasing
12 small button mushrooms
10 sheets filo pastry (very fine pastry available from Chinese and Greek shops) or strudel pastry
250 ml/8 fl oz Lobster sauce (page 102)
40 g/1½ oz clarified butter
salt
cayenne
4 tablespoons whipped cream

Boil the prepared slipper lobsters, one after the other, in fast-boiling court-bouillon for 3–4 minutes. Break open. Remove the tail meat, cut in half and remove the gut. Slice the meat.

Blanch the washed leek leaves in salted water for 1 minute, then cool in iced water. Cut a strip 3 mm/⅛ in wide from the length of each leaf. Cut the washed leek hearts into rings and fry until soft in 40 g/1½ oz butter. Season sparingly with salt.

Trim the mushrooms and cut into thick slices. Halve 2 sheets of pastry. Place 2 whole sheets one on top of the other with a half sheet in the centre, for extra strength. Repeat 3 times with the remaining sheets.

Place the leek rings, mushroom and lobster slices in the centre of each pile of

pastry. Gather up the pastry around the filling. Stick the handle of a wooden spoon into the top and squeeze the pastry around it, then remove the spoon, leaving a hole at the top. Pour a little Lobster sauce into each pocket and tie the pastry together at the top with the reserved strips of leek.

Grease a baking sheet with butter and place the pockets on it. Brush each pocket with the clarified butter. Set the oven at moderate (160 C, 325 F, gas 3). Bake the pockets for about 10 minutes.

Bring the remaining Lobster sauce to the boil. Season with salt and a little cayenne and fold in the whipped cream. Serve the lobster pockets with the sauce.

1 **Lift the boiled slipper lobster out of the court-bouillon** on a skimmer. It should boil in the seasoned stock for only 3–4 minutes, so that the flesh is only partly cooked and will be nice and tender when baked. Leave the lobster to cool slightly in the stock before lifting it out of the pan.

2 **Separate the tail from the body** by twisting it firmly off with your right hand. This is not as easy as it sounds, for the tail of a slipper lobster is fixed more firmly to the body than that of a lobster or crawfish.

3 **Cut open with kitchen scissors**. You will need strong scissors to crack the thick shell. Hold the tail upside down in your left hand and cut along the side; this will give you the best leverage. Remember to cut away from your hand to minimise the risk of injury if the scissors should slip.

6 **To make Slipper lobster in pastry pockets**. The leek, mushroom and lobster filling goes into the centre of 2½ sheets filo pastry. Bring the corners up to the centre. If you use strudel pastry, you will need only one layer, as this is usually thicker. Make sure that there is enough filling to give a plump pocket.

8 **Fill the stuffed pastry pocket with sauce**, using a sauce spoon. First, remove the handle of the wooden spoon carefully. Do not add more than 1 spoon sauce to each pocket, for the extra weight is likely to split the pastry. (The sauce spoon is ideal for this task because its spout enables you to fill the pocket without getting sauce on the outside.)

4 **The tail meat is exposed** when you lift off the underside of the shell. To remove the top, bend back the edges of the upper shell, using both hands and exerting an equal pressure. This brings the firm, white flesh away cleanly and it is then ready for you to proceed. Lay the meat on a clean chopping board.

7 **Stick in the handle of a wooden spoon**. Gather the pastry – three sides of which have already been drawn up – around the handle of a wooden spoon. Using your left hand, bring up the remaining side and press to the spoon so that the pastry sticks together well, leaving an opening at the centre.

9 **Tie up each pocket with a strip of leek**. This is more for decoration than to hold the pastry together. If the pastry has been pressed firmly to the spoon, it will hold its shape unaided. All that remains is to bake the lobster pockets and serve, in a shallow pool of lobster sauce with any remaining filling.

5 **Gently pull out the gut**. To do this, cut the tail meat exactly in half lengthways. In doing so you may cut through the gut several times and then all you have to do is to carefully remove the pieces. Ideally, you should remove the gut in a single piece, however, so cut through the flesh with care.

Seafood stew
with saffron rice

Ragoût de fruits de mer

4 scallops in the shell
200 g/7 oz cockles
20 mussels
4 scampi
200 g/7 oz boiled prawns
200 g/7 oz halibut fillet
40 g/1½ oz carrots
40 g/1½ oz celeriac
40 g/1½ oz leeks
75 g/3 oz butter
250 ml/8 fl oz Fish stock (page 97)
6 tablespoons dry white wine
150 ml/¼ pint cream

2 tablespoons good-quality vermouth
2 teaspoons chopped fresh basil
or tarragon
salt
freshly milled pepper

Prise the scallops open with a strong knife and stand them on the hot hob for a few minutes until completely open. Using a tablespoon, carefully free the meat from the shell, separate the roe from the meat, wash and drain on absorbent kitchen paper. Cut the meat in half. Steam the cockles and mussels as shown on page 148. They can then be used either with or without the shell. Twist the tails off the scampi, halve lengthways with the shell and remove the gut. The boiled prawns can either be peeled or used whole. Cut the halibut into 1.5-cm/½-in cubes.

Finely dice the carrots and celeriac and cut the leeks into fine strips. Melt 25 g/1 oz butter in a large pan and fry the chopped vegetables for 2–3 minutes. Add the halibut and scampi and cook for a further 2

minutes. Add the scallops, with the roes. Add the Fish stock and white wine. Add the steamed cockles and mussels and cook everything together for about 2 minutes. Then tip into a sieve, reserving the stock. Keep the seafood and vegetables hot and reduce the stock by about half. Add the cream and reduce again slightly. Flavour with vermouth and basil or tarragon. Return the seafood and vegetables to the pan, season to taste and thicken with 50 g/2 oz butter. Serve with saffron rice.

Cooked in a crisp coating

Deep-frying is the ideal cooking method for certain crustaceans (and shellfish, of course). The protective coating can be either batter or egg and breadcrumbs. The important thing is that the delicate meat of the seafood should not come into direct contact with the hot oil, but should cook slowly inside its coating. The claw meat of all types of crab deep-fries excellently, but scampi and king prawns are delicious as well – one need think only of the Japanese 'Tempura' (prawns cooked in a rice-flour batter). They are just as good coated in egg and breadcrumbs. For soft-shell crabs, mix the breadcrumbs with a little grated Parmesan cheese and fry in two frying pans. In the first pan, fry the underside in hot oil until brown and crisp (about 2 minutes) and then cook in the second pan at a lower temperature, in plenty of butter, until fully cooked (3 minutes). The buttery flavour goes marvellously with the fine flavour of the crab.

Tempura

Crevettes panées à la Japonaise

This dish, originally from Japan, has justifiably made its way onto menus throughout the world, for these prawns in their thin, crisp batter coating are a real delicacy. Large prawns, such as Tiger Prawns, are ideal for this dish but best of all are Scampi.

24 large prawns
200 g/7 oz French beans
4 tablespoons freshly grated horseradish
½ lemon, cut into wedges
For the batter:
1 egg
6 tablespoons water
6 tablespoons light beer
¼ teaspoon salt
freshly milled white pepper
150 g/5 oz rice or wheat flour
oil, for deep frying
For the sauce:
2 tablespoons vegetable oil
30 g/1¼ oz shallots, chopped
1 small chilli, deseeded and chopped
250 ml/8 fl oz Fish stock (page 97)
freshly milled pepper
generous pinch of ground ginger
1 teaspoon sugar
4 tablespoons light soy sauce

This dish is made with uncooked prawns (fresh or frozen). Peel the prawns, leaving the tail fins attached to the body. Cut open lengthways and remove the gut. Wash and dry on absorbent kitchen paper. Trim, wash and dry the beans and tie into a bundle with a length of cotton. To make the batter, quickly beat together the egg, water, beer, salt and pepper, stir in the flour and leave to stand for 30 minutes. The batter should run off the spoon in a thick stream. If it is too thick, stir in a little water.

To make the sauce, heat the oil in a large frying pan and fry the finely chopped shallots and chilli. Add the Fish stock, season with pepper, ground ginger and sugar and reduce over a low heat to about one-third. Strain through a conical sieve, mix in the soy sauce and reheat.

In a deep pan or deep-fryer, heat the oil to 180 C (350 F). Dip the prawns and beans into the batter, drain off any excess, and drop into the hot oil. Fry until the food stops bubbling (about 3–4 minutes), for this shows that it is cooked. Drain on absorbent kitchen paper and serve hot, with grated horseradish and lemon wedges.

Deep-fried seafood can be a real delicacy. From top to bottom: **1**. King prawns are cut open lengthways before coating. **2**. Soft-shell crabs are delicious coated in breadcrumbs and deep-fried. The thin skin becomes an integral part of the egg and breadcrumb coating. **3**. Clams should be boiled in water for a few minutes, to solidify them before coating. **4**. Peel scampi but leave the end of the tail on, to make them easier to get hold of.

NOTHING
BUT THE BEST

Classic cuisine at its best

The most expensive crustaceans are not everyday foods but it would be wrong to look on them as delicacies reserved for millionaires. To take a case in point, on the east coast of the United States they have become a regular part of the diet and are even eaten off paper plates (a thought that would horrify the *bons vivants* of Europe!). Even so, there is still great emphasis on quality. In Europe, on the other hand, one has to pay a pretty penny for top quality. This chapter gives the best of the crustaceans the attention they so richly deserve. Without neglecting classic dishes, such as Homard à l'Armoricaine or Lobster Thermidor, we concentrate mainly on simpler, more up-to-date methods of preparation. In addition, many of the recipes can be used for preparing less expensive seafood.

1 **Dividing up the lobster**. Top to bottom: Twist the claws off the body. Using a sharp, heavy knife, and starting at the tail end, cut through the body. The liquid that runs out consists of coral, creamy innards and seawater. You should collect the liquid and reserve it for the sauce. Using your hand and a teaspoon to help you, remove the stomach sac. Then, using a sharp knife, separate the tail from the rest of the body.

2 **Cutting up the claws**. Top to bottom: The two claws are first cut lengthways and then separated from the base using a knife. Next, crack the side of the claws with a sharp bang of the knife. Now you can either cut into the base diagonally or beat it flat with the back of the knife. This is necessary if the meat is to cook evenly. You will need to use quite a lot of force when dealing with the claws, for the shell is extremely strong.

3 **Cutting up the tail and separating the legs**. Top to bottom: Using a sharp knife, cut the tail, including the shell, into 2-cm/1-in slices. This is quite easy, as the tail shell is much thinner than the claw shell. Then cut off the legs from both sides of the body. To clarify the process further, the last photograph shows all the individual parts of the dismembered and dissected lobster, laid out in their proper positions – sliced tail, severed legs and cracked claws.

Glazed lobster with brandy

Homard à l'Armoricaine

The dish that many top restaurants now serve as 'Lobster à l'Américaine', is in fact a Breton dish. Brittany has made an important contribution to international cuisine, not the least of her contributions being this fine lobster dish, properly called Lobster à l'Armoricaine. Armorique or Armorica is the old name for Brittany but, because the words sound similar, this famous dish is now often made to appear to be an American speciality.

1 (1 kg/2¼ lb) lobster
salt
ground white pepper
5 tablespoons olive oil
40 g/1½ oz butter
30 g/1¼ oz shallots, finely chopped
50 g/2 oz celeriac, diced
30 g/1¼ oz carrots, diced
½ garlic clove, chopped
5 tablespoons cognac
150 ml/¼ pint dry white wine
200 ml/7 fl oz Fish stock (page 97)
2 tablespoons meat glaze
1 teaspoon dried tarragon
150 g/5 oz tomatoes, peeled and diced
5 tablespoons whipped cream
1 teaspoon chopped parsley
cayenne

Plunge the lobster head first into fast-boiling water or put it in the freezer to kill it (see page 97). Cut the lobster into pieces – follow the step-by-step illustrations. Catch the liquid that runs out – greenish coral, seawater and body liquids. Season all the lobster pieces. Heat the olive oil in a large pan. Add the lobster pieces and fry, turning frequently, until the shells are nice and red.

Pour off the olive oil and add 20 g/¾ oz butter. Add the shallots, celeriac, carrot and garlic and fry until the shallots are transparent. Add the cognac, set alight and allow to burn out. Add the white wine and Fish stock. Stir in the meat glaze, tarragon and diced tomato. Cover the pan and simmer very gently over a low heat for 8–10 minutes. Remove the lobster from the pan and keep hot. Reduce the stock until it begins to thicken.

Meanwhile, mix the remaining 20 g/¾ oz butter with the liquid from the lobster. Press through a sieve into a bowl and then whisk vigorously. Use to thicken the sauce. Stir in the cream and parsley and season with salt, pepper and cayenne. Arrange the lobster pieces on a serving plate and the sauce over the top.

4 **Turning it into Glazed lobster with brandy**. Top to bottom: Fry the lobster pieces in plenty of hot olive oil, until the shell is nice and red. Pour off the oil and add a little butter. Then fry the chopped vegetables and flame the mixture with cognac. Simmer gently with the remaining ingredients. Remove the lobster from the pan. Add the lobster liquid, mixed with butter, and reduce to make a sauce. Pour the sauce over the lobster pieces (right).

Lobster in cream sauce

Homard à la crème

Nothing could be simpler or more delicious than this method of cooking a fresh lobster. An essential factor in the success of this dish – as well as a top-quality lobster – is to use fresh cream of the very best quality. On no account should you use any sort of preserved cream.

Serves 2:
1 (800–1,000-g/$1\frac{3}{4}$–2-lb) lobster
2 tablespoons best vegetable oil
375 ml/13 fl oz fresh cream
(about 30% fat)
parsley sprig
freshly ground white pepper
1 tablespoon lemon juice
salt (optional)

Kill the live lobster by plunging into a large pan of fast-boiling water. After 2 minutes, take the lobster out of the pan and transfer to cold water. Twist off the legs and claws. Break open the claws by banging on a board with the flat side of a meat cleaver and carefully remove the flesh. Twist the tail off the body and – without removing the shell – cut it into 3-cm/$1\frac{1}{4}$-in slices.

Heat the oil in a pan until very hot. Quickly fry the lobster all over, turning it continuously. The strong heat not only gives the meat a good flavour but also breaks down the protein, making the flesh nice and juicy.

Stir in the cream. Add the parsley and a little freshly ground pepper. Reduce the heat and simmer for 12–15 minutes.

Remove the lobster and the parsley sprig from the pan. Whisk up the reduced cream. Season with lemon juice and, if necessary, a little salt. Return the lobster to the pan and serve at once.

Lobster in yellow pepper sauce

Homard à la crème poivron

Serves 2:
2 shallots, diced
20 g/¾ oz butter
1 yellow pepper, deseeded and diced
½ bay leaf
1–2 cloves
2 juniper berries, crushed
2 sprigs thyme
4 tablespoons vermouth
8 tablespoons dry white wine
300 ml/½ pint Fish stock (page 97)
1 (800-g/1¾-lb) lobster,
boiled for 3–4 minutes
4 tablespoons olive oil
salt
2 heaped tablespoons whipped cream
fresh coriander, to garnish

Lightly fry the diced shallots in the hot butter. Add the coarsely diced yellow pepper with the bay leaf, cloves, juniper berries and thyme, and cook gently. Add the vermouth and white wine. Reduce until the vegetables are just moist. Add the Fish stock and simmer for 20 minutes. Remove the bay leaf and thyme. Blend the sauce in a liquidizer or food processor and then strain.

Cut the shelled lobster meat into good-sized pieces. Fry in the olive oil for 3–4 minutes. Arrange on two serving plates. Season the pepper sauce with a little salt, beat in the whipped cream and pour onto the lobster. Garnish with the coriander leaves.

Navarin of lobster

Navarin d'homard

Serves 2:
100 g/4 oz carrots
100 g/4 oz courgettes
10 g/⅓ oz butter
pinch of sugar
salt
1 (800-g/1¾-lb) lobster,
boiled for 3–4 minutes
400 ml/14 fl oz Lobster sauce (page 102)
few drops of cognac
40 g/1½ oz butter
2 heaped tablespoons whipped cream
chopped fresh tarragon or basil leaves

Carve the carrots and courgettes into small ovals. Heat the butter and sugar in a saucepan and toss the carrots in the mixture. Cover with water and simmer for 7–8 minutes in a covered pan. Blanch the courgettes in salted water for about 1 minute and then transfer to iced water. Shell the lobster and cut into bite-sized pieces. Bring the vegetables and lobster to the boil in the Lobster sauce and cook through. Remove the lobster and vegetables from the pan and reduce the sauce to about 300 ml/½ pint. Flavour with a few drops cognac. Thicken with the butter and fold in the whipped cream. Reheat the lobster and vegetables in the sauce. Season lightly with salt and add the tarragon or basil.

Lobster with cucumber and dill

Homard à concombre et aneth

Serves 2:
2 shallots
20 g/¾ oz butter
3 tablespoons vermouth
3 tablespoons white wine
300 ml/½ pint Fish stock (page 97)
200 g/7 oz cucumber, unpeeled
salt
5 tablespoons double cream
1 (800-g/1¾-lb) lobster,
boiled for 3–4 minutes
2 teaspoons chopped fresh dill
pinch of cayenne
few drops of lemon juice
2 tablespoons whipped cream
sprigs of dill

Slice the shallots and fry lightly in the melted butter. Add the vermouth and white wine. Reduce. Add the Fish stock and simmer until velvety.

Cut the cucumber into thick sticks and then carve into ovals. Blanch for 1 minute in salted water and then transfer to iced water. Stir the double cream into the sauce, bring to the boil and strain through a lined, conical sieve.

Shell the lobster and cut into bite-sized pieces. Add to the sauce with the cucumber and chopped dill. Season with cayenne and lemon juice. Fold in the whipped cream and serve, garnished with sprigs of dill.

Boiled lobster

Homard poché vivant

Boiling a lobster is very easy; it is cutting it up and getting at the meat that is the difficult part. With the right tools for the job, however, even this is no problem. The only thing you have to do to boil the lobster is to plunge it – head first – into boiling water, court-bouillon or fish stock. The heat kills it almost immediately.

There are two (if not more) schools of thought on how long to boil a lobster. According to the first, the lobster is boiled for 12 minutes from the time the heat is reduced for the first 500 g/18 oz, 10 minutes for the next 500 g/18 oz, and 5 minutes for each further 500 g/18 oz. Thus, a lobster of 1 kg/2¼ lb would need about 22 minutes. The second method allows only 8–10 minutes for the first 500 g/18 oz. This leaves the tail flesh fairly transparent, rather than cooking it until it is completely white, and many people prefer it cooked like this.

If the lobster is left to cool in the cooking stock, you will have to reduce the cooking time by 15 per cent, since it continues cooking while the water remains hot. All this applies also to crawfish.

Once the lobster has been boiled, it will need cutting up. This is usually done in the kitchen but if you want to do it at the table the method is the same. If you order lobster in a restaurant, it will usually come cut up and with the claws ready-cracked. Occasionally, the waiter will cut it up at the table and serve you the meat. On the American coast, where lobster is preferred plain boiled, there is a slight difference in the method of cutting up the lobster. The claws, tail and legs are removed, but the body is left whole for shelling rather than being cut in half lengthways. Whichever method you use, the lobster will still taste delicious.

Although lobster is usually served sliced and 'cracked', you will still need a lobster fork to get the delicious meat out of every corner of the legs. It is quite all right to suck the meat out of the legs at the table. In either case, you should provide a finger bowl containing water and a slice of lemon whenever you serve boiled lobster.

1 **Twist off the claws**. Hold the breastplate of the boiled lobster firmly in your left hand and twist both claws off the body, one after the other. This is easiest if you hold the claws close to the body. Grip the root of the claw firmly and pull as you twist, to free the strong joint from the body.

2 **Cut open the lobster** with a knife. To make a good, clean cut, hold the lobster firmly on a hard surface, right way up, and cut through it using a large, strong knife. The point of the knife should be placed in the seam between the head and the body and pressed down firmly.

3 **Halve the head**. To do this, turn the lobster round the other way. Hold it firmly on the worktop, push the point of the knife deep into the lobster and cut the head in half in the same way as the body. This will allow you to remove all the flesh from the body with no problems.

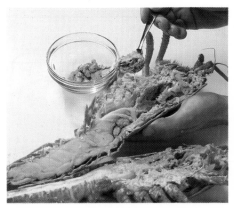

4 **The correctly halved lobster**. Each half should contain half of the delicious green liver. This should be scooped out with a teaspoon and put in a small dish, to be used for flavouring a sauce or stock on some later occasion. Then you should remove the inedible parts of the body, including the feelers.

5 **Remove the gut**. If you have cut the lobster open properly, you will be able to see the canal which holds the gut. It is not for aesthetic reasons alone that it has to be removed – it is also inedible. You should remove it with extreme care, to prevent it breaking, as it may contaminate the meat.

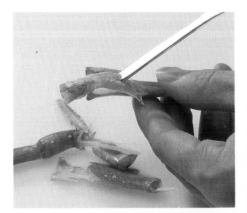

6 **The tender leg flesh is removed** using a lobster fork. First, the thin legs are twisted off the body. Next, they should be hit lightly (to prevent the meat being squashed) with the back of the knife. It is then a simple matter to remove the shell by peeling off the broken pieces and lifting out the meat.

7 **Holding the claws**. To get the meat out of the claws whole and undamaged, first take hold of the curved side of the claw in your left hand and give a sharp downward tug to pull off the smaller half of the pincer. Hold the main part of the claw firmly, pressing down on the outer edge to increase your leverage.

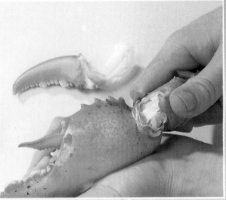

8 **Separating the claw** from the lower section. Hold the claw firmly in your left hand. Hold the lower section in your right hand where it joins the claw and twist off the claw. Repeat for the other claw. Again, you will need to use quite a strong downward and outward pull to break the strong joint.

9 **Gently prise open the joint**. The lower, jointed section of the claw contains delicious meat. All you need to do to get at this is to prise the joint gently apart. The shell is relatively soft here, so this is relatively easy. Try to extract the joint meat in a single unbroken piece – it won't taste any different, but looks better.

10 **Opening the large claw**. The shell of the claw is the strongest part of the whole lobster. Place the claw on its side on the worktop and give it one sharp tap with the knife – at the wider end – to crack it. Be prepared for the fact that when you strike it, the claw will bounce up from the worktop – keep a firm grip on it.

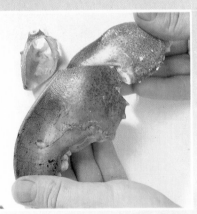

11 **Remove the meat from the claw**. First, break off the cracked piece of claw so that you can get hold of the meat. Then, using your right hand, pull out the meat, moving it gently to and fro as you go. It should come out in one piece if you proceed with care (see next picture).

12 **The claw and its delicious meat**. The broken shell of the lobster claw – the large and small pincers and the joint – clearly shows how the claw is made up. Above it is the meat from the pincer and the joint – completely undamaged, and exactly the same shape as it was in the shell.

Lobster and julienned vegetables

Homard avec légumes divers

There are as many different lobster and vegetable combinations as there are types of vegetable, for there is scarcely a vegetable grown in our fields or gardens that will not go with lobster. One vegetable that does not go very well, however, is strongly flavoured red or white cabbage. You can turn a lobster and vegetable mixture into a special dish by adding poached fish, such as sole or turbot, or other seafoods, such as crayfish or mussels. Give free rein to your imagination in creating new combinations.

Serves 2:
1 (800-g/1¾-lb) lobster
salted water or court-bouillon
6 shallots
1 courgette
1–2 carrots
80 g/3 oz green beans
2 tablespoons vegetable oil
freshly ground white pepper
1 teaspoon chopped parsley
3 tablespoons chopped shallots
5 tablespoons dry white wine
2 teaspoons chopped lemon balm
salt
100 g/4 oz butter
8–10 grapes, peeled and depipped

Plunge the live lobster headfirst into a deep pan of fast-boiling, salted water (or court-bouillon) to kill it. Simmer for 6 minutes and then transfer to cold water.

Break open the lobster. Remove the meat and the gut from the tail. Discard the gut. Remove the claw meat and cut all the meat into slices. Peel the shallots, trim the courgette and carrots and cut into strips. Blanch with the trimmed green beans in salted water. Transfer to iced water and then drain.

Heat the oil in a frying pan and add the vegetables. Season with a very little white pepper and the parsley. Sauté until the vegetables are cooked but are still firm to the bite. Remove the pan from the heat, add the lobster and keep hot in the covered pan.

Bring the chopped shallots to the boil in the white wine and reduce for a few minutes. Flavour with the lemon balm and a little salt and then beat in the butter in flakes, to thicken the sauce. Warm the peeled grapes through in the sauce.

Arrange the lobster and vegetables on two plates and serve with the sauce.

This recipe can also be used for crawfish or crab. You might like to vary it by trying the following mixture of vegetables: cucumber, celery and diced tomatoes. Instead of lemon balm, finely chopped tarragon would suit this dish, or you could just use dill.

Lobster with white wine sauce

Homard à la sauce au vin blanc

A lobster in all its natural glory like this one is the last word in flavour for gourmets. It is simply cooked in court-bouillon and served as it is. Many people prefer to eat it just with bread and butter and a good white wine. Others prefer their fresh-boiled lobster with a tasty sauce, like the one given here.

80 g/3 oz carrots
100 g/4 oz onions
4 shallots
1 garlic clove
sprig of thyme
½ bay leaf
parsley sprig
salt
freshly ground white pepper
375 ml/13 fl oz white wine
200 ml/7 fl oz water
4 (600-g/21-oz) live lobsters
For the wine and butter sauce:
2 tablespoons chopped shallots
150 ml/¼ pint vinegar
300 ml/½ pint white wine
salt
freshly ground white pepper
100 g/4 oz butter

To make the court-bouillon, peel the carrots, onions, shallots and garlic and cut all the vegetables into slices. In a large pan, boil them with the thyme, bay leaf, washed parsley, salt and pepper in the white wine and water for 5 minutes. Add a little more water if necessary and then bring to a rolling boil. Add the lobsters headfirst, one after the other, cover the pan and simmer for 15 minutes.

To make the wine and butter sauce, first bring the chopped shallots, vinegar and half the white wine to the boil in a pan. Season to taste. Reduce until the mixture is thick. Add the remaining wine and bring back to the boil. Strain the sauce, reheat and whisk in the butter, a little at a time, until the sauce thickens.

Drain the lobsters. Cut them in half, crack the claws and serve, with the sauce as an accompaniment.

To shell a boiled lobster tail whole. Top to bottom: Hold the body of the lobster in your left hand and twist out the tail with your right hand. Press on the tail shell to crack it. Pulling from the underside, break the shell open and remove the meat. The meat should be intact, in the shape of the shell.

Lobster Thermidor

Homard Thermidor

The word 'Thermidor' is of Graeco-French origin and is the name of the eleventh month in the French Revolutionary calendar. It means the month of heat, and ran from the 19th July to 17th August. This calendar was introduced by Robespierre and was used in France until 1806, despite the fact that Robespierre was deposed on 9th Thermidor in the year II (i.e. on 27th July) and arrested the following day.

Whoever conceived the name for this dish was obviously thinking, not of the French Revolution, but of midsummer, which is an excellent time for lobster – as is the summer in general. Lobster Thermidor is a country-style dish that goes well with a simple wine. Many people prefer to drink a good beer with it.

Serves 2:
1 (700–800-g/1½–1¾-lb) lobster
For the court-bouillon:
750 ml/1¼ pints water
750 ml/1¼ pints white wine
1 carrot
1 onion
1 small parsley root
¾ celery stick
3 sprigs fresh coriander
sprig of thyme
1 small bay leaf
white pepper
salt
3 tablespoons brandy
1 shallot
1 tablespoon butter
3 tablespoons white wine
400 ml/14 fl oz Fish stock (page 97)
4 tablespoons Béchamel sauce
½ teaspoon English mustard
cayenne
2 tablespoons whipped cream
40 g/1½ oz grated cheese

Prepare the lobster. To make the court-bouillon, first bring the water and white wine to the boil in a pan. Trim and chop the carrot, onion, parsley root and celery. Add to the pan with the coriander, thyme and bay leaf. Season generously with pepper and less so with salt. Simmer for 15 minutes and then bring to a rolling boil.

Plunge the lobster headfirst into the pan and cook for 8–12 minutes, depending on size. Remove from the pan. When it has cooled slightly, cut it in half lengthways, using a strong, sharp knife. Remove the gut, stomach sac and coral. Make the coral into coral butter and keep in the refrigerator. Discard the stomach and gut. Remove the meat from the tail and claws and cut into thick slices, before marinating in the brandy.

Peel and finely chop the shallot. Fry lightly in the heated butter, add the white wine and reduce until just moist. Then add the Fish stock and reduce to one-quarter the volume. Add the Béchamel sauce and whisk vigorously. Strain through a fine sieve. Add the mustard and reduce, whisking continuously. Keep hot.

Rinse the lobster shell under running water and remove any remaining fragments of meat. Wipe the shell dry, pour in a little sauce and then fill with the marinated lobster. Bring the remaining sauce back to the boil and season generously with cayenne. Stir in the whipped cream. Pour the sauce over the lobster, sprinkle with grated cheese and brown under a preheated grill.

Crawfish with two sauces

Langouste aux deux sauces

Serves 2:
For the court-bouillon:
1 litre/1¾ pints water
1 litre/1¾ pints white wine
2 carrots
1 parsley root
1 head fennel
1 onion
3 sprigs fresh coriander
sprig of thyme
1 small bay leaf
white pepper
1 (700-g/1½-lb) crawfish
100 g/4 oz broccoli florets
salt
5 tablespoons White butter sauce (page 99)
½ ink sac from a squid
5 tablespoons White wine sauce (page 106)
few saffron threads
2 tablespoons whipped cream

Boil the water, white wine, chopped, peeled vegetables, coriander, thyme and bay leaf in a large pan for 15 minutes. Season generously.

Plunge the prepared crawfish headfirst into the pan, boil for 2 minutes then reduce the heat and cook for 15 minutes. Remove the crawfish from the pan and remove the shell, starting from the underside (as for lobster). Slice the meat and keep hot.

Blanch the washed broccoli in salted water for about 4 minutes. Transfer to iced water, drain and reserve.

Warm the White butter sauce, colour with the ink, strain through a fine sieve and season with salt and freshly ground pepper. Heat the White wine sauce, add the saffron threads and simmer for a few minutes to make saffron sauce. Fold in the whipped cream and adjust the seasoning.

Quickly steam the broccoli to reheat it. Pour a little of each sauce onto two serving plates, to make a decorative pattern, and top with the broccoli and crawfish.

Lobster Newburg

Homard Newburg

One of the best-known international seafood dishes is Lobster Newburg. Many people believe it to be a French dish but it was, in fact, the creation of a Mr Wenburg, a former head chef at Delmonico's in New York. The first letters of the name Wenburg have been transposed to give Newburg. As is so often the case, you will come across this dish made with a variety of ingredients and by a variety of methods. The following recipe has now become something of a classic.

2 (800-g/1¾-lb) lobsters
3 litres/5 pints court-bouillon
6 tablespoons olive oil
salt
freshly ground white pepper
5 tablespoons brandy or cognac
5 tablespoons dry sherry
250 ml/8 fl oz cream
200 ml/7 fl oz reduced Fish stock
(page 97)
2 tablespoons butter
coral and liquid from the lobsters
2 tablespoons flour

Clean the lobsters. Heat the court-bouillon to a rolling boil in a large pan. Place one lobster headfirst into the pan and remove after 3 minutes. Repeat with the second lobster, once the water has come back to a rolling boil.

Using a heavy, sharp knife, cut each lobster into fairly large pieces. Discard the gut and reserve the corals and the liquid produced.

Heat the olive oil in a pan. Quickly fry the lobster, turning continuously, and season. Pour off the oil. Add the brandy and sherry and reduce by two-thirds. Remove the pan from the heat and stir in the cream and reduced stock. Cover the pan and simmer, over a low heat, for about 15 minutes.

Remove the lobster from the pan. Remove the meat from the shells and place it in a serving dish. Keep hot. Mix the butter, corals, lobster liquid and flour to a smooth paste. Whisk this into the sauce, a little at a time, and simmer for at least 10 minutes. Reduce further, if necessary, until creamy. Then strain it over the lobster.

Instead of the mixture of butter, coral, liquid and flour, other recipes mix Béchamel sauce and egg yolk into the Newburg sauce. This gives a good consistency, but cannot compare with the flavour given by the coral and lobster liquid.

Frying or grilling lobster

Before we discuss these methods, there is one thing that must be made clear. In many countries, it is permissible to chop up live lobsters or other crustaceans when the lobster halves are to be fried or grilled in the shell. This is out of the question in Britain, for it is a heartless practice. Either freeze the lobsters (see page 97) or kill them by plunging into boiling water. For this, a large pan of fast-boiling water should be on hand into which the creatures are plunged headfirst, one after the other. The high temperature kills them very swiftly. If they are to be used in a cooked dish, they are removed from the pan after 2–4 minutes. To fry or grill them, they are then cut in half and the claws cracked, so that the claw meat cooks evenly with the body meat. With both methods, the flesh side is cooked first before turning over to cook the shell side.

There are some people who will only eat their lobster grilled, either from the grill of the stove or the barbecue, and they are not usually put off by the black (burnt) spots produced by careless barbecueing, even when eating lobster.

The preference of those who like their lobster fried is perhaps more easily justified. The lobster is first sealed all over in oil, before butter is added. This makes the noble seafood a real delicacy. The hot oil helps to break down the protein in the meat and to make it juicier.

Whether you grill or fry your lobster, you should always serve it with a good sauce. If eaten hot, classic sauces like Béarnaise, Hollandaise, Choron and Chantilly are excellent. Try accompanying it with a handful of wild rice, too. Alternatively, you might like to try a cold sauce, such as dill mayonnaise, Chantilly mayonnaise or a remoulade.

The method for crawfish is exactly the same. They are killed in boiling water, halved lengthways and then cooked in just the same way, whether grilled or fried.

Lobster from the frying pan – a very simple cooking method but one which is excellent for lobster. When fried in hot oil, the lobster shells give the meat extra flavour and the frying breaks down the proteins to keep the meat juicy.

Allow 500–600 g/18–21 oz uncooked lobster or crawfish per person. Shellfish of these 'ideal' weights are becoming more and more common on the market but, in fact, they often prove to be less than perfect because they contain relatively little meat. It is much better to buy a crawfish or lobster of 1 kg/2¼ lb to serve two, as you get more meat and it works out cheaper.

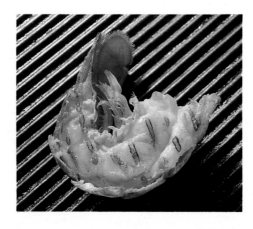

Lobster or crawfish tails can be grilled as well as whole shellfish. If you buy them frozen, make sure that they are completely defrosted before you cut the tail in half. Grill for 6–8 minutes per side, starting with the cut side.

SHELLFISH

Hot dishes with mussels, oysters and snails

'Don't despise my shellfish' . . . when one thinks of their taste, versatility and variety one would like to be able to change the words of the opera! We can't help wondering why it is that such a surprising number of chefs have a low opinion of shellfish (oysters excepted, of course), for they can be really delicious when they are properly prepared. This chapter invites you to embark on a voyage of discovery with mussels and oysters, to try your hand with fine recipes made with cockles, mussels, abalone and clams. You will be shown how to turn simple, inexpensive shellfish into veritable delicacies. The recipes are numerous and varied and provide ample opportunity for you to try out your own variations. The inkfish – cuttlefish and squid – have also been included in this chapter, and with good zoological reason, for they are invertebrate and can be grouped with shellfish. The snails have also sneaked in – although they are not, strictly speaking, seafood, we think they have a right to be included.

Steamed mussels

Moules à la vapeur

This is a basic recipe which can also be used to cook cockles, clams and whelks. Once cooked, the shellfish can either be eaten immediately or used in other dishes, such as Mussel kebabs.

4 kg/9 lb mussels
200 g/7 oz carrots
120 g/4½ oz leeks
2 onions
2 tablespoons oil
2 small garlic cloves
4 sprigs thyme
1 bay leaf
1 litre/1¾ pints white wine

Scrub the mussels under running water and, if thickly encrusted, scrape with a knife. Remove the 'beards' (byssus threads). Wash thoroughly once more. Throw away any mussels that are open, for these are bad. Drain the mussels in a sieve or colander.

Trim the carrots and leeks, peel the onions and chop all the vegetables. Heat the oil in a large pan and, over a low heat, fry the vegetables until transparent. Add the mussels and then the peeled, halved garlic cloves, the thyme and crumbled bay leaf. Pour on the white wine. Cover the pan and steam the mussels over a moderate heat for 6–8 minutes. The shells will open as they cook. Discard any that remain closed.

Now the mussels are ready to eat. Place them in bowls, add a little of the stock, and eat with bread and butter.

If you are going to use the mussels in another recipe, remove the flesh from the shells. Leave the stock to stand for 10 minutes, so that any sand or shell particles can settle, and then drain thoroughly.

Washing and debearding. Mussels must be thoroughly washed under cold, running water to remove any particles of sand or shell. It is a good idea to use a scrubbing brush for this. Remove the 'beards' – these are the byssus threads by which the creature attaches itself to posts or rocks. Hold the beard between thumb and index finger and pull it off.

Frying the vegetables and draining the cooked mussels. In a large pan, fry the diced vegetables in a little oil until transparent. Pile the cleaned mussels into the pan and add the herbs and wine. Cover the pan and steam for 6–8 minutes. They are now ready to eat. If you are going to use them in another recipe, drain in a sieve.

Whether you are cooking whelks or other univalves, the recipe is the same. Bring the whelks to the boil in a stock made with plenty of water, onion, leek rings and flat-leafed parsley, cover the pan and simmer for 15–20 minutes. Then drain in a sieve but catch the stock. To eat immediately, serve the whelks with a little stock. Alternatively, shell the whelks – preferably using a lobster fork – and filter the stock for use in another recipe.

Steamed cockles

Bucardes à la vapeur

2 kg/4½ lb cockles
100 g/4 oz onions
50 g/2 oz carrots
150 g/5 oz leeks
100 g/4 oz celery
1 garlic clove
4 tablespoons oil
2 bay leaves
½ parsley sprig
sprig of thyme
glass of white wine (optional)

Wash the cockles thoroughly several times in cold water and drain. Peel the onions. Trim the carrots, leeks and celery. Slice the onions. Dice the carrots, leeks, celery and peeled garlic. Fry the vegetables quickly in hot oil, until they begin to colour. Add the cockles and then the bay leaves, parsley and thyme. Add a glass of white wine, if you like. Cover the pan and steam, over a high heat, for 5–10 minutes, until the cockles have opened.

To serve, remove half of the shell from each cockle and arrange the cockles on plates.

To use the cockles in another recipe, remove them from the shells. Leave the stock to stand for 10 minutes and then pour off slowly, to get rid of sediment.

Steamed clams

Palourdes à la vapeur

1 kg/2¼ lb clams (Venus shells)
50 g/2 oz onions
50 g/2 oz carrots
100 g/4 oz leeks
2 tablespoons oil
sprig of thyme
1 bay leaf
6 tablespoons water
6 tablespoons white wine

Wash the clams thoroughly several times in cold water. Drain in a sieve. Peel and dice the onions. Peel the carrots, trim the leeks, wash and slice. Pour the oil into a pan and add the clams. Sprinkle with the chopped vegetables. Add the thyme and the crumbled bay leaf. Pour on the water and white wine. Cover the pan and steam for 8–10 minutes, until all the clams have opened.

Now the clams are ready to serve. Present them in the stock, with bread and butter.

Alternatively, if you are going to use them in another recipe, shell the clams and leave the stock to stand for 10 minutes. Then drain off carefully. Clams can be used to make delicious soups.

Cockle and Mussel pie

Ragoût de moules

A spicy stew of shellfish covered with puff pastry is one of the popular old-fashioned dishes that has recently been rediscovered. This recipe uses cockles, but it is just as good with any shellfish. Larger types of shellfish will, however, need to be cut up before steaming. One general point to watch is not to overcook the shellfish, or it will become tough. Nowadays, you can buy such good frozen puff pastry for the lids that you can leave it to the professional chefs to make their own.

1 (300-g/11-oz) packet frozen puff pastry
80 g/3 oz shallots, finely chopped
120 g/4½ oz carrots, finely diced
40 g/1½ oz celery, finely diced
80 g/3 oz leeks, finely diced
40 g/1½ oz butter
1 garlic clove, finely chopped
2 sprigs thyme, chopped
600 ml/1 pint mussel stock
400 g/14 oz shelled cockles
12 medium button mushrooms
flour and water, to coat
4 teaspoons finely chopped parsley
salt
freshly ground pepper
flour
2 egg yolks

Thaw the puff pastry, following the instructions on the packet. Meanwhile, fry the vegetables in the hot butter. Add the garlic and chopped thyme and cook for a few minutes more. Stir in the stock and reduce by about one-third. Remove the pan from the heat and stir in the cockles. Trim the mushrooms, dip in a mixture of flour and water (to prevent them turning brown), drain and slice. Add to the cockles with the parsley. Season to taste and then spoon the mixture into four cups or small moulds.

On a floured board, roll out the puff pastry to 5 mm/¼ in thick and leave to stand for 30 minutes. Cut rounds 2 cm/1 in larger than the diameter of the cups. Brush the edges carefully with beaten egg yolk and leave to dry for 5 minutes. Place the pastry lids on the cups and press firmly but carefully to the rims. Take care not to tear the pastry, for the steam formed during baking should not be able to escape. Brush the pastry lids with egg yolk.

Heat the oven to moderately hot (200 C, 400 F, gas 6) and bake the pies for 12 minutes, until golden-brown. The essential thing is for the pastry lid to remain intact, so that the trapped steam makes it rise like a soufflé.

Mussel ravioli with tomatoes and basil

Ravioli de moules à la crème de basilic

60 g/2¼ oz butter
4 tablespoons each finely diced carrots, shallots and leeks
275 ml/9 fl oz white wine
650 ml/22 fl oz Fish stock (page 97)
12 mussels, cleaned
4 egg yolks
salt
freshly ground white pepper
12 green pasta (ravioli verdi) cases
2 shallots, finely diced
4 tablespoons good-quality vermouth
60 g/2¼ oz chilled butter
4 large tomatoes, diced
4 teaspoons coarsely chopped basil
4 teaspoons whipped cream

Heat 40 g/1½ oz butter and quickly fry the vegetables. Add 6 tablespoons white wine and a scant 250 ml/8 fl oz Fish stock and reduce. Add the mussels, cover the pan and steam for 4–5 minutes. Remove and shell the mussels.

Reduce the stock further until the vegetables are just moist. Stir in the egg yolks. Heat until the mixture thickens, then add the mussels and season to taste. Wrap the mussels in green pasta to make ravioli and cook in fast-boiling, salted water for 5 minutes.

Heat 20 g/¾ oz butter in a frying pan and lightly fry the diced shallots. Add the vermouth, and the remaining white wine and Fish stock. Reduce to about one-

quarter and strain. Thicken the sauce with the chilled butter. Fold in the diced tomatoes, basil and cream and season to taste.

Mussels with olives and anchovies

Moules aux anchois

4 large tomatoes
2 shallots
1 garlic clove
50 g/2 oz butter
8 black olives
8 green olives
4 anchovy fillets, in oil
48 mussels, cooked in a little Fish stock for 2–3 minutes and shelled
4 teaspoons coarsely chopped fresh coriander

Scald the tomatoes with boiling water, cool in cold water and then peel and quarter them. Remove the seeds and dice the flesh. Peel and very finely chop the shallots and garlic. Fry in 10 g/½ oz butter for 10 minutes, without allowing them to colour.

Stone the olives, if necessary, and chop as finely as the shallots. Cut the drained anchovies into small pieces or purée in a food processor. Add both to the shallots and braise for 3–4 minutes, over a low heat.

Add the diced tomatoes and mussels. Heat through and thicken with the remaining butter. Arrange on individual plates and sprinkle with the coriander.

This dish is delicious with fresh white bread but many prefer to eat it with garlic bread, which goes well with most seafood dishes.

Mussels in white wine

Moules au vin blanc

Mussels steamed in white wine and water are as easy to make as they are delicious. If you use fish stock instead of water, you can add even more to the rich flavour created by the other ingredients in this recipe.

3 kg/6½ lb mussels
40 g/1½ oz butter
or 4 tablespoons olive oil
8 tablespoons finely diced carrots
8 tablespoons finely diced shallots
3 garlic cloves, finely diced
8 tablespoons finely diced leeks
8 tablespoons vermouth
400 ml/14 fl oz white wine
400 ml/14 fl oz Fish stock (page 97)
sprig of thyme

Carefully scrub the mussels under cold, running water. Remove the beards and drain in a sieve.

Heat the butter or oil in a large pan. Fry the diced carrot, shallots and garlic and then add the leek. Tip the mussels into the pan. Pour on the vermouth, white wine and fish stock. Top with the thyme and cover the pan. Steam the mussels for 7–8 minutes. Arrange the cooked mussels in soup plates and pour on a little of the stock to serve.

Oysters gratin

Huîtres au gratin

Serves 1:
6 good-quality, firmly closed oysters
coarse salt
4 tablespoons Fish stock (page 97)
4 tablespoons White wine sauce
(page 106)
dash of champagne or dry sparkling wine
1 tablespoon whipped cream
1 tablespoon Hollandaise sauce
salt
pinch of cayenne
1 tablespoon caviare
parsley, to garnish

Wash the oysters thoroughly and open them carefully. Remove the oyster flesh from the shells, pour the liquid into a bowl and reserve. Clean the lower halves of the shells, arrange on coarse salt in a suitable dish and place to warm.

Bring the Fish stock and oyster liquid to the boil in a small pan. Poach the oysters for only 5 seconds and keep them hot in the shells.

Reduce the stock by half. Add the White

wine sauce and reduce until smooth and thick. Cool slightly and flavour with champagne or sparkling wine. Gently fold in the whipped cream and Hollandaise sauce. Do not allow to boil from this point on. Season lightly with salt and cayenne. Pour the sauce over the oysters and grill until golden brown. Top with the caviare and garnish with parsley.

If you have no ready-made Hollandaise sauce, you can replace it with $\frac{1}{2}$ egg yolk beaten with 2 teaspoons melted butter.

Mussels with almond butter

Moules au beurre d'amande

Serves 1:
12 mussels
6 tablespoons breadcrumbs
4 tablespoons white wine
$\frac{1}{4}$ garlic clove, finely chopped
$\frac{1}{2}$ teaspoon finely chopped parsley
50 g/2 oz soft butter
1 teaspoon coarsely chopped almonds
salt
freshly ground white pepper
lemon slices, to garnish (optional)

Wash the mussels thoroughly, remove the beards and then steam (see page 148). Remove the upper half of the shells and keep the mussels hot in the lower half, in a suitable dish.

Soak the breadcrumbs in the white wine. Squeeze out the breadcrumbs and mix with the garlic, parsley and butter. Whisk until light and fluffy and then add the almonds. Season to taste and spread thickly over the mussels.

Brown in a hot oven or under the grill until golden. Serve immediately. Garnish with lemon slices, if liked.

Clams in curried cream

Gratin de palourdes épicées au curry

Serves 1:
6–8 clams
coarse salt
10 g/½ oz butter
½ teaspoon curry powder
250 ml/8 fl oz White wine sauce (page 106)
1 tablespoon whipped cream
1 tablespoon Hollandaise sauce
salt
freshly ground white pepper

Wash the clams thoroughly. Steam for 5–6 minutes (see page 149). Shell the clams and carefully remove the two strings attached to the muscle and the beards (gills). Wash both the meat and shells thoroughly once more and pat dry.

Fill a suitable dish with coarse salt. Return the clams to the shells, stand in the salt and keep hot. Heat the butter in a saucepan until frothy and lightly cook the curry powder. Add the White wine sauce and boil for 4–5 minutes. Allow to cool slightly. Fold in the whipped cream and Hollandaise sauce. Do not allow the sauce to boil from this point on. Season to taste.

Cover the hot clams with the sauce and brown under the grill. Serve immediately.

Scallops on spinach and mushrooms

Coquilles aux champignons et épinards

Serves 1:
2 scallops
10 g/½ oz butter
3 medium mushrooms, trimmed and sliced
100 g/4 oz spinach, blanched
salt
cayenne
5 tablespoons White wine sauce (page 106)
1 tablespoon Hollandaise sauce
1 tablespoon whipped cream

Prepare and open the scallops (see page 156). Remove the top shells. Take out the meat and the roes and keep separate. Place the lower halves of the shells to warm. Heat the butter in a saucepan until frothy and quickly fry the sliced mushrooms. Squeeze the excess moisture from the spinach, coarsely chop and add to the mushrooms. Braise and season with salt and cayenne. Spoon into the warm shells. Slice the scallop meat. Season the meat and roes and arrange on the spinach.

Bring the White wine sauce to the boil and then allow to cool slightly. Stir in the Hollandaise sauce and gently fold in the whipped cream. Do not allow the sauce to boil from this point on. Season with salt and cayenne. Spoon the sauce over the scallops and brown under the grill.

Venus clams with garlic butter

Petites palourdes au beurre d'ail

Serves 1:
2 tablespoons finely chopped parsley
1½ teaspoons chopped garlic
1 tablespoon chopped shallots
80 g/3 oz soft butter
salt
freshly ground white pepper
12 uncooked Venus clams
or other small clams
coarse salt

In a basin, work the parsley, garlic and shallots into the soft butter. Season to taste with salt and freshly ground white pepper. Whisk to give a uniform texture.

Carefully clean the Venus clams and steam as for mussels (see page 148). Remove the top halves of the shells and keep the bottoms, which contain the meat, hot in a dish of coarse salt (to keep them upright). Spread generously with the garlic butter. Brown in the oven or under the grill and serve hot.

Oyster kebab with bacon

Huitres à la broche

These oyster kebabs are based on the world-famous dish of oysters wrapped in bacon, known as 'Angels on horseback' or 'Anges à cheval'. One can't be sure, but the name may have been invented by some keen equestrian who was so taken with the dish that he made this evocative comparison.

Serves 1:
6–8 oysters, depending on size
6–8 thin rashers bacon
boiling water
5 tablespoons White wine sauce
(page 106)
saffron threads or powdered saffron
salt
freshly ground white pepper
1 tablespoon whipped cream
few drops pastis (optional)

Open the oysters and collect the juice. Derind the bacon, add to boiling water, return to the boil and then drain. (This makes the bacon less salty and helps it keep its shape under the grill.) When the bacon is cool, wrap each oyster in a rasher of bacon. Thread the rolls onto a skewer, stand on buttered aluminium foil and brown lightly for 3–4 minutes, under a preheated grill.

Bring the White wine sauce to the boil and add the oyster juice. Colour with the saffron and season. Reduce, and then fold in the whipped cream. If you like, add a little pastis (aniseed aperitif) for extra flavour. Drain the kebab on absorbent kitchen paper and serve on a bed of sauce.

Mussel kebab

Moules en brochettes

Serves 1:
8–10 mussels, depending on size
salt
freshly ground white pepper
lemon juice, to taste
flour
1 egg, beaten
sifted breadcrumbs
small parsley sprig
3 tablespoons remoulade sauce
good-quality vinegar or white wine
1 teaspoon chopped parsley

Steam the cleaned mussels in a wine and vegetable stock (see page 148). Shell and season the mussels with salt, pepper and

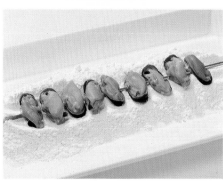

Coating mussel kebabs in breadcrumbs. This is not difficult but it is worth knowing a few tricks. When you thread the steamed mussels onto the skewer, leave a small space between so that you can get the breadcrumbs all around them. First, pour the flour, beaten egg and breadcrumbs into three shallow dishes. Then dip the kebabs in turn in the flour, egg and breadcrumbs, taking care not to miss any part of the mussels, so that they will brown evenly all over. Use a spoon to distribute the coatings evenly over the mussels.

lemon juice and thread onto a skewer. Dip in turn in flour, egg and breadcrumbs. Cook in a deep-fryer at 180 C/350 F until golden-brown. Alternatively, the kebab is delicious fried in butter in a frying pan.

Wash the parsley and pat dry. Deep-fry very quickly – count up to three and then remove from the oil. Drain and lightly salt.

Flavour the remoulade sauce with vinegar or white wine and chopped parsley. Serve the kebab on the sauce, with the fried parsley as a garnish.

Grilled scallops

Coquilles grillées

Serves 1:
4 scallops, preferably fresh, in the shell
salt
freshly ground white pepper
For the chive butter:
½ shallot
3 tablespoons dry white wine
150 ml/¼ pint Fish stock (page 97)
30 g/1¼ oz ice-cold butter
salt
white pepper
½ tablespoon chopped chives

Open the scallops (see page 156) and wash well. Drain on kitchen paper. Cut off the grey edge and separate the white meat (nut) from the roe (coral). Thread the nuts and corals alternately onto a skewer. Brown under the grill for 4 minutes. Season sparingly.

To make the chive butter, finely dice the half shallot. Bring to the boil in the white wine, reduce and add the Fish stock. Reduce to about one-third. Strain through a small sieve – a tea-strainer is best. Bring the sauce back to the boil. Add pieces of ice-cold butter and stir in. Bring back to the boil, season to taste, stir in the chives and serve with the kebab.

Oyster kebab with bacon, a world-famous delicacy. Threaded individually onto small cocktail sticks before grilling, these make a delicious starter or canapé with cocktails. Served as a kebab, they are equally good as a starter or main course. Serve with saffron sauce and rice or white bread.

Mussel kebab. This inexpensive shellfish is often described as the poor man's oyster, but one should not underestimate its fine flavour. Coated in breadcrumbs and deep-fried or – even more delicious – fried in butter, you will enjoy them to the full with a fine remoulade sauce.

Grilled scallops. Scallops are also one of the finest shellfish. The creamy-white meat, or nut, is threaded alternately onto skewers with the reddish-gold corals before grilling and seasoning sparingly. They are served with an extremely flavoursome chive butter.

Scallops

Scallops, which have become deservedly famous under their French name – Co-quilles St-Jacques – are one of the most popular shellfish in gourmet circles. Since they are found in large numbers in the sand and coral of the Mediterranean, most scallop recipes come from the Mediter-ranean countries. Top chefs throughout Europe like to have scallops in their kitchens and they turn them into the finest starters, savouries or even main courses. This says a great deal about the quality of these generously sized shellfish.

Whether intended for use by a pro-fessional chef or prepared at home, scallops must be absolutely fresh. If you cannot find live scallops, they are available frozen. If you are using live scallops, it is essential to prepare them properly before cooking. They take in sand with their food and will have to expel this before cooking. To encourage them to do this, once you have thoroughly cleaned the shells, stand them in salted water for several hours.

Opening scallops. After carefully washing and cleaning the scallops, hold them firmly in your left hand in a tea-towel, flat side uppermost. Slide a short, strong, pointed knife between the shells and cut through the muscle on the inside of the flat half (top left). Lift off the upper shell. Hold the lower half in your left hand. Using the knife.

loosen around the grey edge of the scallop and lift out of the shell (top right). Pull the grey edge away from the white meat and orange roe (bottom left). Carefully separate the white meat (known as the nut) from the roe (coral). Use the grey edge in fish stock.

Scallops with vegetables and garlic sauce

Coquilles aux légumes sauce d'ail

Serves 2:
30 g/1¼ oz carrots
30 g/1¼ oz celeriac
20 g/¾ oz turnips
30 g/1¼ oz courgettes
20 g/¾ oz cucumber
6 garlic cloves
300 ml/½ pint milk
40 g/1½ oz butter
10 g/½ oz onion, finely chopped
1 tablespoon good-quality vermouth
3 tablespoons Fish stock (page 97)
4 tablespoons crème fraîche
6 scallops, shelled
salt
freshly ground white pepper

Trim and wash the vegetables and carve into ovals. Blanch the carrots, celeriac and turnip for 8–10 minutes and the courgettes and cucumber for 3–5 minutes. Cool in iced water, drain and reserve in a covered bowl.

Cook the peeled garlic in the milk until soft and then blend in a liquidizer or food processor. Heat 20 g/¾ oz butter and fry the finely chopped onion until transparent. Add the vermouth and then the Fish stock. Reduce by half, stir in the crème fraîche and bring back to the boil. Season the shelled scallops and add to the boiling sauce. Remove the pan immediately from the heat and leave on the edge of the hob for 4–5 minutes, to cool slightly.

Lift the scallops out of the sauce and keep hot. Strain the sauce and then add the remaining butter and the liquidized milk and garlic. Warm the vegetables and scallops through in the sauce and serve immediately.

Scallops in spring greens

Coquilles en bette bouillie

12 unblemished leaves spring greens
salt
160 g/5½ oz white fish fillet, e.g. burbot
8 scallops, fresh or frozen
1 egg
cayenne
160 ml/5½ fl oz cream
fish, vegetable or chicken stock
dill, tarragon or parsley (optional)
2–3 juniper berries
1 onion, sliced
250 ml/8 fl oz White wine sauce (page 106)
salt and cayenne, to taste
40 g/1½ oz Lobster butter (page 104)

Wash the spring greens. Blanch for 5 seconds in fast-boiling, salted water and transfer immediately to iced water. Drain on a tea-towel. Cover and keep in the refrigerator.

To make the filling, first trim the fish. Shell fresh scallops or defrost and shell frozen ones. Trim them and separate the nuts from the roes.

Season the egg with salt and cayenne and then beat. Blend the white fish, scallop roes and egg in a liquidizer or food processor, strain through a fine-mesh sieve, place on ice and stir in the cream.

Cut the thick stalks out of the blanched spring green leaves and place a half leaf over the opening that this leaves in the centre of each leaf. Cover with the filling, leaving about 1.5 cm/¾ in free around the edge. Place a scallop at the wider end of each leaf. Fold the sides of the leaf over and roll up.

Fill a steamer to a depth of about 2 cm/1 in with fish, vegetable or chicken stock. Add dill, tarragon or parsley to taste, the juniper berries and onion and bring to the boil. Place the green rolls in the steamer basket, cover the pan and steam for 5–6 minutes.

Bring the White wine sauce to the boil. Adjust the seasoning with salt and cayenne. Work in the Lobster butter. Pour the sauce onto plates and serve two scallop rolls on each.

Cut out the thick stalks, once the spring greens have been blanched and cooled. Cover the gap with a half leaf. Cover with the filling to 1.5 cm/¾ in from the edge. Place a scallop at the wider end and roll in the leaf. Cook in a steamer.

Scallops in saffron

Coquilles au safran

16 large scallops, in the shell
7 g/¼ oz shallots, finely chopped
20 g/¾ oz butter
salt
freshly ground white pepper
5 tablespoons Fish stock (page 97)
5 tablespoons white wine
3 tablespoons cream
generous pinch of saffron threads
60 g/2¼ oz tomatoes, diced
1 tablespoon chopped parsley

Open the scallops using a strong, pointed knife, cut through the muscle and lift off the top half of the shell. Using a knife, remove the meat and roe and wash thoroughly. Remove the grey rim. Carefully separate the meat (nut) and roe (coral). Halve the nuts and leave to drain on a tea-towel.

Fry the finely chopped shallots in the hot butter in a sauté pan, without allowing them to colour. Season the scallop meat and roes and add to the pan. Pour in the Fish stock and white wine and simmer for 2 minutes. Remove the scallops and roes from the pan and keep hot.

Reduce the stock. Stir in the cream and saffron threads and reduce until nice and thick. Add the tomatoes and parsley, heat through and adjust the seasoning. Return the scallops and roes to the sauce, transfer to a serving dish and serve.

Clams with tomatoes and parsley

Petites palourdes à la tomate

Serves 2:
1 kg/2¼ lb vongoli (Venus clams)
2 firm, ripe tomatoes
2 tablespoons good-quality oil
40 g/1½ oz shallots, finely chopped
5 tablespoons white wine
5 tablespoons shellfish or fish stock
100 g/4 oz tomato purée
1 tablespoon chopped parsley
salt
freshly ground white pepper

Wash the clams and rinse under cold, running water. Discard any open or cracked shells and drain the rest in a colander. Cut a cross in the tomato skins, scald with boiling water, chill in cold water, peel and dice. Heat the oil in a large frying pan and fry the shallots until transparent. Add the clams, cook for a few minutes and then pour in the white wine and stock. Stir in the tomato purée. Bring to the boil, cover the pan and cook for about 5 minutes. Remove the clams from the pan.

Reduce the stock slightly. Reheat the clams in the sauce with the chopped tomatoes and parsley. Season to taste and arrange on two serving plates.

Razor clams in wine and shallot butter

Couteaux au vin blanc et au beurre d'échalote

Serves 2:
16–20 Razor clams
2 tablespoons olive oil
20 g/¾ oz shallots, finely chopped
3½ tablespoons white wine
3 tablespoons Fish stock (page 97)
60 g/2¼ oz butter
salt
freshly ground white pepper

Soak the Razor clams in cold water to clean them, rinse under running water and pat dry with absorbent kitchen paper. Heat the olive oil in a frying pan. Add the clams and fry for a few minutes. Add the shallots and fry until golden-brown. Pour on the white wine and Fish stock and bring quickly to the boil. Remove the razor clams from the pan.

Strain the stock and reduce by half. Melt the butter in the stock, a little at a time. Season to taste. Reheat the clams in the butter and serve immediately.

Tartufi di mare with fennel and garlic

Petites palourdes au fenouil

Serves 2:
1 kg/2¼ lb tartufi (Venus clams)
80 g/3 oz onions
50 g/2 oz carrots
3 tablespoons olive oil
6 whole garlic cloves, peeled
150 g/5 oz fennel, sliced
250 ml/8 fl oz light, dry red wine
6 tablespoons cream
½ teaspoon salt
1 tablespoon paprika
1 tablespoon chopped dill

Because of their rough shells, the Venus clams must be scrubbed very thoroughly under cold, running water. Peel and very finely chop the onions and carrots. Heat the oil in a large pan and fry the onion and carrot for a few minutes. Add the peeled,

whole garlic cloves and the sliced fennel. Cook for 3–4 minutes. Pour in the wine. Pile the clams into the pan, cover and steam until the clams have opened. Pour the cream over the clams. Season with salt and paprika and cook, uncovered, for a further 5 minutes. Sprinkle with dill and serve.

Trough shells with julienne vegetables and thyme

Mactres à la thym

Serves 2:
1 kg/2¼ lb trough shells
60 g/2¼ oz carrots
60 g/2¼ oz courgettes
1 tablespoon olive oil
200 ml/7 fl oz water
3½ tablespoons white wine
2 garlic cloves
1 teaspoon chopped fresh thyme
salt
freshly ground white pepper

Soak the trough shells in cold water and rinse under cold, running water. Drain in a colander. Trim and wash the carrots and courgettes and cut into fine strips. Heat the olive oil in a large pan and quickly fry the julienne carrots, stirring frequently. Add the trough shells, water, white wine, unpeeled garlic and thyme. Cover the pan, bring to the boil and cook, shaking the pan from time to time so that all the shellfish cook evenly. When the shellfish begin to open, add the courgettes. Cover the pan and steam for a further 30 seconds. Take the garlic out of the pan and season the trough shells. Arrange on two serving plates, with the stock.

Abalone with Chinese mushrooms

Oreilles de Saint-Pierre aux champignons

Serves 2:
200 g/7 oz fresh abalones, shelled
20 g/¾ oz dried Chinese mushrooms
10 g/½ oz butter
10 g/½ oz shallots, finely chopped
1 tablespoon Port
salt
freshly ground white pepper

200 ml/7 fl oz White butter sauce, made with red Bermuda onion (page 99)
cayenne

Boil the abalones for 5–6 hours, until tender, changing the water several times. Soak the mushrooms in lukewarm water. Clean the abalones, using a soft brush, and remove the gills and guts. Finely slice the meat (after cleaning, you will have about half the original weight). Squeeze all excess moisture from the mushrooms.

Heat the butter in a saucepan. Fry the shallots and then pour on the Port. Lightly season, cover the pan and cook until tender. Stir in the abalone slices, adjust the seasoning and arrange on two serving plates.

Stir the White butter sauce into the stock. Season with salt and cayenne. Pour the sauce over the abalones and serve with the mushrooms.

Abalones are not unlike calf's tongue in flavour and consistency.

Snails in Meursault make a delicious light starter. For a starter, half a dozen snails per person will be enough. For a main course, you will need a dozen or even more. You can buy snail pans to take either half a dozen or a dozen.

Bourgogne snails

Bourgogne and spire snails really deserve a chapter to themselves, for they do not really fit into any group. Since it is impossible to ingore them, we have boldly included them in this chapter. Since sea snails obviously find their rightful place here, we have taken the liberty of including land snails along with them – for, whilst they are not shellfish, they undeniably also have shells!

Snails are prepared for cooking in the following way. Live snails should be kept for three days in a closed, but not airtight basket. This will allow the gut to be emptied. The snails should then be washed and scrubbed several times before pre-cooking in fast-boiling water for 15 minutes. Using a snail fork, the snails are then removed from the shells. Cut off the head and the black part at the other end. Rub the flesh several times with coarse salt, but not too vigorously, rinsing it off each time with a mixture of vinegar and water. There should be no slime left on the snail at this point. Clean the shells thoroughly. Alternatively, you can buy excellent conserved snails, including spire snails from Southeast Asia and frozen Bourgogne snails.

The cooked snails are now ready to eat. They are easiest to eat with special cutlery sets, consisting of a pair of specially shaped tongs and a two-pronged fork. You hold the shell in the tongs in one hand and use the fork to pull out the snail.

Snails in Meursault

Escargots au vin blanc

48 live or conserved snails
2 tablespoons oil
60 g/2¼ oz shallots, diced
1 garlic clove, chopped
¼ teaspoon salt
1 bouquet garni (1 piece leek, 1 piece celeriac, ½ onion, 2 cloves and thick parsley sprig)
500 ml/17 fl oz white wine (preferably Meursault)
250 ml/8 fl oz chicken stock
1 slice bread, with crust removed
3 tablespoons Marc du Bourgogne (grape spirit)
48 snail shells
For the snail butter:
300 g/11 oz soft butter
40 g/1½ oz shallots, finely chopped
2 garlic cloves, crushed
1–2 tablespoons chopped herbs (parsley, basil, thyme, sage and rosemary)
salt
freshly ground pepper

Prepare live snails or drain conserved ones. Heat the oil in a large pan and fry the shallots and garlic. Add the salt, the bouquet garni and the snails. Stir until hot, then add the white wine and chicken stock. Simmer very gently over a low heat, so that the surface of the liquid barely ripples. Soak the slice of bread in the Marc de Bourgogne and crumble it into the stock 5 minutes before the end of the cooking time. Remove from the heat and leave to cool. Cook canned snails for only half the time, in only half the amount of liquid.

Spoon ½ teaspoon shallot mixture into each snail shell and then put in the snails. Beat together the ingredients for the snail butter and season to taste. Fill the opening of the shells with the butter. Set the oven at moderately hot to hot (200–220 C, 400–425 F, gas 6–7). Place the snail shells in a snail pan and bake in the hot oven until the butter is frothy.

Snails Provençal

Escargots Provençals

2 dozen Bourgogne or spire snails (boiled or canned)
2 tablespoons vegetable oil
40 g/1½ oz shallots, diced
1 garlic clove, chopped
50 g/2 oz red pepper, finely chopped
50 g/2 oz mushrooms, thinly sliced
50 g/2 oz boiled ham, finely diced
6 tablespoons dry white wine
2 tablespoons sweet (cream) sherry
250 ml/8 fl oz fish or chicken stock
2–3 leaves basil, finely chopped
2 leaves sage, finely chopped
parsley sprig, finely chopped
1–2 rosemary leaves, crumbled
sprig of thyme
100 g/4 oz tomatoes, diced
salt
white pepper
paprika
4 tablespoons crème fraîche

Drain the Bourgogne or spire snails. Heat the oil in a pan and fry the shallots and garlic. Then add and fry the red pepper, mushrooms and ham. Add the white wine, sherry and stock. Add the snails and herbs and simmer for 20 minutes. Warm through the tomatoes in the mixture. Season with salt, pepper and paprika and serve with a spoonful of crème fraîche for each portion.

Ink fish

While squid, cuttlefish and octopuses are obviously not shellfish, zoologically speaking they belong to the same group – the molluscs – so we have taken the liberty of including ink fish here. In some ways, it would be more correct to think of them as ink snails.

The flesh of these creatures, which are plentiful in all the world's seas, is especially popular in the Far East, the Middle East and the Mediterranean. They have recently become popular in the United States, too, where squid in particular is eaten more and more.

The mild, fishy flavour of ink fish goes really well with highly flavoured ingredients such as onion, garlic, tomato, green pepper and olive oil. The best-flavoured ingredient of all, and one that comes naturally with most ink fish, is the ink itself – a brownish-black liquid produced through the ink jet. This is excellent for use in sauces to serve with the ink fish, for it not only adds flavour and colour but also helps thicken the sauce. Cooking 'en su tinta' (in its own ink) is the best-known method of cooking ink fish.

Squid and cuttlefish are also the ideal shape for stuffing. The bodies are sack-shaped and smaller ones, of around 15–20 cm/6–8 in long are the ideal size for one portion. In addition to the stuffings given in the following recipes, you can try prawns, fish or other sorts of vegetables.

Ink fish in its own ink

Calamares en su tinta

1 kg/2¼ lb ink fish (cuttlefish or squid)
120 g/4¼ oz onions
2 garlic cloves
4 tablespoons oil
40 g/1½ oz fresh, white breadcrumbs
salt
freshly ground white pepper
pig's caul, for wrapping
250 ml/8 fl oz dry white wine
2 large tomatoes, peeled and chopped
pinch of chilli powder
potato starch
dash of Armagnac (brandy)

Wash the ink fish thoroughly and prepare as shown in the step-by-step illustration.

Empty the ink into a basin. Keep the bag to one side and cut the tentacles into thin pieces or strips.

Peel the onions and garlic. Reserve 1 onion and 1 garlic clove. Heat 2 tablespoons oil and quickly fry the pieces of ink fish with the finely chopped onions and crushed garlic. Cover the pan and cook over a low heat for 30 minutes. Add a dash of water, if necessary. Add the breadcrumbs and season to taste.

Stuff the bag of the ink fish with this mixture. Sew up the opening or wrap in pieces of pig's caul. Heat the remaining oil and fry the stuffed bags with the onion and garlic you kept back, both chopped. Add the white wine and then the tomatoes and season sparingly with chilli powder. Simmer, uncovered, for about 30 minutes.

Stir a little potato starch into the ink. Stir this mixture into the ink fish juices, to flavour and thicken the sauce. Flavour with Armagnac and adjust the seasoning.

Ink fish in batter

Sépia frites

1 kg/2¼ lb cuttlefish or squid
For the batter:
3 eggs
150 g/5 oz flour
1 tablespoon oil
200 ml/7 fl oz light beer
½ teaspoon salt
freshly ground white pepper
vegetable fat, for frying

Prepare the cuttlefish or squid, as demonstrated in the step-by-step illustrations. Cut the tentacles into strips and the body into even rings. Drain thoroughly on absorbent kitchen paper.

To make the batter, first separate the eggs. Beat the yolks with the flour and oil until smooth and then gradually beat in the beer. Season and leave to stand for about 30 minutes. Whisk the egg whites until stiff and fold into the mixture. Heat the frying fat to around 175 C/350 F.

Coat the pieces of ink fish in batter, drain slightly and deep-fry in the hot fat for about 5 minutes, until crisp and golden. Lift out of the fat using a slotted spoon and drain on absorbent kitchen paper. Keep hot and serve on white paper serviettes.

1 **Cut open the ink fish**. First, cut off the head and the tentacles with a sharp knife. Cuttlefish are normally prepared in the same way as squid (pages 164/165), but if you need the ink they must be carefully slit open lengthways.

2 **Take out the cuttlebone**. To do this, carefully open out the slit along the ink fish, so that you can see and get hold of the bone. At the base of the body, you will now see the ink sac and inside it the dark-coloured ink – be careful not to break it.

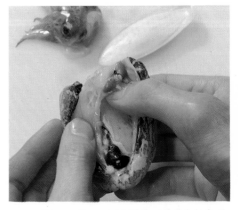

3 **Remove the gut**. Hold the ink fish in both hands and, using one thumb, carefully loosen the gut, taking care not to damage the ink sac. The ink is used to flavour and slightly to thicken sauces. Lift out the gut in a piece and discard it.

4 **Squeeze out the ink**. This is best done between thumb and index finger. Squeeze the dark liquid into a bowl and keep until required. To squeeze out the ink, hold the ink fish in both hands and squeeze the ink sac between your thumb and index finger.

5 **Cut the bag-shaped body into even strips**, after first washing the ink fish. Also, cut the tentacles off the head in such a way as to leave them joined by a narrow ring of flesh. Pat dry carefully on absorbent kitchen paper, so that the batter will stick.

8 **Put the pieces of ink fish into hot fat**, one at a time, using the carving fork. It is best to use pure vegetable fat, for this can be heated to a high temperature without burning. The fat should be heated to 175–180 C (345–355 F). Obviously, you should keep an eye on the pan throughout to avoid the ink fish colouring too much. You should be able to fry 15 to 20 pieces in one batch, added one after the other, depending on the size of the deep-fryer. They should be taken out of the pan in the same order that they went in and thoroughly drained.

6 **Fold the whisked egg white into the batter**. Beat together the egg yolks, flour, oil, light beer, salt and white pepper to make a batter. Leave to stand for 30 minutes and then fold in the whisked egg whites. This makes the batter light, so that it will fry really crisply.

7 **Coat the inkfish pieces** in batter. Spear the pieces one at a time on a carving fork and dip in the batter to cover completely. If you dip each piece of ink fish in flour first, the batter will stick better and coat the ink fish more evenly.

9 **Fresh, fried ink fish** – a real delicacy that doesn't cost much. Cold, spicy sauces such as paprika chutney, or even a sweet and sour mango chutney, go excellently with fried ink fish.

Skinning squid. First, thoroughly wash the squid. Then hold the body firmly in one hand and, grasping the skin in your other hand, pull it off. Next, get hold of the tentacles and pull them out of the body cavity. Using a sharp knife, cut off the tentacles just above the eyes, so that they remain joined by a narrow band of flesh. Hold the tentacles upside down at the centre and, using your index finger, push out and remove the beak.

Remove the transparent whalebone. Then carefully wash the edible parts, i.e. the tentacles and body with the fins. Pull the fins off the body and use with the tentacles for the stuffing. If you plan to fry the squid in batter (see pages 162/163), the body will have to be cut into even strips and the fins and tentacles into pieces. If it is to be stuffed, the bag-shaped body must be left whole.

To make the stuffing, finely dice the fins and tentacles with a sharp knife. Make sure that you dry the legs and fins well before chopping. Seal the pieces of squid in hot olive oil, stirring continuously. Fry diced white bread in hot butter until golden, turning continuously. Add both to a mixture of leek, onion, carrot and garlic, cooked in fish stock and reduced until just moist.

Stuffed squid

Calmar farci

4 (250-g/8¾-oz) squid
200 g/7 oz crustless white bread
120 g/4½ oz butter
200 g/7 oz onions
4 garlic cloves
200 g/7 oz leeks
200 g/7 oz carrots
600 ml/1 pint Fish stock (page 97)
8 tablespoons olive oil
4 tablespoons chopped parsley
4 egg yolks
salt
freshly ground white pepper
1 piece pig's caul, soaked in water
Vegetable butter sauce (page 118),
to serve

Wash, skin and clean the squid. Keep the body, fins and tentacles to use later. Finely dice the bread and fry slowly in 80 g/3 oz melted butter until golden-brown, stirring continuously. Drain in a metal sieve. Peel the onions and garlic. Trim and wash the leeks and carrots. Dice all the vegetables and then fry them in a pan in 40 g/1½ oz butter, without allowing them to colour. Add the Fish stock and reduce until the vegetables are just moist.

Wash the squid tentacles and fins once more, then wipe dry and cut into small cubes. Heat 4 tablespoons olive oil in a frying pan and quickly fry the squid pieces, over a high heat. Remove from the pan immediately and add to the vegetables, with the fried bread. Mix in the parsley and egg yolks and season to taste.

Cut the soaked pig's caul into four equal pieces. Spread them out and pat dry with absorbent kitchen paper. Fill the squid bodies with the stuffing and wrap in the caul. Heat the remaining 4 tablespoons olive oil in an ovenproof dish and seal the stuffed squid. Heat the oven to moderately hot to hot (220–220 C, 400–425 F, gas 6–7) and roast the squid for 20 minutes.

Serve with the Vegetable butter sauce recommended for Marron with cockle stew (see page 118) and saffron rice. Leaf spinach and parsley rice would also go well with this dish.

One important tip: always serve ink fish immediately, for the flesh can become tough if left to stand.

Stuffing the body. Add egg yolk and chopped parsley to the stuffing. Mix thoroughly and season sparingly, to taste. Hold the body of the squid in one hand and spoon in the stuffing with a teaspoon. Do not overfill, as the stuffing swells slightly as it cooks. Wrap the stuffed squid in a piece of pig's caul that you have first softened in water. If you cannot obtain pig's caul, you can secure the end of the body with a wooden cocktail stick or sew it up with kitchen twine. Fry in olive oil to seal and then roast in a moderately hot to hot oven.

REGIONAL SEAFOOD DISHES

Local specialities from around the world

This chapter includes tasty savoury dishes with an international flavour and brings together local dishes from all around the world. These seafood specialities are a far cry from the elitism of Nouvelle or Haute Cuisine, yet fulfil all our modern culinary requirements. Here, once more, success is dependent upon the quality and freshness of the ingredients. While this is desirable for the vegetables used, it is absolutely essential for the seafood cooked with them. In any part of the world, on any coastline – in countries bordering the Atlantic, the Pacific, the seas of Asia or inland seas – in every coastal region, seafood is part of the everyday fare. Yet the dishes which are taken for granted in these areas can become real delicacies in other parts of the world. It is all a question of availability, price and rarity.

One example is Cioppino, a staple dish in San Francisco and thought to be Mexican in origin. This stew of clams, Dungeness crabs and root vegetables is as much a part of everyday life in San Francisco as Zarzuela, with its ink fish, scampi, mussels, fish, tomatoes and garlic, is in Spain – or Paella, which could never be the same without seafood. Jambalaya, a Creole lobster dish, is a familiar dish around New Orleans. How lucky one would be to live in a place where lobsters could be bought cheaply from the local fish market!

Clam chowder

Clam chowder is typical of most regional specialities in that there is no one authentic recipe – instead we have numerous variations on the same theme, each admittedly containing the same basic ingredients. The basic ingredients of a clam chowder are – in addition to clams – onions and potatoes, and bacon or ham, which gives the dish its distinctive smoky flavour. For a richer chowder, you can replace some of the milk with cream. In Manhattan clam chowder, however, there is neither milk nor cream, but plenty of fresh vegetables.

24 chowder clams (total weight
6–8 kg/13–18 lb)
6 rashers rindless bacon, diced
300 g/11 oz potatoes, diced
250 g/9 oz smoked pork, diced
100 g/4 oz onions, diced
250 g/9 oz fresh sweetcorn
1 teaspoon salt
½ teaspoon coarsely ground pepper
1 slice bread, diced
750 ml/1¼ pints milk

Scrub the clams thoroughly under running water. Open them and catch the liquid in a jug to use later. Remove the clams from the shells and then finely chop or mince them. Continue as shown in the step-by-step illustrations.

Clambake

A good example of how geography determines what constitutes everyday fare. The coasts of New England, so rich in seafood, are not merely a source of cheap clams. The famous Maine lobster is another local speciality and is a popular feature of a real clambake.

The baking of shellfish in the ground, a primeval cooking method that modern-day Americans have learnt from the Indians, has become a popular pastime. Along the east coast of the United States, a clambake is now a regular feature of holiday weekends by the sea.

The procedure is quite simple. You need to dig a pit about 30 cm/1 ft deep in the sand (or in your garden) and half-fill it with large stones. You then pile dry wood on top of the stones, light the fire and keep it going for three to four hours, until the stones are really hot. The ash is then raked out, aluminium foil spread over the stones and clams and corn cobs baked on the foil. For special occasions, add a small (600-g/21-oz) lobster per person. The east coast fishermen call these individual-sized lobsters 'chickens'. You then cover the whole thing with lots of damp seaweed and/or a damp groundsheet. After about an hour, you can uncover the food. Be sure to allow yourself time to enjoy the aroma before you start on your lobster.

1 **Open the clams**. This looks more difficult than it is. When you have scrubbed the clams under running water, dry them and grip firmly. Push the blade of a strong knife into the front end of the shell and then turn the shell so that the knife runs all around it.

2 **Remove the flesh**. Using the knife, cut through the muscle on the upper shell. Cut to the hinge and open the clam. Catch the liquid. Run the knife around the lower shell to loosen the flesh and remove it from the shell.

3 **Arrange the ingredients in layers**. First fry the diced bacon to bring out its full flavour, and then cover with layers of the remaining ingredients. First the potatoes, then pork, onion and sweetcorn. Lastly, add the chopped clams with their liquid.

4 **Season well**. Season each layer with salt and freshly ground pepper. As you add the layers, shake the pan occasionally to settle the ingredients. Unless they are fairly densely packed, they will absorb too much liquid and become mushy.

5 **Fill up with milk**. First cut the bread into tiny cubes and sprinkle over the pan. This gives the chowder a little body. Then add enough milk almost to cover. Cover the pan and place in a preheated moderately hot oven (200 C, 400 F, gas 6).

6 **Clam chowder is a cross between a soup and a stew.** All the ingredients should be cooked through but the potatoes should be intact and the chowder should be neither too runny nor too dry. It is served with fresh, farmhouse bread.

Zarzuela de Mariscos

Translated into English, the name of this dish means 'seafood operetta'. It is a dish that can taste different every time you cook it. The Catalonians, who invented it, say that it *should* taste different every time. This is not difficult in an area with such a varied supply of seafood. You can use almost any type of seafood, provided that you keep the ratio of fish, crustaceans and shellfish more or less the same.

1 kg/2¼ lb mussels
500 g/18 oz prawns
500 g/18 oz swordfish
(or other firm-fleshed fish)
6 tablespoons olive oil
400 g/14 oz squid
120 g/4¼ oz onions, finely diced
2 garlic cloves, crushed
500 g/18 oz ripe tomatoes
1 chilli, finely chopped
6 tablespoons dry white wine
6 tablespoons fish or chicken stock
2 tablespoons Spanish brandy
1 bay leaf
a few saffron threads
1 teaspoon salt
freshly ground pepper
juice of ½ lemon
2 tablespoons chopped fresh herbs
(thyme, parsley and marjoram)
3 tablespoons black olives

Prepare as shown in the accompanying step-by-step illustrations, but first scrub and debeard the mussels and then boil them until they have opened. Remove the heads and the gut from the prawns. Cut the fish into cubes and stir in the heated oil for about 2 minutes.

1 **Prepare the squid**. Cut off the head. Remove the innards and ink sac (see page 164). Wash thoroughly. Cut the tentacles off the head and press out the beak. Skin the body and cut the flesh into strips 1 cm/½ in wide.

2 **Fry the onion, then add the squid**. Heat 2 tablespoons oil in a frying pan and lightly fry the diced onion with the crushed garlic, stirring with a wooden spatula. After about 6–8 minutes, add the cleaned, even-sized pieces of squid.

Cioppino

This seafood stew from California is made with the best the Pacific can provide. You can use any seafood available, provided one of them is crab. Here is a typical recipe:

4 tablespoons vegetable oil
100 g/4 oz onions, finely chopped
1 garlic clove, crushed
100 g/4 oz green peppers
150 g/5 oz celery
4 tomatoes, peeled and deseeded
½ teaspoon salt
pepper
2 Dungeness crabs or Common crabs
(total weight about 1 kg/2¼ lb)
300 g/11 oz Gaper clams or scallops,
shelled
1 kg/2¼ lb mussels
1 tablespoon chopped parsley
500 ml/17 fl oz dry white wine

3 **Add the tomatoes**. First blanch them in boiling water, then peel them and cut into pieces. Remove the seeds. Finely chop the chilli (after scraping out the seeds) and add to the tomatoes. Cook gently for 3–4 minutes over a low heat, stirring occasionally.

4 **Add the wine and stock**. Add the wine first and simmer for 2–3 minutes, then add the fish stock and brandy. Cook for a further 6–8 minutes, uncovered, stirring from time to time. Add the bay leaf and saffron threads, and stir.

Heat the oil in a pan and lightly fry the onion and garlic. Dice the green peppers and celery and add to the onion. Simmer for 5–6 minutes. Add the tomatoes and season to taste. Add only the cracked claws and the body meat from the crabs. Add the clams or scallops, with the roes. Scrub the mussels under running water, debeard and add to the pan. Sprinkle with the parsley and pour on the wine. Cook over a low heat, on the hob or in the oven for about 15 minutes.

5 **Season the Zarzuela**. Season sparingly, as the seafood is naturally quite salty. Add a little salt at a time and taste each time to make sure you do not over-season. Finally, add the lemon juice and chopped herbs and stir well.

6 **Add the prepared seafood**. First the fish, then the prawns and mussels. Stir in carefully and simmer over a low heat for a further 6–8 minutes. If necessary, adjust the seasoning with salt, pepper and lemon juice. Add the olives just before serving.

Paella Valenciana

An everyday Spanish dish that has become an international speciality, born of the Spaniards' love of stews and anything that comes out of the sea. The ingredients of a Paella can vary considerably but the nearer you are to the coast, the more seafood it will contain. Nevertheless, it should also contain chicken and pork (even in the form of sausage or ham), for only the right combination can produce the typical flavour of a Paella Valenciana. To bring out the full flavour of the sausage, it should be added immediately after the onion. Alternatively, it is added at the end, just before the dish goes into the oven.

500 g / 18 oz mussels
300 g / 11 oz trough or Venus shells
300 g / 11 oz ink fish
(small cuttlefish or squid)
400 g / 14 oz medium-sized prawns
200 g / 7 oz red peppers
200 g / 7 oz tomatoes
3 tablespoons olive oil
120 g / 4¼ oz onions, finely chopped
1 garlic clove
150 g / 5 oz garlic sausage (chorizo)
½ chicken (about 750 g / 1½ lb)
375 ml / 13 fl oz chicken stock
6 tablespoons dry white wine
200 g / 7 oz short-grain rice
a few saffron threads
½ teaspoon salt
pepper
150 g / 5 oz fresh peas, shelled

Prepare the Paella as shown in the accompanying step-by-step photographs, but first wash the shellfish under running water and remove the beards. Prepare the ink fish (see page 162) and cut into pieces. Use only the tails of the prawns and remove the gut from each one. Halve the peppers, remove the seeds and cut into strips. Peel and dice the tomatoes. *NB:* The Paella needs sufficient liquid to cook properly, so check after the first 15 minutes to see if you need to add any extra.

1 **Fry the onion and garlic sausage.** Heat the olive oil in a frying pan and lightly fry the chopped onion and crushed garlic until the onion is transparent. Add the sliced sausage and fry over a high heat, stirring continuously, to prevent the sausage from sticking to the bottom of the pan.

2 **Add the chicken, squid and vegetables.** First add the chicken in large chunks and seal over a high heat. Then add the prepared squid, followed by the peppers and tomatoes. Cook gently for 5 minutes before adding the stock and white wine. Stir well to combine all the ingredients.

3 **Stir in the rice and saffron, and season.** Then bring the mixture to the boil. After about 10 minutes, gently fold in the peas, prawns and shellfish. Transfer the pan to a preheated moderate oven (180 C, 350 F, gas 4) and bake for 15–25 minutes, adding extra stock if necessary.

Jambalaya

This is a Creole dish found in many different forms in the southern states of America and in Central America. Rice, tomatoes and crustaceans are, however, essential ingredients. The dish is typified by its hotness (provided by pepper and chillies). Often, the fleshy oysters found in the Gulf of Mexico are included. These are shelled and arranged over the rice a few minutes before the end of the cooking time, so that they solidify but remain tender.

2 medium green peppers
500 g/18 oz tomatoes
100 g/4 oz boiled ham
250 g/8¾ oz prawns, shelled
4 crab claws (Stone or Common crab)
2 (150–200 g/5–7 oz) crawfish tails
4 rashers rindless smoked streaky bacon
80 g/3 oz onions, finely chopped
1 garlic clove, crushed
200 g/7 oz long-grain rice (parboiled)
½ teaspoon salt
freshly ground pepper
sprig of thyme
1 teaspoon lemon balm
1 chilli, finely chopped
2 teaspoons lime or lemon juice
chicken stock, to cover

The step-by-step photographs alongside show how Jambalaya is made but first the ingredients have to be prepared. Halve, deseed and dice the green peppers. Blanch, peel and quarter the tomatoes. Cut the ham into 1-cm/½-in strips. Remove the gut from the prawns. Crack the crab claws with a heavy knife or weight, so that they will cook evenly. Cut the crawfish into 2–3-cm/¾–1-in slices and remove the gut.

While the Jambalaya is baking, check from time to time that there is sufficient liquid and add a little more stock as and when necessary.

1 **Fry the vegetables.** First, dry-fry the diced bacon and then lightly fry the onions in the bacon fat, over a moderate heat. Add the crushed garlic and finally the diced peppers. Simmer the vegetable mixture for about 5 minutes, or until the peppers are tender and the onion transparent.

2 **Sprinkle in the rice** and stir until it is transparent and beginning to swell. Add the salt, pepper, thyme and lemon balm. Marinate the finely chopped chilli in the lime juice for 10 minutes before adding it to the other ingredients in the pan. Make sure that the chilli is well distributed through the dish.

3 **Stir in the ham and tomatoes.** Pour on the chicken stock and cook over a high heat for 5 minutes. Then fold in the prawns, crab claws and crawfish. Set the oven at moderate (180 C, 350 F, gas 4). Place the pan in the preheated oven and cook for about 20 minutes.

Empanada de Mariscos

They, say that the empanada originated in Galicia, but it is found everywhere throughout the Spanish-speaking world. Seafood empanadas are at their best in La Coruna or Vigo in Spain, where the shellfish, prawns and squid are fresh and of top quality. Empanadas can take the form of individual pasties but it is more usual to make them as large, round pies. They can be served as a main course or as a snack, depending on the size of the portions.

For the pastry:
500 g/18 oz flour
30 g/1¼ oz yeast
200 ml/7 fl oz milk
30 g/1¼ oz butter
1 egg
1 teaspoon salt
For the filling:
500 g/18 oz prepared ink fish (page 162)
1 kg/2¼ lb mussels
300 g/11 oz peeled prawns
4 tablespoons olive oil
100 g/4 oz onion, diced

2 garlic cloves, crushed
2 red peppers, diced
200 g/7 oz tomatoes, peeled and diced
2 small chillies, finely chopped
1 teaspoon salt
2 teaspoons paprika
6 tablespoons red wine (preferably Rioja)
1 tablespoon chopped herbs
(thyme, sage and parsley)
1 egg yolk, for pastry
butter, for greasing
salt
freshly ground black pepper

Sift the flour into a basin. Make a well in the centre and crumble in the yeast. Stir into the flour, with the lukewarm milk. Leave to stand for 15 minutes. Beat the lukewarm butter with the egg and salt, add to the yeast mixture and beat to give a smooth, dry yeast dough.

Prepare the filling as shown in the accompanying illustrations. Cut the cleaned inkfish into pieces. Boil the mussels in salted water until they open, and shell. Remove the gut from the prawns. Braise in the

vegetable mixture and leave to cool. Fill the empanada, as shown in the photographs. Set the oven at hot (220 C, 425 F, gas 7) and bake the empanada in the hot oven for 30–35 minutes.

1 **Fry the onions, then add the peppers**. Heat the oil in a frying pan and lightly fry the onion and garlic over a moderate heat. Then add the diced peppers, deseeded and peeled tomatoes and finely chopped chillies. Season with salt and paprika.

2 **Add the prepared ink fish** and braise for 3–4 minutes over a high heat. Then add the boiled, shelled mussels and peeled prawns. Add the red wine. Cook for a further 3–4 minutes and, finally, sprinkle with the chopped herbs.

3 **Fill the empanada**. Halve the pastry and roll out both halves. Use one half to line a buttered, 25-cm/10-in pie tin. Add the filling and level the surface. Brush the edge with egg yolk and cover with the second sheet of pastry. Press gently down.

4 **Decorate with a lattice pattern** by thinly rolling the left-over pastry and cutting into thin strips. Brush the top of the empanada with egg yolk, arrange the pastry strips on the top and brush again with egg yolk. Sprinkle with salt and pepper.

Seafood Gumbo

A Gumbo is a nourishing Creole soup or stew and a real delicacy if made with fresh seafood.

600 g/21 oz okra
salted water
100 g/4 oz carrots
100 g/4 oz celery
150 g/5 oz spring onions
4 tablespoons vegetable oil
3 chillies
2 garlic cloves, crushed
juice of 1 lime or lemon
500 ml/17 fl oz chicken stock
200 g/7 oz tomatoes
250 g/8¾ oz shrimps
1 crawfish (about 200 g/7 oz), shelled
500 g/18 oz mussels
1 teaspoon salt
2 tablespoons fresh herbs
(thyme, basil, parsley)

Cut off the stalk ends of the okra. Then cut into pieces and boil in salted water for 3 to 4 minutes. Drain and pour away the water. Clean and chop the carrots, celery and spring onions. Heat the oil in a deep pan and lightly fry the finely chopped and deseeded chillies with the garlic. Add the prepared vegetables and braise for 3–4 minutes. Add the lime juice and chicken stock. Add the peeled, deseeded and diced tomatoes and the okra and simmer for a further 4–5 minutes. Add the whole shrimps, the sliced crawfish and the scrubbed, debearded mussels. Season with salt and add the fresh herbs. Cover the pan and simmer very gently over a very low heat for about 15 minutes.

COLD DELICACIES

The best cold cuisine nowadays depends on the freshness and quality of its ingredients. Best-quality fresh seafood and fresh-picked vegetables and salads are the main ingredients of the many light and easily digestible cold delicacies that have become popular recently. Classic cold dishes, such as Crawfish Bellevue or Lobster cocktail have not, however, lost their appeal – so this chapter contains examples of both old and new, although the main emphasis is on the more modern, light, simple creations.

Seafood served ice-cold

Many would agree that nothing tastes as good as fresh seafood served ice-cold, just as they come out of the sea. Served uncooked, they have only their own natural flavour and that of the sea. So there are many connoisseurs of oysters who assiduously slurp down their favourite food by the dozen (for slurping is the only way to eat them), with only a few drops of fresh lime or lemon juice to flavour them. Nothing else is needed.

Such lovers of pure flavour like to experiment and are always ready to try other seafood in the same way – raw. Amongst the species that delight the palate without any preparation are carpet shells, dog cockles, periwinkles, mussels and sea urchins. For many people, this is enjoyment in its purest form.

On the other hand, there are many who are not impressed by raw shellfish or who refuse even to try them. It is not our intention to make a futile attempt to convert such people, for cooked seafood can also be served cold. The selection of iced seafood illustrated on this page includes live oysters, Venus shells and winkles as well as cooked crab, scampi, prawns and mussels. Mussels, as we have already said, can also be served raw.

Preparation of iced seafood is easy, as you might guess. You cover a serving plate with crushed ice and serve the seafood on it. To garnish, all you need is a few slices of lime or lemon and possibly a sprig of dill. Alternatively, you can cover the ice with seaweed and serve the seafood on that. Of course, you can also serve it on individual plates if this is more convenient. You should also supply wedges of lime and lemon for squeezing onto the seafood. Further suitable accompaniments include crisp, white bread or tasty wholemeal bread and butter,

or mayonnaise or aïoli. Many people like a sprinkling of pepper or a lump of cheese.

A good, dry white wine (Meursault, Sancerre or Chablis, for example), a quality sparkling wine or even champagne are usually drunk with seafood. English gourmets are said to prefer oysters with a mixture of dark and light beer. In Ireland and the United States, the preference is for unmixed beer straight from the barrel. Many find any drink unnecessary.

If seafood is to be eaten raw, it is essential to select it carefully. Freshness must be the main consideration. In coastal areas this is no problem, for here seafood comes straight from the sea to one's plate. It is, of course, possible to serve a platter of raw seafood even if you don't live by the sea, but you should buy only from a fishmonger you can trust. Nowadays, there is no problem in covering hundreds of kilometres in only a few hours and, if handled properly, seafood will survive such a journey with no ill effects.

Before serving, it is best to stand the live shellfish in lightly salted water for a few hours, so that they expel any sand or impurities. Then they should be washed, scrubbed, any irregularities or growths on the shell scraped off and mussels debearded. It is essential to leave opening oysters and other shellfish until just before serving. To do this you can use a short, strong kitchen knife or special oyster opener.

When choosing the ingredients of a seafood platter, you can please yourself what you include – although you will find your choice determined by what the market can provide on any one day. For, as we have said, any shellfish to be served raw must be absolutely fresh. Lobster, crawfish and even prawns can be boiled one or even two days in advance and then refrigerated. If you are able to buy a good variety, you can serve a platter consisting entirely of uncooked shellfish, including, for instance, oysters (Belons and Fines de Claires), small cockles, winkles, small Venus shells and, of course, mussels. You can add a little variety with sea urchins or sea squirts. The quantity per person depends largely upon whether the seafood platter is to be a starter or a main course.

Opening dog cockles. Hold the shell firmly in a cloth in your left hand. Push a strong, sharp knife into the join and run it all around the shell, including the hinge. Keep the shell horizontal, to prevent the liquid running out.

Cutting open sea urchins. Hold the sea urchin in the palm of your hand and, from the underside, which curves slightly inward, cut out a round opening. You can then remove the inedible mouth and innards. Pour the juice of the sea urchin into a small pan, as it makes an excellent flavouring for cooked fish dishes. The ovaries or gonads, usually referred to as the 'tongue', are spooned out and eaten raw.

Open oysters with a special knife. Hold the oyster in a cloth in your hand with the rounded side underneath. Grip firmly. Push the special knife through the hinge, then run it around the shell and lift off the top, making sure you don't lose any of the liquid in the shell. Loosen the oyster flesh with the knife and serve, on ice, in the lower half of the shell.

Crawfish Bellevue

Langouste Bellevue

This delicious sea creature has a distinguished past. The crawfish, more impressive than the lobster with its long feelers, has traditionally been the centrepiece of a cold buffet at an elegant party, and so it remains today. Without detracting from the decorative possibilities of crawfish and lobster, the emphasis nowadays tends to be more upon their wonderful flavour than their appearance. This is not to say, however, that they cannot be made visually attractive as well.

10–12 leaves gelatine, soaked
500 ml/17 fl oz Fish consommé (page 109)
For the court-bouillon:
4.5 litres/8 pints water
185 ml/6½ fl oz vinegar
60 g/2½ oz salt
450 g/1 lb sliced carrot
300 g/11 oz onion rings
100 g/4 oz chopped parsley
2 bay leaves
1½ tablespoons crushed peppercorns
1 (3-kg/6½-lb) crawfish
1 cucumber
2 large, firm tomatoes
1 black truffle
sprig of chervil, to garnish

Dissolve the gelatine in the highly seasoned Fish consommé and leave to set in the refrigerator.

Boil all the ingredients for the court-bouillon, up to and including the bay leaves, in a fish kettle for 40 minutes. Shortly before the end of the cooking time, add the crushed peppercorns.

Prepare the crawfish (see accompanying illustrations). Place headfirst in the fast-boiling court-bouillon and boil for 30 minutes. Lift out of the pan and leave to cool. Break open and cut into slices. Thickly peel the cucumber and tomatoes and remove the flesh from the skin. Thinly slice the truffle and cut all three vegetables into petal shapes.

Gently warm the chilled fish aspic and glaze the crawfish shell. Place on a serving plate. Lay the slices of crawfish along the shell and cover with aspic. Garnish with flowers made with the cucumber, tomato and truffle (see picture) and glaze. Garnish with a sprig of chervil.

1 **Tie the crawfish to a piece of wood** to keep it in shape as it cooks. The wood will need to be the same size as the crawfish and should be covered in aluminium foil, to prevent the flavour of the wood being transmitted to the crawfish. Starting at the tail end, tie the crawfish to the board at regular intervals.

2 **Tie up the feelers.** If the crawfish is to be used as the centrepiece for a cold buffet, you can tie the feelers to a vertical stick as shown here. Alternatively, they can be laid alongside the lobster as we have done for our finished Crawfish Bellevue (far right, main picture).

3 **Place the crawfish in the stock.** Gently slide the crawfish into the pan, headfirst. The stock should be at a rolling boil, so that the crawfish is killed almost immediately. For Lobster Bellevue, allow 30 minutes cooking time. If the crawfish is to be left to cool in the stock, 20 minutes will suffice.

4 **Using carving forks, lift the serrated shelf out of the fish kettle.** A large fish kettle like this is much the best way of cooking crawfish. To remove the crawfish from the kettle, simply place two carving forks in the handles of the shelf and lift out the shelf, complete with the cooked crawfish.

5 **Cut the crawfish open with scissors.** Place the crawfish upside-down and cut along the sides of the soft under-shell. This will allow you to lift the meat out in one piece. The shell remains intact, too, and can be used as a base to display the slices of crawfish, as in our main picture.

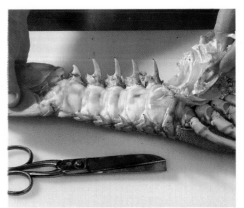

6 **Lift off the shell.** First, gently loosen the meat so that none of it is sticking to the shell, as this will spoil the finished shape of the medallion slices. Hold the tail in one hand and pull the shell off with the other. Pull the shell with an even, steady movement to avoid breaking the flesh.

7 **Slide your hand between the shell and the meat**. First, carefully loosen the meat with a knife to ensure that it comes out whole and in a piece. Hold the body lightly in the other hand as you go, making sure that the shell remains intact. Lift out the meat and place it on a chopping board or worktop.

8 **Slice the meat**. Using a sharp knife, cut the meat into attractive even slices. This is how it is served in Crawfish Bellevue, but you should also aim at cutting even, regular slices if you are going to serve the crawfish in a salad. Arrange the slices, slightly overlapping, on the back of the shell or on a serving platter.

Crawfish Salad

Salade de langouste

1 (1.5-kg/3¼-lb) crawfish, freshly boiled
juice of 1 orange
6 tablespoons crawfish stock
4 tablespoons tarragon vinegar
6 tablespoons olive oil
2 shallots, finely chopped
salt
white pepper
4 handfuls curly endive
4 tablespoons peeled, diced tomato
4 tablespoons diced cucumber
4 black truffles, finely sliced
4 sprigs chervil

Cut the crawfish tail into 12 slices. Beat together the orange juice, crawfish stock, tarragon vinegar, olive oil and finely chopped shallots and season to taste. Toss the endive in this dressing. Arrange on four serving plates, each with three slices of crawfish. Scatter the diced tomato and cucumber into the dressing on each plate. Sprinkle with thin strips of truffle and garnish with chervil.

Cocktails and salads

The cold seafood dishes described on the following pages are often found on menus and in books under a wide variety of different names. Nowadays, fantastical names are a thing of the past and one tends to name these fine creations more appropriately after the main ingredients (for example, 'Lobster on yellow-pepper sauce', named after the ingredient that determines the dominant flavour). Nevertheless, the names still do not tell us much. The terms 'salad' or 'cocktail' usually indicate only a fairly tart or lemony dish, while the terms 'seafood platter' or even 'surprise' tell us very little. In some ways this is not a bad thing, for the real gourmet enjoys surprises (so long as they are pleasant ones) and a

good chef can create the impression that each dish has been thought up specially for each individual diner.

There are unlimited possibilities for endless new creations in the area of cold starters, savouries and snacks, but while enjoying this creative freedom, it is necessary to work within certain parameters when combining different flavours. You should see what fresh ingredients you can buy, for freshness is an essential element of cold cuisine, but don't be afraid to use frozen crustaceans. Many of these, such as snow crabs, king crabs or prawns are hardly ever available fresh. Frozen products are often pre-cooked and therefore good to use in cold dishes, provided that they are used in dishes that do not call for absolutely top quality.

Frozen, uncooked shellfish can be used in just the same way as fresh, after thawing, but only if correctly thawed – not by standing in hot water but slowly, at room temperature. Microwave ovens are excellent for thawing frozen food quickly. If in doubt, have a careful look at the instructions so that you don't cook the frozen food by mistake!

Prawn cocktail on oak-leaf lettuce

Salade de crevettes à la crème de piment

2 tablespoons vegetable oil
30 g/1¼ oz shallots, finely diced
5 tablespoons dry white wine
5 tablespoons chicken stock
150 g/5 oz fresh, shelled peas
¼ teaspoon salt
250 g/9 oz cooked, peeled prawns
1 head oak-leaf lettuce
For the vinaigrette:
4 tablespoons olive oil
2 tablespoons sherry vinegar
salt
freshly ground pepper
1 tablespoon chopped fresh dill
For the chilli cream:
1–2 fresh chillies
2 tablespoons mayonnaise
2 tablespoons crème fraîche
4 tablespoons cream
1 tablespoon tomato purée
salt
generous pinch of sugar

Heat the oil in a large pan and lightly fry the shallots. Add the wine and chicken stock, tip in the peas and salt sparingly. Simmer for 3–4 minutes, uncovered. Remove from the heat, strain the stock and reduce to about 4 tablespoons.

To make the vinaigrette, whisk the reduced stock in a basin with the oil and vinegar until velvety. Season to taste and add the chopped dill. Marinate the peas and prawns in the sauce, in the refrigerator, for about 30 minutes.

To make the chilli cream, deseed the chillies, crush with a knife and press through a fine-mesh sieve. Whisk all the ingredients until frothy and season to taste.

Line four bowls or plates with the washed and dried oak-leaf lettuce and arrange the peas and prawns in the centre, sprinkling a little of the vinaigrette over the lettuce. Top with the chilli cream.

Lobster in Chablis aspic

Homard en gelée de Chablis

250 ml/8 fl oz clarified Fish stock
(page 97)
6 tablespoons Chablis (or other dry
white wine)
1 teaspoon lemon juice
salt · white pepper
12 g/⅓ oz powdered aspic or gelatine,
soaked in 2 tablespoons tepid water
1 (750-g/1½-lb) lobster, boiled
50 g/2 oz cooked peas
sprig of chervil, to garnish
For the herb cream:
2 tablespoons mayonnaise
4 tablespoons crème fraîche
few drops Tabasco sauce
2 teaspoons lemon juice
1 tablespoon chopped fresh herbs
(parsley, chervil and tarragon)

Stir together the Fish stock, wine, lemon
juice and seasoning, warm slightly and
thicken with the gelatine. Set aside to cool.
Slice the lobster and arrange in four glasses,
with the peas. Pour on the almost-cold aspic
and refrigerate until the cocktail is completely set. Whip the herb cream ingredients
to make a dressing and spoon onto the jelly.
Serve ice-cold, garnished with chervil.

Lobster cocktail

Salade d'homard à la sauce épicée

1 (750-g/1½-lb) lobster, boiled
1 lettuce heart
For the dressing:
100 g/4 oz best mayonnaise
2 teaspoons tomato purée
1 tablespoon cognac, or brandy
2 teaspoons lime or lemon juice
generous pinch of ground ginger
12–15 drops Tabasco sauce
1 teaspoon sweet paprika · salt
175 ml/6 fl oz whipped cream
To garnish:
4 slices lime
4 slices truffle

Shell and slice the lobster. Arrange the
lettuce leaves in four glasses and top with
the lobster slices. Beat the mayonnaise with
the tomato purée, cognac or brandy and
lime or lemon juice and season with ginger,
Tabasco, paprika and salt before stirring in
half the whipped cream.

Pour the dressing over the lobster and
garnish with the remaining cream, the lime
and the truffle.

Seafood salad

Salade de fruits de mer

1 (600-g/21-oz) lobster, boiled
4 cooked scampi
1 heart curly endive
12 cooked mussels
12 raw winkles
For the dressing:
3 tablespoons olive oil
30 g/1¼ oz shallots, finely diced
80 g/3 oz celery
1 tomato
30 g/1¼ oz green pepper
30 g/1¼ oz yellow pepper
3 tablespoons Fish stock (page 97)
2 teaspoons good-quality vinegar
salt
freshly ground pepper

Shell the lobster and slice the tail and claw meat. Halve the scampi lengthways, in the shell. Wash and shake dry the endive.

To make the dressing, heat the olive oil in a large frying pan and fry the diced shallots for 1–2 minutes. Cut the celery into thin sticks, dice the tomatoes and cook both with the shallots for a further 2 minutes. Leave to cool. Finely dice the peppers and add to the dressing. Pour on the Fish stock and season with vinegar, salt and pepper.

Arrange the seafood and salad on four plates, as shown above, and pour on the dressing.

Lobster, scallop and avocado salad

Salade d'homard et coquilles à l'avocat

1 tablespoon olive oil
1 tablespoon diced shallots
4 tablespoons dry white wine
4 tablespoons Fish stock (page 97)
¼ teaspoon salt
freshly ground white pepper
8 scallops (without coral)
4 medium prawns, cooked and peeled
1 (250-g/9-oz) avocado
1 large tomato
60 g/2¼ oz courgettes
1 (600-g/21-oz) lobster, boiled
120 g/4¼ oz green beans, boiled
1 heart cos lettuce
For the dressing:
½ teaspoon Dijon mustard
3 tablespoons sherry vinegar
6 tablespoons olive oil
salt
pepper

Heat the olive oil in a saucepan and quickly fry the shallots. Add the wine and Fish stock and season to taste. Add the thickly sliced scallops and simmer for 1 minute, then remove from the heat. Add the peeled prawns, cover the pan and set aside to cool slowly.

Cut the avocado flesh into balls or small cubes. Finely dice the tomato flesh and courgettes. Slice the lobster meat and arrange on four plates with the other ingredients.

Beat together the mustard, vinegar, oil and seasoning to make a smooth vinaigrette and pour over the salad.

Oyster salad with spinach

Salade d'huîtres vinaigrette

24 medium oysters
4 tablespoons dry white wine
2 teaspoons finely chopped shallots
2 small courgettes
2 carrots of similar length
sugar
100 g/4 oz tender leaf spinach
finely chopped chives, to garnish
For the vinaigrette:
½ teaspoon Dijon mustard
6 tablespoons olive oil
2 tablespoons sherry vinegar
salt
pepper

Scrub the oysters well under running water, open them and remove from the shell, using a knife. Heat the wine with the shallots and reduce by half, add the oysters and bring quickly to the boil. Remove immediately from the heat, place the pan on a bed of ice and leave the oysters to cool in the stock.

When cool, remove the oysters from the pan and reduce the stock to about 2 tablespoons. Beat with the mustard, oil, vinegar and seasoning to make a vinaigrette.

Wash the courgettes and remove the centre with an apple corer. Bring quickly to the boil in salted water and allow to cool. Cook the carrots in salted water with a little sugar until cooked but still crisp, and cool. Trim the carrots so that they will fit exactly into the middle of the courgettes. Slide a carrot into the centre of each courgette and slice the courgettes and carrots together.

Arrange the uncooked or blanched spinach on four plates with the oysters and courgette slices. Beat the vinaigrette and sprinkle over the salad. Sprinkle with the chives, to garnish.

Snow crab and fennel salad

Salade d'araignée de mer au fenouil

250 ml/8 fl oz Fish stock (page 97)
3 tablespoons dry sherry
4 leaves unflavoured gelatine, soaked in
3 tablespoons tepid water
salt
freshly ground white pepper
150 g/5 oz fennel
salted water
24 snow crab claws, thawed if frozen
3 tablespoons mayonnaise
1 tablespoon cognac
2 tablespoons fresh cream
6 drops Tabasco sauce
salt
For the dressing:
2 tablespoons sherry vinegar
6 tablespoons sunflower oil
salt
pepper
finely chopped dill

Reduce the Fish stock by half, add the sherry and soaked gelatine and season to taste. Pour the jelly into a large bowl in a layer no deeper than $\frac{1}{2}$ cm/$\frac{1}{4}$ in and leave to set. When set, cut into cubes.

Thinly slice the fennel and cook in salted water until cooked but still crisp, then remove from the pan and cool. Remove the meat from half the crab claws and shred it finely. Beat it with the mayonnaise, cognac and cream and season to taste with Tabasco and salt.

Scatter cubes of fish stock jelly across each of four serving plates. Arrange the fennel on top, with three cracked crab claws on each plate. Sprinkle with a dressing made with the vinegar, oil, salt and pepper and dill. Spoon a little crab mayonnaise into the centre of each plate.

Lobster on yellow-pepper sauce

Homard au piment jaune

Saltwort is a sea plant found on the French Atlantic and North Sea coasts. It makes a most attractive accompaniment for lobster.

250 g/9 oz saltwort
500 ml/17 fl oz water
6 tablespoons white wine
1 tablespoon lemon juice
$\frac{1}{2}$ teaspoon salt
1 (600-g/21-oz) lobster, boiled
2 tablespoons diced red pepper
chervil
For the sauce:
2 tablespoons olive oil
2 tablespoons chopped shallots
$\frac{1}{2}$ garlic clove, chopped
1 large (120-g/4$\frac{1}{4}$-oz) yellow pepper
6 tablespoons chicken stock
$\frac{1}{4}$ teaspoon salt
4 tablespoons whipped cream

Carefully sort the saltwort. You should be left with at least 150 g/5 oz. Bring the water to the boil, add the wine, lemon juice and salt and simmer the saltwort for 3–4 minutes. Remove from the pan and leave to cool.

Heat the olive oil for the sauce and lightly fry the shallots and garlic. Carefully trim and deseed the yellow pepper to leave only the pure flesh. Add to the shallots, pour on the stock and season with salt. Braise for about 15 minutes, until the pepper is soft, remove from the heat and blend in a liquidizer. Strain through a fine-mesh sieve and leave until completely cool.

Stir the whipped cream into the sauce and pour onto four serving plates. Shell the lobster, slice the meat and arrange with the saltwort on top of the sauce. Garnish with diced red pepper and chervil.

Scallop and oyster salad

Salade d'huîtres et coquilles

12 oysters
12 scallops
1 tablespoon finely chopped shallots
4 tablespoons dry white wine
6 tablespoons Fish stock (page 97)
1 teaspoon dry vermouth
1 teaspoon lemon juice
6 drops Tabasco sauce
$\frac{1}{2}$ head Batavian endive
80 g/3 oz green beans, boiled
For the dressing:
2 teaspoons good-quality vinegar
6 tablespoons olive oil
salt
coarsely ground pepper
30 g/1$\frac{1}{4}$ oz courgettes, finely diced

Scrub the oysters well under running water. Open them and pour the liquid into a saucepan. Remove the oysterflesh from the shells. Shell the scallops but use only the muscle, which should be thickly sliced. Add the chopped shallots, wine, Fish stock and vermouth to the oyster liquid and reduce by about half. Add the oysters and scallops and return to the boil. Remove from the heat, season with lemon juice and Tabasco and leave to cool.

Remove the oysters and scallops from the stock and refrigerate. Reduce the stock again (to about 2 tablespoons) and then strain through a fine-mesh sieve. Beat with the vinegar and olive oil until thick, season and stir in the diced courgette.

Arrange the endive, beans, oysters and scallops on four serving plates and sprinkle with the dressing.

Colourful scampi salad

Langoustines avec salade vinaigrette

1 heart oak-leaf lettuce
1 heart curly endive
8 bunches lamb's lettuce
4 tablespoons red-wine vinegar
8 tablespoons olive oil
salt
freshly ground black pepper
4 teaspoons diced tomato
4 teaspoons blanched carrot,
cut into flowers
4 tablespoons olive oil
12 fresh scampi, shelled

Sort the oak-leaf lettuce, endive and lamb's lettuce, then wash them and shake dry in a tea-towel.

Beat the red-wine vinegar and olive oil with salt and freshly ground black pepper to make a dressing and adjust the seasoning. Toss the lettuce and endive in the dressing and arrange on four serving plates. Add the tomato and carrot.

Heat the olive oil in a frying pan and quickly sauté the scampi. Season lightly with salt. Arrange three scampi tails on each plate and sprinkle lightly with black pepper. Sprinkle the remaining dressing over the salad and serve immediately.

Scampi salad with green asparagus

Langoustines aux asperges

40 spears tender, green asparagus
2 carrots
salted water
12 fresh scampi, shelled
3 tablespoons olive oil
salt
4 teaspoons chopped tarragon
4 sprigs tarragon to garnish
For the marinade:
4 tablespoons tarragon vinegar
8 tablespoons olive oil
salt
freshly ground black pepper

Trim the asparagus. Use only the tips and keep the rest to serve as a vegetable. Peel the carrots and cut into 12 even slices, with a serrated knife. Blanch the asparagus and carrots separately in salted water for 3–4 minutes. Cool in iced water and drain in a sieve or colander.

Beat the tarragon vinegar with the olive oil, salt and freshly ground black pepper to make a marinade and adjust the seasoning. Marinate the asparagus and carrot slices.

Meanwhile, quickly sauté the scampi in the hot oil in a frying pan or small saucepan. Season lightly with salt.

Arrange the asparagus and carrot slices on four serving plates with three scampi tails on each. Sprinkle with tarragon, then with the remaining marinade. Garnish with sprigs of tarragon before serving.

Scampi and artichoke salad

Langoustines avec coeurs d'artichaut

4 small, young artichokes
4 tablespoons flour
salted water
4 tablespoons sherry vinegar
6 tablespoons salad oil
2 tablespoons walnut oil
salt
freshly ground black pepper
1 walnut, shelled and coarsely chopped
16 fresh scampi, shelled
4 tablespoons olive oil
1 heart oak-leaf lettuce
1 heart curly endive
1 large mushroom

Twist the stalks off the artichokes. Cut off the outer leaves and the tops of the hearts. Stir the flour into salted cold water and bring to the boil. Blanch the artichoke hearts for 8–10 minutes. Cool in cold water, to prevent them cooking any further.

Meanwhile, beat the vinegar with the salad and walnut oils, salt and freshly ground black pepper and adjust the seasoning. Add the coarsely chopped walnut. Thinly slice the artichoke hearts into the marinade. Toss and marinate for 5 minutes.

Quickly sauté the scampi in the hot olive oil in a saucepan and season lightly.

Arrange the marinated artichoke hearts on four serving plates. Toss the lettuce and endive in the marinade and add to the plates, with four scampi tails on each. Cut the mushroom into very thin sticks and sprinkle over the salad.

Scampi and broccoli salad

Salade de langoustines et brocoli

16 broccoli florets
salted water
4 tablespoons sherry vinegar
6 tablespoons olive oil
2 tablespoons walnut oil
salt
freshly ground white pepper
12 fresh scampi, shelled
3 tablespoons olive oil
1 small heart oak-leaf lettuce
½ heart curly endive

Blanch the broccoli for 2 minutes in salted water and cool in iced water.

Beat the sherry vinegar with the olive oil, walnut oil, salt and freshly ground white pepper, to make a dressing.

Quickly sauté the scampi in a pan in the hot olive oil and season lightly with salt.

Toss the broccoli, lettuce and endive in the dressing. Arrange on four serving plates with three scampi tails on each. Sprinkle with the dressing before serving.

Lobster with cos lettuce

Salade d'homard et romaine

1 large piece pale-green leek
salted water
2 hearts cos lettuce
1 heart curly endive
4 tablespoons sherry vinegar
few drops good-quality white vinegar
4 teaspoons truffle juice
6 tablespoons olive oil
2 tablespoons walnut oil
salt
white pepper
20 slices lobster claw meat
4 tablespoons olive oil
4 sprigs chervil
4 slices black truffle, cut into thin sticks

Cut the leek into 16 slanting slices and blanch in boiling, salted water. Choose 20 nice heart leaves from the cos lettuce. Sort the endive heart and wash with the lettuce.

Beat the vinegars with the truffle juice, olive and walnut oil, salt and white pepper to make a tasty dressing.

Quickly sauté the lobster in the hot olive oil in a frying pan, and salt lightly. Toss the leek, lettuce and endive in the dressing.

Arrange on four serving plates with five slices of lobster on each. Sprinkle with the dressing and garnish with the chervil and truffle.

Crab salad

Salade de tourteau

4 (400–500 g/14–18 oz) crabs
For the court-bouillon:
3 litres/5 pints water
6 tablespoons vinegar
45 g/1½ oz salt
350 g/12 oz carrots, sliced
200 g/7 oz onions, cut into rings
50 g/2 oz chopped parsley
1 bay leaf
1 tablespoon crushed peppercorns
For the filling:
2 tablespoons oil
60 g/2¼ oz shallots, chopped
1 garlic clove, chopped
50 g/2 oz celery, chopped
1 tablespoon chopped herbs
(parsley, thyme, sage)
½ teaspoon salt
white pepper
livers and corals (if available) of crabs
4 hard-boiled egg yolks
2 teaspoons hot Dijon mustard
juice of 1 lemon
6–8 tablespoons olive oil
For the garnish:
1 hard-boiled egg, sliced
4 bunches lamb's lettuce
For the dressing:
1 tablespoon wine vinegar
2 tablespoons finely chopped onion
1 tablespoon finely chopped chives
salt
white pepper

Wash and scrub the crabs well. To make the court-bouillon, boil the water with the vinegar, salt, carrot, onion, parsley and bay leaf in a large pan for 40 minutes. Just before the end of the cooking time, add the crushed peppercorns and bring to a fast boil. Add the crabs, one after the other, simmer for 20 minutes and leave to cool in the stock.

Break open the crabs, keeping the shells intact for filling (see page 120). Remove the meat from the body and legs and use only the white meat.

To make the filling, heat the oil in a saucepan and fry the shallots, garlic and celery until transparent. Add the herbs and seasoning and cook for 5–6 minutes, then leave to cool. In a mortar, purée the livers and corals, if using, with the egg yolks, mustard and lemon juice. Work in the olive oil, a few drops at a time, to give a smooth, uniform sauce. Fold in the vegetables and half the crabmeat and spoon the mixture into the crab shells. Top with the remaining white crabmeat.

Place each crab, with its claws (cracked to make them easier to eat), on a serving plate. Garnish with egg slices and lamb's lettuce. Beat together the ingredients for the dressing and pour over the crabs.

Mixed shellfish salad

Grande salade de fruits de mer

2 kg/4½ lb mixed shellfish (mussels, trough
shells, small Venus shells and cockles)
250 ml/8 fl oz Fish stock (page 97)
6 tablespoons dry white wine
50 g/2 oz onion, chopped
50 g/2 oz leek, chopped
100 g/4 oz celery, chopped
½ teaspoon salt
freshly ground white pepper
3 tablespoons olive oil
1 tablespoon lemon juice
1 tablespoon wine vinegar
1 tablespoon chopped herbs
(tarragon and parsley)
½ head curly endive

Wash and scrub all the shellfish several
times, in cold water. Debeard the mussels.
Bring the Fish stock to the boil in a large
pan and add the white wine, onion, leek and
celery. Season with salt and freshly ground
pepper and return to the boil. Add all the
shellfish, cover the pan and boil until they
have opened. Remove from the pan and
leave to cool.

Strain the cooking stock into another
pan, boil to reduce by about half and leave
to cool. Beat the olive oil, lemon juice and
wine vinegar into the reduced stock and add
the chopped herbs. Tear the washed and
drained endive into pieces, mix with the
shellfish and the dressing and serve.

Crawfish salad with noodles

*Langouste aux truffes
avec nouilles blanches*

Serves 2:
1 (300-g/11-oz) crawfish tail, boiled
40 g/1½ oz noodles
salted water
1 heart curly endive
1 tomato
1 truffle, cut into thin strips
For the dressing:
250 ml/8 fl oz defatted meat stock
1 tablespoon dry sherry
½ teaspoon good-quality vinegar
2 teaspoons finely chopped shallots
salt
freshly ground pepper

Break open the crawfish tail and remove the
meat in one piece (see pages 180–181). Cut
into slices, removing the gut.

Boil the noodles in salted water until 'al
dente' and rinse. Tear the endive leaves into
bite-sized pieces.

Reduce the meat stock to about one-
quarter of the original quantity. Leave to
cool, then stir in the sherry, vinegar and
shallots. Refrigerate for 30 minutes.

Blanch, skin and deseed the tomato, then
dice the flesh. Arrange the noodles, endive
and crawfish slices on two serving plates and
sprinkle with the diced tomato. Season the
dressing and sprinkle over the salad.
Garnish with the truffle.

An extra special individual dish of seafood in a dry Riesling jelly. For a less expensive dish, you can replace the lobster with inexpensive crab or frozen king crab.

Seafood in Riesling aspic

Fruits de mer en gelée de Riesling

A really delicious way of serving cold crustaceans and shellfish. This refreshing dish can be served in small cocktail glasses as a starter, or left to set in small moulds and turned out onto a plate when cold and garnished with leaf spinach. The following recipe will make a delicious savoury for four people and should be served in soup plates. Serve with toast and fresh butter and a chilled, dry Riesling, the same one that you have used in the aspic.

18–20 g/$\frac{1}{2}$–$\frac{3}{4}$ oz aspic or unflavoured
gelatine powder, soaked in about
2 tablespoons tepid water
375 ml/13 fl oz clarified Fish stock
(page 97)
6 tablespoons dry Riesling
(or other white wine)
1 tablespoon dry vermouth
1 tablespoon lemon juice
$\frac{1}{2}$ teaspoon salt
(if the Fish stock is unsalted)
1 (700-g/1$\frac{1}{2}$-lb) lobster, boiled
4 scampi
1 kg/2$\frac{1}{4}$ lb fresh shellfish (to give about
200 g/7 oz when boiled)

150 g/5 oz medium prawns, cooked and
peeled
2 tomatoes
50 g/2 oz carrots, cut into strips
50 g/2 oz leeks, cut into strips
salted water
$\frac{1}{2}$ lettuce
1 hard-boiled egg, sliced

The amount of gelatine you need will depend on how solid you like your aspic. 18 g/$\frac{1}{2}$ oz should give just the right consistency for this amount of liquid.

Tip the aspic or gelatine powder into a small basin with just enough tepid water to allow it to swell. If you use leaf gelatine, soak it in plenty of water and squeeze out firmly before use. Add the Fish stock, wine, vermouth and lemon juice to the soaked gelatine and heat sufficiently to melt the gelatine. Season with salt, if required, and leave to cool.

If you buy fresh lobster rather than ready-boiled, cook it in court-bouillon (see page 180) for 5–6 minutes and leave to cool in the stock. Fresh scampi should also be boiled in court-bouillon, for a maximum of

3 minutes. Steam the shellfish as described on page 148 and then shell them. Shell and slice the lobster and halve the shelled scampi lengthways.

Scald, skin and deseed the tomatoes and dice the flesh. Quickly blanch the strips of carrot and leek in salted water. Wash the lettuce and shake dry.

Line four soup plates with a few lettuce leaves and top with all the other ingredients, attractively arranged. Garnish with sliced egg. Chill in the refrigerator for 30 minutes and then pour on the almost-cold but still liquid aspic. Leave until fully set before serving.

Crayfish mousse

Mousse d'écrevisses

350 g/12 oz cooked, shelled crayfish
2 leaves unflavoured gelatine, soaked in
1 tablespoon tepid water
350 ml/12 fl oz strong Crayfish stock made
from the shells (page 100)
salt
cayenne
250 ml/8 fl oz whipped cream
aspic made from Fish consommé
(page 97)
crayfish heads, to garnish
sprigs of dill

Tip the crayfish meat into a liquidizer. In a small frying pan, dissolve the soaked gelatine in the soaking water and stir in the Crayfish stock. Gradually add to the crayfish meat and blend in the liquidizer for about 2 minutes. Then strain through a fine-mesh sieve and season generously with salt and cayenne (slightly over-season if anything, for the cream that is to be added later will cancel out the effect to some extent). Place in a basin over crushed ice and whisk until completely cool and slightly thickened by the gelatine.

Gradually fold the whipped cream into the crayfish mixture and transfer to a mould about 3 cm/1 in deep. Dip a palette knife in water and smooth the top. Cover and refrigerate for 2–3 hours, until set.

Spoon out the mousse, using a dessert spoon or teaspoon dipped each time in hot water. Serve 2 spoonsful on each plate, with 2 tablespoons finely diced aspic and garnished with a crayfish head and a sprig of fresh dill.

1 **Ladle the stock into the liquidizer**. It is added a little at a time to the crayfish. The stock should first be mixed with the dissolved gelatine. The ingredients should not be ice-cold, or the gelatine will set. Blend to give a fine purée.

2 **Strain the mixture through a sieve**. Spoon a little at a time onto a fine-mesh sieve and push through with a pastry scraper, slowly and carefully. This will remove any tough crayfish fibres or lumps of gelatine. Season well with salt and cayenne.

3 **Whisk the crayfish mixture** until almost cold. Place the bowl in a larger bowl of ice cubes. Whisk the mixture evenly, making sure that it does not begin to set at the bottom of the bowl. It will begin to feel stiffer as the gelatine begins to set.

4 **Fold in the whipped cream**. The mixture should now be cold but not yet set. Fold in the whipped cream gently, so that it keeps its volume and the mousse remains light. Transfer to a mould, smooth the top and refrigerate.

5 **Spoon out** with a dessert spoon or teaspoon, dipping the spoon each time into hot water to prevent it sticking to the mousse. Dip the spoon vertically into the mousse and turn to get an even shape. Use a deep spoon for a domed effect.

FROM THE FAR EAST

Culinary delights from an exotic world

Varying geographical, climatic and cultural conditions mean that the national cuisines of the Asian countries have little in common. Yet they all make good use of seafood and often in masterly fashion – the coastal Chinese are particularly notable for this. They have developed really simple recipes for unbeatable results, based entirely on the wonderful tastes of fresh, high-quality crustaceans and shellfish. Quality and freshness are also basic criteria in Japanese cooking, for the Japanese love to eat both fish and shellfish raw. In contrast to the seafood dishes of the moderate zones, on the tropical coasts of Asia seafood dishes are usually highly spiced. There is good reason for this traditional method of preparation – seafood soon goes off in the hot climate and spices help to preserve it. Regional recipes from India to Indonesia include many amazing dishes using native vegetables, spices and fruits. These include combinations that are quite new to outsiders, as well as dishes that may appear more familiar, influenced as they are by the European presence in Asia over the centuries.

Three prawn dishes from the wok

There is no quicker or tastier way of cooking this fine seafood than in a wok, or Chinese frying pan. The following recipes, for four people, require a large wok of at least 50-cm/20-in diameter. If you have only a small pan, it will be easier to prepare them in two batches.

Braised prawns

6 tablespoons vegetable oil
100 g/4 oz spring onions, diced
3 garlic cloves
20 g/¾ oz fresh root ginger, sliced
16 prawns
2 teaspoons sugar
½ teaspoon salt
2 tablespoons rice wine
2 teaspoons vinegar
freshly ground black pepper
2 teaspoons cornflour
2–3 tablespoons tomato juice

Prawns in sherry

16 prawns
375 ml/13 fl oz Fish stock (page 97)
½ teaspoon salt
2 teaspoons sugar
freshly ground black pepper
6 tablespoons dry sherry
1 tablespoon cornflour

Chilli prawns

16 prawns
1 egg white
salt
3 tablespoons cornflour
oil, for frying
3 fresh chillies, deseeded and chopped
2 garlic cloves, sliced
¼ teaspoon monosodium glutamate
1 teaspoon sugar
30 g/1¼ oz fresh root ginger, sliced
4 tablespoons light soy sauce
4 tablespoons sherry

Braised prawns. Heat the oil in a wok and fry the diced onions, the peeled, whole garlic cloves and the sliced ginger. Add the prawns and fry for 2 minutes, turning from time to time. Add the sugar, salt, rice wine, vinegar and pepper. Stir the cornflour into the tomato juice, pour over the prawns and braise for 5 minutes. Arrange the prawns on serving plates, reduce the sauce slightly and pour over the prawns.

Prawns in sherry. Cook the prepared prawns in the Fish stock for 2 minutes and remove from the pan. Season the stock with salt, sugar and pepper and add 5 tablespoons sherry. Dissolve the cornflour in 1 tablespoon sherry and stir into the sauce. Simmer until the sauce is clear. Return the prawns to the pan for 3 minutes and then serve, with a vegetable. Broccoli is an excellent accompaniment for this dish.

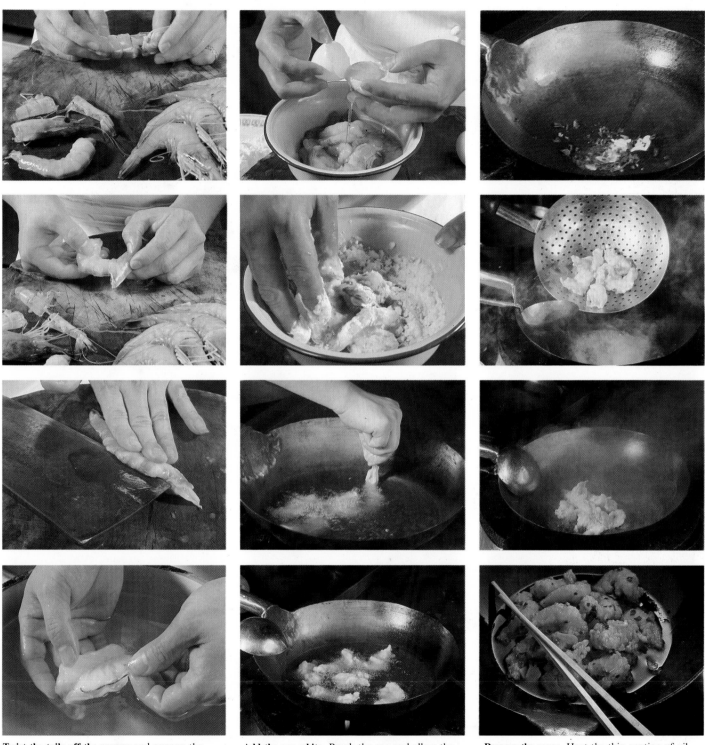

Twist the tails off the prawns and remove the shell. Lay the prawns flat on a board and, using a meat cleaver or knife, cut halfway through the length of the prawns. Rinse and remove the gut. Dry the prawns on absorbent kitchen paper and place in a bowl.

Add the egg white. Break the egg and allow the white to run into the bowl (the yolk is not used). Season with salt, add the cornflour and mix in until the prawns are covered by a solid layer. Fry in the hot oil for 3–4 minutes. Remove the prawns from the pan and drain. Pour the oil out of the wok but do not rinse.

Prepare the sauce. Heat the thin coating of oil still in the wok and quickly fry the chopped chillies and sliced garlic. Add the remaining ingredients and bring to the boil, stirring continuously. Then add the prawns and simmer for a few minutes before serving.

Chilli crabs

This method of cooking crabs can be used for other seafood – for instance, prawns or crayfish. The technique is simple, the results outstanding. The pieces of crab are pre-cooked by deep-frying and then flavoured in a sauce. For best results, you will need to use a wok (round Chinese frying pan) and a gas hob, for you need a really high heat for this cooking method.

In Asia, this dish is usually made using Mangrove Crabs, Pacific Crabs or Striped Crabs. The European Common Crab gives equally good results, however.

4 (400-g/14-oz) crabs
salt
flour
vegetable oil, for frying
50 g/2 oz spring onions, finely chopped
3 garlic cloves, crushed
1 tablespoon fresh chillies, chopped
1 teaspoon sugar
1 tablespoon light soy sauce
1 teaspoon fresh root ginger,
finely chopped
250 ml/8 fl oz water or chicken stock
1 teaspoon fresh coriander leaves,
finely chopped

Prepare the crabs as shown on the facing page and deep-fry. In a wok, first fry the finely chopped spring onions and crushed garlic, add the finely chopped chillies and fry quickly. Season with sugar, soy sauce and ginger. Tip the water or stock all at one go into the hot wok and reduce over a high heat for about 1 minute. Add the crab and coriander leaves and simmer over a low heat for 4–5 minutes.

Crab claws in spicy sauce

4 (400-g/14-oz) Mangrove or
Common Crabs
salted water
¼ teaspoon salt
½ garlic clove, crushed
1 small chilli, deseeded and
finely shredded
1 tablespoon soft-cooked rice
½ egg white
4 tablespoons vegetable oil
50 g/2 oz spring onions, chopped
1 chilli, chopped
1 tablespoon fresh root ginger, grated
1 tablespoon dark soy sauce
6 tablespoons chicken stock
1 tablespoon fresh coriander leaves,
chopped

Drop the crabs into boiling, salted water, boil for 1 minute and then reduce the heat and simmer for 8 minutes. Remove the crabs from the pan and leave until completely cool. Then break off the claws, crack the thick part with a meat cleaver and carefully remove the shell, taking care not to damage the meat and to leave it attached to the smaller half of the claw. Remove all the remaining crabmeat from the legs and body and crush in a mortar with the seasoning

(salt, garlic, chilli) until you have a smooth paste.

Add the rice and egg white and continue pounding until the rice is completely worked in. Use this mixture to coat the crabmeat attached to the claws. Leave to dry slightly on an oiled plate.

Heat the oil in a wok, add the onions and chopped chilli and fry quickly. Add the

claws and fry for 2–3 minutes, turning them continuously but carefully to avoid breaking them up. Remove the claws from the pan. Add the ginger, soy sauce, chicken stock and coriander and reduce the sauce slightly over a low heat. Return the claws to the pan and reheat for a few minutes. Serve with bamboo shoots, mushrooms and plain boiled rice.

Cut up the crabs. In Europe, they must first be killed with a skewer or in boiling water. Chop into the underside, using a meat cleaver, and break away the shell from the centre. Remove gills and intestine.

Leave the crabmeat and coral on the shell. The legs too are left on the shell. The upper shell is left whole. Crack the claws and cook quickly. Season lightly with salt.

Dip the pieces of crab in flour until evenly coated all over. Shake off excess flour. Deep-fry in hot oil (about 180 C/350 F) for 5–6 minutes. Remove the crabs from the oil and tip the oil away.

Quickly fry the onion and garlic. The oil left adhering to the pan is as much as you will need. Then add the seasonings, followed by the water and return the pieces of crab to the pan.

Sea cucumber and prawns in egg white

This is a good example of how this sea creature – most unusual in Europe – can be prepared in a really tasty way.

60 g/2¼ oz dried sea cucumber (Trepang)
8 prawn tails (250 g/9 oz)
4 tablespoons peanut oil
1 tablespoon onion, very finely chopped
2 tablespoons rice wine
6 tablespoons chicken stock
6 egg whites
salt
pepper

Carefully wash the sea cucumber and soak in water for 1–2 days, until it swells to its original size (to compare sizes before and after soaking, see page 91). Cut open lengthways, remove the innards and wash out thoroughly. Cook in plain water for about 20–30 minutes, or until soft, and then cut into slices.

Shell the prawn tails, cut in half lengthways and remove the gut. Cut across into two or three pieces.

Heat the oil in a wok and fry the sea cucumber slices for 2–3 minutes. Add the finely chopped onion and cook for a few minutes before adding the rice wine and stock. Simmer over a low heat for 6–8 minutes. Mix the egg whites with the prawns, salt and pepper and stir into the ingredients in the wok. Continue stirring until the egg white solidifies but remove it from the heat before it becomes too dry.

Abalones with vegetables

600 g/21 oz shelled fresh abalones or
400 g/14 oz canned abalones
salted water
3 tablespoons peanut oil
50 g/2 oz spring onions, chopped
½ teaspoon salt
1 tablespoon vinegar
80 g/3 oz dried Tongu mushrooms,
soaked to original size
250 ml/8 fl oz chicken stock
1 teaspoon sugar
1 teaspoon dark soy sauce
few drops sesame oil
1 teaspoon cornflour
300 g/11 oz broccoli (the best substitute
for the authentic Chinese cabbage)

Remove the abalones from the shells, take out the gills and intestines, and thoroughly scrub them with a soft brush under running water. Cook until soft in lightly salted water for 5–6 hours, changing the water from time to time.

Heat the oil in a wok and fry the onions for 2 minutes. Add the salt, vinegar and soaked mushrooms and cook for a further 2–3 minutes. Add the chicken stock, season with sugar, soy sauce and sesame oil and stir in the cornflour, dissolved in a little water. Cut the abalones into ½ cm/¼ in slices, add to the stock and simmer gently for about 10–12 minutes. Boil the broccoli in lightly salted water until tender and set aside. Remove the abalones and mushrooms from the wok, strain the sauce and warm through the boiled broccoli in the strained sauce for 2–3 minutes. Serve with the abalones and mushrooms.

Prawns and peppers from the wok

Serves 2:
8 Tiger Prawns
cornflour
oil for deep-frying, plus 4 tablespoons
50 g/2 oz spring onions, diced
1 garlic clove, crushed
½ green pepper
½ red pepper
1 onion, diced
1 teaspoon vinegar
2 tablespoons light soy sauce
½ teaspoon salt
1 teaspoon coarsely ground black pepper

Twist the tails off the prawns, remove the shells and cut lengthways halfway through the back of the prawns to remove the gut. Coat the prawns in cornflour and shake off excess. Deep-fry in hot oil (180 C/350 F) for 2 minutes, remove from the pan and drain.

Heat 4 tablespoons oil in a wok and fry the diced spring onions and crushed garlic. Remove the seeds from the peppers and cut into pieces. Add to the wok with the diced onion. Cook for 2–3 minutes and then season with vinegar, soy sauce, salt and pepper. Simmer for a further 2–3 minutes and then add the prawns. Cook for 1 minute before serving.

Shanghai crabs

In Chinese cuisine, these freshwater crabs are considered a real delicacy – probably because they are in season for only a short time in autumn and are rare even then. The price in the markets of Hong Kong and Singapore for these crabs with 'woolly gloves' on their claws, which are imported from northern China, is continually rising. These crabs are very aptly named Chinese Mitten Crabs.

Despite the popularity of this crab in China, it has never caught on in Europe and the fishermen of the Elbe, where it is plentiful, would be only too pleased if they could find a market for it. Maybe one day this will happen and it will be as familiar to the gourmet as to the fisherman. This delightfully flavoured crab could fill a gap in our culinary experience.

The ingredients given here will serve four people as a snack or savoury. For a main course, allow four or five crabs per person.

8 Chinese Mitten Crabs
8 spring onions
8 sprigs fresh coriander
salted water
50 g/2 oz green Chinese tea
For the dip:
6 tablespoons light soy sauce
juice of ½ lemon
30 g/1¼ oz fresh root ginger, grated
generous pinch of cayenne
1 teaspoon sugar

Rinse the crabs under running water. Cut the spring onions in half lengthways and then into 6–8-cm/2½–3-in pieces. Arrange the onion with the coriander on the underside of each crab and then tie the crabs into a neat parcel with a piece of twine or raffia. (In Europe, they must first be killed by spearing the nerve ganglia with a skewer or boiling in water for 2 minutes.)

In a large pan, suspend a strainer or sieve 3–4 cm/1–1½ in above the base of the pan. Fill the bottom of the pan with salted water. Bring to the boil and sprinkle the tea into the sieve. Cover the pan and, when the water is boiling vigorously and producing plenty of steam, place the crabs in the sieve and steam for 15–20 minutes.

The crabs are served whole. Everyone cracks their own and takes out the meat, including the delicious coral. Only the gills and intestines are inedible. Serve simply with a light soy sauce or make a dip, using the ingredients listed.

A PRACTICAL GUIDE TO COOKING SEAFOOD

Equipment for seafood cookery

For most seafood cooking, the standard equipment of any well-stocked kitchen will suffice – with few exceptions, the preparation of shellfish and crustaceans requires no special equipment. But for those who like to do things properly and for whom quality is paramount, there are a few items that may be worth considering, since they make the job slightly easier. A glance into a well-equipped restaurant kitchen would be a useful guide to many an amateur cook, for it is often little things that make the difference between fair and fine results.

You should have a large saucepan holding at least 12–15 litres/21–26 pints, for you need a lot of liquid when boiling large crustaceans (lobster, crawfish, large crabs, etc.). If you want to boil crawfish stretched out straight, as shown on page 180, then a large fish kettle is ideal.

A good choice of knives is an essential item of standard equipment but you will also need a large, heavy knife for crustaceans and shellfish, to crack the shells. Many prefer to use a solid nut-cracker, which can also be used at the table to allow guests to crack the claws of lobster. Modern, all-purpose scissors can be a great help for cutting up crustaceans in the kitchen.

One of the few special tools the seafood cook needs is a short, strong oyster knife for opening oysters and other large shellfish.

While you can use a variety of kitchen implements to get the meat out of a lobster, at the dining table you will need special crockery and cutlery. For crustaceans a lobster fork, for snails the special cutlery consisting of snail tongs to hold the shell and a two-pronged fork for taking out the meat, and also a special plate with indentations on which to serve your snails. These are also available on a larger scale for oysters.

1 Fish kettle
2 Large saucepan
3 Conical sieve
4 Straining cloth, preferably muslin
5 A range of sharp knives, and a sharpener
6 Metal scraper
7 Plastic scraper
8 Rubber spatula
9 Two styles of all-purpose scissors
10 Oyster knife
11 Oyster plate
12 Snail plate and cooking pan
13 Nut-cracker
14 Lobster fork
15 Snail tongs and fork

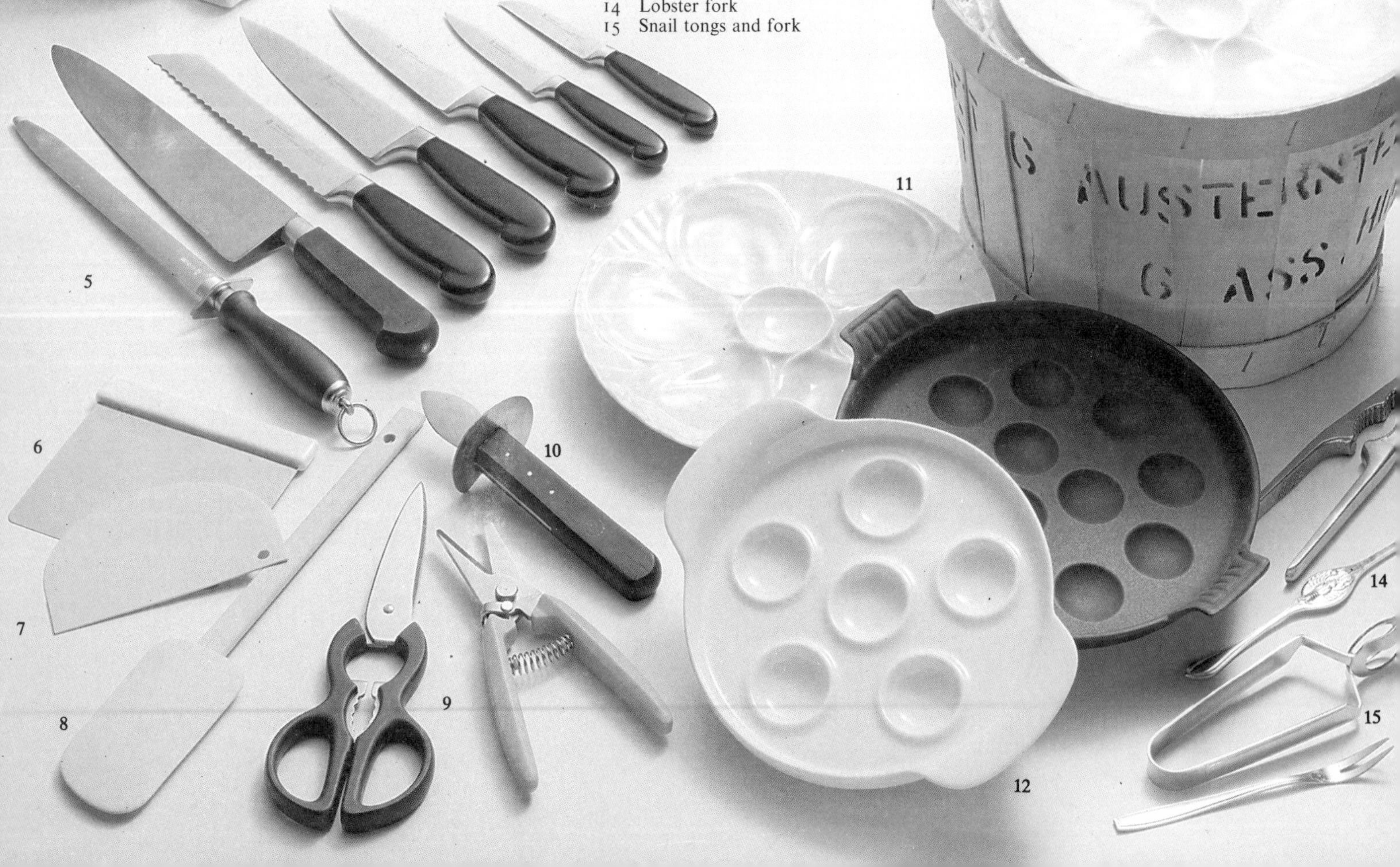

Glossary

al dente – firm to the bite, of pasta.

aspic – a savoury jelly made from fish, seafood or meat stock.

bain-marie – a container part-filled with hot water in which delicate dishes, such as sauces, can be kept hot or gently warmed. An inner container holding the sauce is supported to prevent it touching the base of the pan. The water should not boil.

bake blind – to bake pastry cases without their filling to help them keep their shape. They should be lined with greaseproof paper or aluminium foil and filled with dried peas or beans. Both are removed after baking.

bard – to wrap in or cover with rashers of bacon.

beard – in shellfish, the outer edge of the mantle, which is usually removed. In mussels, the byssus threads anchoring them to the ground. They should be removed before cooking.

bind – to thicken with a binding agent (such as flour or cornflour).

blanch – quick boiling of vegetables in simmering, salted water to remove unpleasant flavours or impurities or to facilitate peeling.

bouquet garni – small bunch of various herbs, vegetables and seasonings used to flavour stocks and sauces.

braise – to cook in a little liquid, fat and its own juice; mid-way between frying and stewing.

carcass – bones of fish and poultry, shell of crustaceans.

carve – to cut up meat or fish to be served in slices.

ciseler – to cut notches, e.g. in the skin of small fish to prevent splitting. Also, to finely chop.

clarify – to remove any cloudy particles from stock or jelly. Egg white and finely chopped meat or fish are added to bind and remove impurities.

consommé – a concentrated clear stock (Fr. *fond*) made from crustaceans, fish, poultry or meat.

coral – (Fr. *corail*), roe of female lobster, crawfish and other crustaceans, which turns from dark green to coral pink when cooked. A great delicacy and also an excellent flavouring agent (e.g. for butter). The orange roe of scallops is also called the coral.

court-bouillon – highly flavoured stock, usually made of water, vinegar, white wine, vegetables and seasoning, used to boil seafoods and fish.

debeard – to remove the mantle edge (beard) from shellfish, or the byssus threads from the shells of mussels.

deep-fry – to fry floating in plenty of hot fat, until golden brown.

dégorger – to soak in water to remove blood from brains, sweetbreads, hearts or liver.

dessécher – to dry by draining or wiping.

dress – to give food a particular shape (e.g. using a piping bag) or to serve tastefully.

duxelles – a mince of mushrooms, shallots and herbs, used for coating or as pie filling.

fines herbes – various combinations of finely chopped herbs for sauces and soups; may include chopped shallots.

flamber – to pour alcohol over a dish and set it alight, for added flavour.

fond – stock obtained by cooking shellfish, crustaceans, fish, meat or vegetables. Used as a base for sauces and soups.

forcemeat – stuffing for pies, terrines, fish, crustaceans, joints or vegetables consisting of finely chopped or minced meat, fish, vegetables, etc. with seasoning and a binding agent.

fumet – essence, stock.

garnish – to decorate a dish. Also, something served with a dish or included in a soup or sauce, which often gives the dish its name.

gelatine – pure, tasteless bone extract in powder or sheet form, used for setting liquids and light desserts.

glaze – highly reduced, unsalted stock from fish, seafood, veal, chicken or game, used to flavour sauces or to give food a shiny coating. When cold, it becomes solid enough to cut. Also, to cover a dish with glaze; to line a mould thinly and evenly with jelly or other fine mixture before adding the filling.

gratin, au gratin – a dish cooked under a grill to give a brown crust.

jelly – various clarified liquids left to set.

julienne – fine strips of vegetable or truffle, used to decorate or in soups.

liaison – thickening agent (e.g. egg yolk, cream).

marinade – liquid (wine, lemon juice, vinegar or buttermilk) with herbs and spices used to preserve, season or tenderize meat and fish. Salad dressings are also sometimes known as marinades.

marinate – to steep in a marinade.

mask – to cover in sauce or jelly.

mince – to finely chop or reduce in a mincer.

mirepoix – fried vegetables, used to flavour sauces. Also, finely chopped root vegetables, onions, possibly streaky bacon, lightly fried with herbs and bay leaf.

mousse – light, frothy dish made with crustaceans, fish, meat or poultry and gelatine or with fruit purée and cream.

mousseline – mousse made in individual moulds.

nut – the firm, white flesh of the scallop.

panada – a basic thickening mixture for stuffings.

poach – to cook boneless foods by simmering very gently.

quenelles – small fish or meat balls.

ragoût – fish, meat, vegetable or seafood stew with a highly seasoned sauce. Can be used as pie filling.

reduce – to boil liquids such as stocks, soups or sauces to the required concentration or until thickened. Reduces the liquid content and increases flavour.

sauté – quick-fried small pieces of meat, fish or poultry. Also, to fry quickly in shallow fat.

skim – to clear stocks and sauces of protein and impurities which rise to the surface, using a serrated spoon.

steam – to cook in water vapour, without the food coming into contact with the water.

strain – to pour or press a liquid through a fine sieve or through a cloth.

stuff – to fill with a highly flavoured mixture.

velouté – basic white sauce (see page 107).

Seafood Index

Recipe Index

The authors and publishers would like to thank the following for photographs used in this book:

Large photograph page 15: G and J Fotoservice/Axel Carp; *page 26 top left:* New Zealand Fishing Industry Board, Wellington, New Zealand; *photographs page 27, centre, page 41 (2), page 53 and page 88 bottom:* Dr. Michael Türkay, Senckenberg Research Institute, Frankfurt, West Germany; *page 44 top left:* Dr. Johannes Kinzer, Institute for Oceanography, University of Kiel, West Germany; *page 45 top left:* National Marine Fisheries Service, Auke Bay Laboratory/William R. Heard, Auke Bay, Alaska, USA; *page 48 bottom right, page 89:* Yim Chee Peng, Singapore; *page 61 below:* New Zealand Marine Farms Limited, Christchurch, New Zealand; *page 85:* Ulla Mayer-Raichle, Kempten, West Germany.

We should like to thank the following scientists and consultants: Dr. Nicolaus Antonacopoulos, Scientific Director at the Institute of Biochemistry and Technology, Federal Research Institute for Fisheries, Hamburg, West Germany; Dr. Rudo von Cosel, mollusc specialist, Gießen, West Germany, currently working at the Museum of Natural Science in Paris; Prof. Peter Kaiser, former head of the mollusc section in the Zoological Institute and Museum of the University of Hamburg, West Germany; John F. Karinen, Supervisory Oceanographer, National Marine Fisheries Service, Auke Bay Laboratory, Auke Bay, Alaska, USA; Dr. Rudhard Meixner, Scientific Consultant at the Institute of Coastal and Inland Fisheries, Federal Research Institute for Fisheries, Hamburg, West Germany; Hans Petersen, documentalist at the Zoological Institute of the University of Hamburg, West Germany; Dr. Hjalmar Thiel, senior scientific consultant at the Institute of Hydrobiology and Fishery Science at the University of Hamburg, West Germany.

We should like to express special thanks to Dr. Michael Türkay, head of the crustacean section at the Senckenberg Research Institute, Frankfurt, West Germany.

Moreover we should like to thank all those who contributed to the success of this book through their help and support: René Acklin, Fundación Chile, Santiago, Chile; Vladimir Durussel, Hotel-College, Lausanne, Switzerland; Paul M. Earl, National Marine Fisheries Service, Gloucester, Massachusetts, USA; Derrick S. Holker, Freshwater Lobsters of W. A., Wellington Mills, Western Australia, plus The West Australian Marron Growers' Association; Hotel Inter-Continental Maui, Wailea, Maui, Hawaii, USA; Ben Hugman, Red Bank Oyster Company Ltd., Burrin, Ireland; Mandarin Hotel, Singapore; Moon Gate, 10 Tanglin Road, Singapore; New Zealand Fishing Industry Board, Wellington, New Zealand; Produktschap voor Vis en Visprodukten, Bergen op Zoom, Netherlands; Sepp Renggle, "The Four Seasons" restaurant, New York, USA; The Dorchester Hotel, London, England; The Mark Hopkins Inter-Continental Hotel, San Francisco, USA; Céline Vence, journalist, Neuilly, France.

This edition published by
The Hamlyn Publishing Group Limited,
Bridge House, 69 London Road, Twickenham, Middlesex, England.
First published 1987
Copyright © The Hamlyn Publishing Group Limited 1987

First published under the title
Das Grosse Buch Der Meeresfrüchte
Copyright © 1985 by Teubner Edition
Postfach 1440. D-8958 Fussen

ISBN 0 600 32605 5

Set in Monophoto Times
by Tameside Filmsetting Ltd

Printed in Hong Kong

WS660